THE DIVINE FEUDAL LAW

NATURAL LAW AND
ENLIGHTENMENT CLASSICS

Knud Haakonssen
General Editor

Samuel Pufendorf

NATURAL LAW AND
ENLIGHTENMENT CLASSICS

The Divine Feudal Law: Or, Covenants with Mankind, Represented

Samuel Pufendorf

Translated by Theophilus Dorrington

Edited and with an Introduction by
Simone Zurbuchen

The Works of Samuel Pufendorf

LIBERTY FUND

Indianapolis

This book is published by Liberty Fund, Inc., a foundation established to encourage study of the ideal of a society of free and responsible individuals.

The cuneiform inscription that serves as our logo and as the design motif for our endpapers is the earliest-known written appearance of the word "freedom" (*amagi*), or "liberty." It is taken from a clay document written about 2300 B.C. in the Sumerian city-state of Lagash.

© 2002 Liberty Fund, Inc.
All rights reserved

Frontispiece portrait of Samuel Pufendorf is to be found at the University of Lund, Sweden, and is based on a photoreproduction by Leopoldo Iorizzo.

Printed in the United States of America

06 05 04 03 02 C 5 4 3 2 1
06 05 04 03 02 P 5 4 3 2 1

Library of Congress Cataloging-in-Publication Data

Pufendorf, Samuel, Freiherr von, 1632–1694.
[Jus feciale divinum. English]
The divine feudal law, or, Covenants with mankind, represented/
Samuel Pufendorf; translated by Theophilus Dorrington;
edited and with an introduction by Simone Zurbuchen.
p.   cm.   (The works of Samuel von Pufendorf)
(Natural law and enlightenment classics)
Includes bibliographical references and index.
ISBN 0-86597-372-5 (alk. paper)   ISBN 0-86597-373-3 (pbk.: alk. paper)
1. Lutheran Church—Relations—Reformed Church.
2. Reformed Church—Relations—Lutheran Church.
3. Unionism (Lutheranism)
I. Title: Divine feudal law.   II. Title: Covenants with mankind, represented.
III. Dorrington, Theophilus, d. 1715.
IV. Zurbuchen, Simone.   V. Title.   VI. Series.

BX8063.7.R4 P8413   2002
284—dc21   2002022570

LIBERTY FUND, INC.
8335 Allison Pointe Trail, Suite 300
Indianapolis, Indiana 46250-1684

CONTENTS

Introduction   ix

THE DIVINE FEUDAL LAW: OR, COVENANTS
WITH MANKIND, REPRESENTED   I

Selected Bibliography   227

Index   229

INTRODUCTION

The present work is a translation of Samuel Pufendorf's *Jus feciale divinum sive de consensu et dissensu protestantium*,[1] a treatise on the reunification of Protestants in Europe. The fact that Pufendorf considered himself a layman in theology helps to explain why the work was first published posthumously in 1695. By then Pufendorf was already renowned in Europe as one of the founding fathers of the modern theory of natural law. His main works in that field are *The Law of Nature and Nations* (1672) and its abridgment, *The Whole Duty of Man According to Natural Law* (1673). In addition, Pufendorf published important political writings as well as a number of historical works that he wrote as court historiographer in the service of King Charles XI of Sweden and later of Frederick William I and Frederick III of Brandenburg-Prussia. From his student days at the University of Leipzig, questions of religion and theology continued to interest Pufendorf. Despite his efforts to separate natural law from moral theology, which put him in opposition to Lutheran orthodoxy, he remained faithful to the Lutheran creed up to the end of his life. This is clearest in his late writings that deal with problems of religion and toleration. The first of these appeared in 1687 under the title *De habitu religionis christianae ad vitam civilem* (literally, "On the Relation of Christian Religion to Civil Life").[2] This treatise was composed in reaction to the revocation of the Edict of Nantes in 1685. With this measure the French king,

---

1. Concerning the difficulties of translating this title, see section V of the Introduction.

2. This was translated as *Of the Nature and Qualification of Religion in Reference to Civil Society* (1698), ed. Simone Zurbuchen (Indianapolis: Liberty Fund, 2002).

Louis XIV, renounced the laws that had granted toleration to the Huguenots, or Calvinists, in France. On the basis of his theory of natural law, Pufendorf denounces the revocation as an illegitimate and tyrannical act and advocates toleration.[3] *The Divine Feudal Law* can be seen as a complement to the treatise on toleration. In the former work, Pufendorf clarifies that toleration is just one means of dealing with religious dissent. It should be applied only when the reuniting of religions or denominations proves impossible. Pufendorf attempts to demonstrate in *The Divine Feudal Law* that union of Lutherans and Calvinists is possible on the basis of a theological system containing the fundamental articles necessary for salvation. In contrast, reconciliation between Protestants and Catholics is declared to be impossible.

II

In the introductory sections of *The Divine Feudal Law,* Pufendorf approaches the problem of religious dissent from a general perspective. He first insists that differences in religion should never be settled in such a way that concern for truth is laid aside. For that reason it is neither desirable that all religious parties join into one body nor that they should be held in the same esteem. The aim is not to eliminate disagreements in religion but to take away the evils that arise from those disagreements. Pufendorf proposes two methods that can be used for this purpose: toleration and reconciliation (p. 15). Toleration is held to be twofold, either "political" or "ecclesiastical" (p. 16). *The Divine Feudal Law* is concerned mainly with the latter, though it contains important conceptual clarifications of the former, dispelling some of its ambiguities. Concerning political toleration, Pufendorf argues, on one hand, that respect for religious freedom is one of the duties of the sovereign; on the other hand, he expounds the opinion that, depending on time and circumstances, sovereigns may either banish dissenters or tolerate subjects who do not adhere to the established reli-

---

3. Cf. the introduction to my edition of this work.

gion. For this reason, it has been questioned whether Pufendorf in fact developed a principled defense of toleration.

The opening sections of *The Divine Feudal Law* are especially pertinent with regard to that question. In section 4 Pufendorf distinguishes two ways of enjoying liberty of religion: subjects have their liberty "either in their own Right, or by the Concession and Favour of those who have Possession of the Government" (p. 16). The former applies wherever liberty of religion is granted by contract. Pufendorf points to the examples of the Lutheran, Calvinist, and Catholic communities in the German Empire, whose rights were guaranteed by the Peace of Westphalia. He also points out that when in any state a prince departs from the publicly received religion, both he and the people enjoy liberty of religion in their own right. The Huguenots in France, whose liberty of conscience had been granted by the Edict of Nantes, provide another example. Commenting on these cases, Pufendorf states, "Those who in this manner enjoy the Liberty of their Religion, cannot properly be said to be tolerated" (p. 17 f.).

Toleration in the proper sense of the term applies only to those communities that have their liberty granted "by the Concession of the Government" (p. 18), as, for example, when foreigners of a different religion are admitted into a state or when a minority of people departs from an ancient religion. In more general terms, Pufendorf explains that toleration should be taken not as a good in itself but rather as a temporary means of overcoming religious diversity. It is "of the Nature of a Truce in War, which suspends the Effects of it, and the actual Hostilities, while the State and Cause of the War do remain" (p. 15). While controversies about the articles of faith persist and continue, they are no longer accompanied by hatred and persecution. Where toleration applies, religious parties "live together as if there were no Dissention among them" (p. 15); that is, they do not hinder each other "from the publick Profession of their different Opinion" (p. 15). Depending on time and circumstances, toleration may be either universal or limited (p. 18). It is universal when all religious parties have equal liberty to the public exercise of their religions and enjoy all the rights and privileges of subjects of the state. It is limited when the exercise of religion is restricted to private realms or when religious minorities are excluded from some benefits of the state, such as the right to bear offices of honor and profit.

III

As Pufendorf goes on to explain, toleration has yet another aspect that leads into the domain of theology. Under the title of "ecclesiastical" toleration, Pufendorf examines the possibility that different religious parties may consider each other members of the same particular church and come together to the Lord's Supper (sec. 7). Pufendorf first insists that reconcilement of differences in religion should always be based on truth. It is of no help to declare that all religions are equally useful for the salvation of men. For this "were to make the Christian Religion altogether Irrational" (p. 22). In theology as elsewhere, where there is a contradiction between two propositions, one or the other must be false. To bring about reconciliation, "one Opinion must of necessity be declar'd and approv'd for Truth, and the other be rejected as false" (p. 21). Pufendorf is convinced that the truths of Christianity can be established on the basis of the Holy Scriptures. However, because of the obstinacy of prejudices and of "the Pride of Humane Nature, which disdains that others should seem wiser than ourselves" (p. 22), reconciliation cannot be obtained on all points of dispute. Thus he proposes, "a *Reconcilement* mixed with a *Toleration*" (p. 23). In the first place, agreement has to be established upon those articles of faith that are necessary to salvation. In the second place, toleration should be granted with regard to those opinions that do not belong to the foundations of faith.

This leads to the "grand Question" whether a disputed religious article belongs to the essentials of the faith or not (sec. 16). As Pufendorf observes, some religious parties extend the fundamentals further, while others bring them within stricter bounds. Moreover, not all parties view them in the same manner. Given such disagreement, Pufendorf proposes to take those principles on which both sides agree and "to compose of them a full and compleat System of Theology, which . . . should hold together, in a well connected Series of those Principles, from End to End" (p. 59). This "System, or Body of Divinity" (p. 59), has to contain everything that a complete Christian should know, and it must therefore "include all the Articles which would make up the whole due Chain of the Faith" (p. 59). As Pufendorf explained in a letter to his brother Esaias in 1681, he wished to develop theology according to the mathematical method that he had already applied in the domain of natural law.[4]

The bulk of *The Divine Feudal Law* contains the theological system on which Pufendorf wished to base reconciliation of the Lutheran and Calvinist Churches. In the first place, "a rude Draught" (p. 127) of the required system of theology is established. It consists of a series of covenants between God and men that Pufendorf uncovers in the Holy Scriptures: The first covenant, concluded with Adam in the state of Paradise, was broken with the Fall. Out of goodness, God established a new covenant with man by the interposition of a mediator. From this a new religion arose that consisted "in the observance of the Law of Nature, both towards God, and towards Man" (p. 78). Because of man's corruption after the Fall, faith and hope in the savior were added. This new covenant was announced by a number of particular covenants (one with Abraham, one with Moses), which testify to God's concern that the knowledge of a savior to come into the world might be lost among dispersed nations. According to Pufendorf, the new covenant consists of a double agreement: "the one of God the Father with the Son, the other of the Son, as Mediator, and Saviour with Men" (p. 87). Its proper understanding depends on explication of the Trinity and the double nature of Christ as God and as man.

The draft of the theological system is followed by a series of paragraphs devoted to the main points of controversy between Lutherans and Calvinists. The most important issues concern the questions of

---

4. Letter to his brother Esaias Pufendorf, Feb. 17, 1681. A revised version of the same letter dates from Feb. 24, 1681. Both of them are printed in Samuel Pufendorf, *Gesammelte Werke,* vol. 1: *Briefwechsel,* ed. Detlef Döring (Berlin: Akademie Verlag, 1996), 122–27.

grace and predestination. They are treated separately because they cannot be integrated into the proposed system. In Pufendorf's judgment,
it is "to imply a Contradiction that a Covenant should be made by
God with Men, and yet that they should be sav'd or damn'd by virtue
of a certain absolute Decree," by which God decides beforehand about
the salvation of men (p. 127). If theology is taken to be a "Moral
Discipline," at least a minimum of freedom of will has to be admitted:
"this at least must be left to our Will, that it can resist and refuse the
offer'd Grace of God [by the covenants]; since without this all Morality
would be utterly extinguish'd, and Men must be drawn to their End
after the manner of working of Engines" (p. 145).

The main part of the work concludes with a detailed examination
of a proposal to reunite the Protestants that was launched from the
Calvinist side. In 1687 Pierre Jurieu (1637–1713)[5] published his *De Pace
inter Protestantes ineunda* (Consultation about Making Peace among
Protestants). As Pufendorf observes, the work fell into his hands while
he was composing *The Divine Feudal Law*. In fact, he takes Jurieu's
paper as an opportunity to explain in greater detail why "the Opinion
of the *Reform'd* upon the Article of Grace and Predestination" (p. 157)
seems unacceptable to him (secs. 70–89), as well as to discuss the four
ways of reconciling and uniting divided parties that Jurieu proposed
(secs. 90–94).

IV

As noted above, Pufendorf's proposal for reconciling different religious
parties is restricted to the union of just two parties; namely, the Lutherans and the Calvinists. We thus have to ask why Pufendorf did not
propose a more comprehensive system of theology that might have
served also to unite Protestants with Roman Catholics. This question
is of special interest, because Pufendorf witnessed in his own time

---

5. Jurieu was a French Calvinist theologian who became pastor of the Walloon
Church in Rotterdam after he had to leave France. He is well known for his con-
troversial writings in defense of the Huguenots.

important attempts to reunite Protestants and Catholics in the German empire.[6] From the early 1670s on, the Spanish Franciscan Cristoforo Rojas y Spinola, Bishop of Tina in Croatia and later of Wiener-Neustadt, acted as an agent of Emperor Leopold. As the emperor's diplomat, Spinola toured various Protestant courts, where he expounded upon church unity and endeavored to stimulate discussion of ways to bring about a reunion between Protestants and the Catholic Church. His negotiation efforts were also supported by Pope Innocent XI. In Hanover, as early as 1679, Spinola negotiated secretly for four months with the Lutheran theologian Gerard Wolter Molanus (1633–1722), Abbot of Loccum. Like Spinola, Molanus was to play a crucial role in a second round of negotiations in 1683. A church "union conference" was convened with a number of Protestant theologians, to whom Spinola submitted his plan of reunion, a work entitled *Regulae circa christianorum omnium ecclesiasticam reunionem* (Rules concerning the Ecclesiastical Reunion of All Christians). On the instruction of Duke Ernst August of Hanover, Molanus drafted *Methodus reducendae unionis ecclesiasticae inter Romanenses et Protestantes* (Method to Restore an Ecclesiastical Union between the Romanists and the Protestants), in which he laid out the Protestant proposals for reunion. These were then examined in comparison with Spinola's plan. Although a second conference round was convened in the same year, no agreement was reached. Later attempts to overcome the Roman Catholic and Protestant division proved equally abortive.

Another participant in the union conference was the philosopher Gottfried Wilhelm Leibniz, who repeatedly raised the issue of the reunification of Protestants and Catholics in his works and extensive correspondence. In the early 1690s Leibniz entered into correspondence on the subject with the leading French theologian Jacques Bénigne

6. For details about attempts to reunite the churches in the late seventeenth and early eighteenth centuries, see *Union–Konversion–Toleranz. Dimensionen der Annäherung zwischen den christlichen Konfessionen im 17. und 18. Jahrhundert,* ed. Heinz Duchhardt and Gerhard May (Mainz: Philipp von Zabern, 2000). *Die Reunionsgespräche im Niedersachsen des 17. Jahrhunderts. Rojas y Spinola–Molan–Leibniz* (Göttingen: Vandenhoeck & Ruprecht, 1999).

Bossuet, Bishop of Meaux and privy councillor to Louis XIV, but he soon became disappointed with the discussion. Leibniz wrote a commentary to *The Divine Feudal Law*,[7] and his sharp criticism of the work was a result of the contrasting philosophical and political perspectives of the two authors.[8]

With a view to *The Divine Feudal Law*, the "union conference" at Hanover is of particular significance insofar as Pufendorf takes a critical view of Molanus's *Methodus*, which he cites in full in the preliminary sections of the work.[9] Before discussing the text itself, Pufendorf explains in general terms the reasons why union between Protestants and Catholics is impossible. The main reason is that the controversies are concerned not with "principles" or "opinions" but rather with "the Establishment and Support of the Authority, Power and Revenues" (p. 28) of the Roman Catholic Church, which Pufendorf also calls the "Empire of the Pope" and the "Pontifical Monarchy." Controversies about "emoluments" cannot be determined, because demonstration of the falsehood of the "Popish principles" would only confirm those of the Protestant party. As the pope will never renounce his pretense of dominion over others, reconciliation would require that Protestants return to subordination "under their former Yoke" (p. 29).

In his critical commentary on Molanus's proposal, Pufendorf repeats the same arguments regarding reconciliation with Catholics in more

---

7. Leibniz's "Epistola ad Amicum super exercitationes posthumas Samuelis Puffendorfii De consensu et dissensu protestantium" is printed in Detlef Döring, *Pufendorf-Studien: Beiträge zur Biographie Samuel von Pufendorfs und zu seiner Entwicklung als Historiker und theologischer Schriftsteller* (Berlin: Duncker and Humblot, 1992), 205–10. See also Detlef Döring, "Leibniz als Verfasser der 'Epistola ad amicum super exercitationes posthumas Samuelis Puffendorfii de consensu et dissensu protestantium,'" in *Zeitschrift für Kirchengeschichte* 104/2 (1993), 176–97. Leibniz's and other commentaries on *The Divine Feudal Law* are discussed by Döring in *Pufendorf-Studien*, 130–42.

8. The contrasting aspects of the two philosophies are analyzed in Ian Hunter, *Rival Enlightenments: Civil and Metaphysical Philosophy in Early Modern Germany* (Cambridge: Cambridge University Press, 2001).

9. This part of the work has recently been analyzed by Martin Ohst, "Gerard Wolter Molan und seine Stellung zum Projekt einer kirchlichen Union," in *Union–Konversion–Toleranz*, ed. H. Duchhardt and G. May, 194–97.

polemical terms. Thus he expresses his conviction that "the far greater Part of the Protestants do believe the Papal Empire to be that Apocalyptical Beast, whose Tiranny by the great Favour of God they have thrown off" (p. 38). He also observes that the Catholic Church "is degenerated from its Primitive Purity . . . into a most pestilent Sink of Superstitions" (p. 39). Moreover, the proposed union with the Catholics is held to be "an empty Fiction" (p. 40) because Protestants could never accept the infallibility of the pope, the principle on which the Church of Rome is founded.

V

Despite the limited scope of Pufendorf's project of reconciliation, it was later used in the attempted reunion of Protestants in England and on the continent, as shown by the English translations of the work. Neither the title of this nor of the second English edition of 1714[10] is faithful to the Latin original. The Latin title is in fact difficult to understand. In Roman law, *jus feciale* (literally, "fecial law") is the law of negotiation and diplomacy. It remains unclear how the reunion of Protestants is related to this particular law. This may explain why the English translator, Theophilus Dorrington,[11] did not follow the original. The title of his first edition ("The Divine Feudal Law") refers to the specific nature of the covenants between God and man. As Pufendorf explains in section 25, the original covenant between God and Adam was of the nature of "feudal" covenants among men, in which no proportion is observed between the matter of the crime and the severity of the punishment; rather, the right to benefit from the contract depends on a condition insignificant in itself. Thus the great condition

---

10. The second edition, also published by Dorrington, bears the title *A View of the Principles of the Lutheran Churches; shewing how far they agree with the Church of England: Being a Seasonable Essay towards the Uniting of Protestants upon the Accession of His Majesty King George to the Throne of these Kingdoms.*

11. The son of nonconformist parents, Dorrington turned against the Dissenters and became a member of the Church of England. In 1710 he obtained his M.A. at Magdalen College, Oxford. He died in 1715.

of the original covenant between God and man was placed in abstinence from the fruit of the tree of knowledge. This explains the severity
of the sanction annexed to the prohibition of eating the fruit.

As Dorrington observes in the "Advertisement" to *The Divine Feudal Law,* his translation is intended to serve two purposes. In his view,
Pufendorf wrote the treatise to promote peace and union among the
Protestant churches in Germany. Finding the state of the church in
England much the same, Dorrington suggests that the book may be
of similar use in his own country as well. What Dorrington must have
in mind here is the much-disputed relationship between the Church
of England and the Dissenters. As the so-called Toleration Act of 1689
had lifted the penalties of only some of the laws on which the former
discrimination of dissent had been based, "orthodox" Protestant Dissenters (Presbyterians, Independents, Baptists) remained in a politically
inferior position, while no other "sects" benefited from the act. In
Pufendorf's terms, Dissenters in Great Britain were at best granted
"limited" toleration. While some authors advocated full toleration of
religious dissent, others pleaded for "comprehension"; that is, they proposed to receive Dissenters as members of the established church.

In the second place, Dorrington recommends Pufendorf's treatise
as a means of better understanding the principles and practices of the
Lutheran Church. In Dorrington's view, the latter was usually depicted
falsely and injuriously by its adversaries. The reasons a proper understanding of the principles of the Lutheran Church seemed important
to him are spelled out more clearly in the second edition of 1714.
Dorrington there introduces the work as a demonstration of the extent
to which the principles of the Lutheran Church "agree with the Church
of England." He considers it "a Seasonable Essay towards the Uniting
of Protestants upon the accession of His Majesty King George to the
throne of these Kingdoms." What made this so "Seasonable" was the
fact that only with the death of Queen Anne and the accession of
George I did the succession to the British throne switch from the
Stuarts to the Hanovers, as provided for at the Glorious Revolution.
What is more, George I had been brought up a Lutheran.

Although Dorrington wished to further strengthen the Protestant alliance by uniting the Church of England with the Protestants on the Continent, some of the Anglican divines still persisted in their opposition to the Protestant succession. Among them was Thomas Brett (1667–1743), an eminent divine who took the accession of George I as an opportunity to join in communion with the "non-jurors." That was the name given to the Anglican churchmen who in 1689 refused to take the oath of allegiance to William and Mary and their successors under the Protestant Act of Succession of that year. Their leaders on the episcopal bench who persisted in their refusal were suspended.

At the time of his ordination, in 1690, Brett had complied with the oath. However, when upon the accession of George I an act of Parliament was passed obliging all divines to refresh their oaths, Brett refused. This helps explain why Brett responded to Dorrington's translation with *A Review of the Lutheran Principles,* in which he attempted to show "that Baron Puffendorf's essay for uniting of Protestants, was not design'd to procure an union between the Lutherans and the Church of England." The *Review* was published in two editions in 1714.[12] In the same year appeared *A Second Review of the Lutheran Principles,* composed by "a Lover of King George" in answer "to Dr Bret's late insolent libel against the Lutheran Churches."[13] The publication of these pamphlets suggests that the influence of Pufendorf's treatise was not restricted to debates on reunification in the German empire. Despite its limited scope, it could also be employed as a model for reconciling Protestants in Europe.

12. Thomas Brett, *A Review of the Lutheran Principles; shewing, how they differ from the Church of England, and that Baron Puffendorf's essay for uniting of Protestants, was not design'd to procure an union between the Lutherans and the Church of England, as is insinuated in the title of the late edition of that book. In a letter to a friend* (London, 1714). The second edition with a postscript containing remarks on a pamphlet titled *Two letters to . . . Viscount Townsend* (London, 1714).

13. *A Second Review of the Lutheran Principles: or, an Answer to Dr Bret's late insolent libel against the Lutheran Churches: shewing that there is no essential difference between them and the Church of England* (London, 1714). Anonymously published by John Lewis (1675–1747).

THE
Divine Feudal Law:
OR,
Covenants with Mankind,
REPRESENTED.
Together with
MEANS
FOR THE
Uniting of Protestants.
In which also
The Principles of the *Lutheran* Churches
are Stated and Defended.

By *SAMUEL* Baron *PUFENDORF.*

Translated from the Latin by *Theophilus Dorrington,*
Rector of Wittresham in *Kent.*

LONDON:
Printed for *John Wyat,* at the *Rose*
in St. *Paul's* Church-yard, 1703.

The Works of this Excellent Author need no Man's Recommendation, nor can I think fit to pretend to give them any Advantage by mine. It shall suffice therefore barely to advertise concerning this, That it is the last Work of this Famous and Great Man, and so may be reckon'd the Product and Fruit of his utmost Improvements in Wisdom, Piety and Learning. He had consider'd it, as he thought, sufficiently, and was about to make it publick when he was prevented by a sudden Sickness; the Issue of which, at first, was doubtful, but which, in a little time, prov'd fatal. When this was expected, he left it in Charge with his Friends to publish this Work after his Death, who fulfill'd his Will in doing so. He wrote it with the Blessed Design to serve and promote Peace and Union among the Protestant Churches in *Germany,* and thought it might be of some Use towards this happy Effect. And then the State of the Church being much the same with us in *England,* as it is with them, we may reckon upon it as his Opinion or Judgment, that such an Essay or Endeavour to Reconcile and Unite Protestants, is very seasonable and proper, and may be useful to us. I thought also that it might be of Use to us in *England,* to understand and know the Principles and Practices of the *Lutheran* Churches (which are the true Protestant Churches beyond the Seas) better than for ought I can find we commonly do: And these are represented here fairly and distinctly in their true and genuine Lustre, and freed from the false and injurious Representations which are commonly made of them by their Adversaries. We may also I think see by this Book, that if any sober and judicious Persons in the *Lutheran* Churches have any Disesteem of the Church of *England,* or Prejudice against it, this comes to pass by their not knowing it exactly. Which may well be, inasmuch as it has been the Fortune of our Church to be more industriously, and more represented abroad by its Enemies than by its Friends. And I believe it may be of great Use to us to know this. For these Reasons I thought it worth my Time and Labour, and agreeable enough with my Duty, and the earnest Desire I have, according to it, to serve Truth, and Piety, and Peace, among us, or, which includes all that in one Word, the Church of *England,* to turn this Book into our common Language; by which Means I judge it will become more known, and so be more useful among us than it was likely to be while it remain'd in the Original Latin. Now this is done, I pray God it may be serviceable to all those good Purposes mention'd, to whom be Glory for ever.

Amen.

AN
EPITOMY
Of the following
BOOK.

Page

Sect. 1. *The Wickedness of Mankind a Cause of many Calamities among them.*   11

Sect. 2. *Religion abused to encrease the Miseries of Mankind.*   12

Sect. 3. *How far it may be endeavoured to reconcile the Dissentions in Religion.*   14

Sect. 4. *The Toleration of Dissenting Parties is either Political;*   15

Sect. 5. *And that either Universal or Limited.*   18

Sect. 6. *Or Ecclesiastical.*   21

Sect. 7. *Of the Reconciliation of differing Opinions.*   21

Sect. 8. *The Dissention is either about Principles or Emoluments.*   24

Sect. 9. *The Controversies about meer Principles may be entirely decided.*   25

Sect. 10. *The Controversies which concern Emoluments seem to be irreconcileable.*   28

Sect. 11. *Of solid and superficial Religion.*   31

Sect. 12. *It is vain to attempt a Reconcilement between the Protestants and Papists.*   35

Sect. 13. *An Examen of a certain Form of a Reconciliation between the Protestants and Papists.*   37

Sect. 14. *Some differ in the whole System.*   57

Sect. 15. *Some differ only upon a few Articles.*   58

Sect. 16. *A Specimen of a System of Divinity, in which it seems that all Protestants may agree.*   60

Sect. 17. *Things presupposed to it.*   61

Sect. 18. *It is agreeable to Reason that there should be a revealed Religion.*   62

Sect. 19. *There are no good Reasons to call in Question the Divine Revelations.*   62

Sect. 20. *In true Religion there is included a Covenant.*   63

Sect. 21. *The peculiar Nature of Covenants between God and Man.*   66

Sect. 22. *The Original Covenant of God with Man.*   67

Sect. 23. *The Will of the first Man.*   68

Sect. 24. *The Heads of the first Covenant of God with Man.*   69

Sect. 25. *Of the Forbidden Tree.*   72

Sect. 26. *Of the State of Man after the Fall, and of Original Sin.*   73

Sect. 27. *The Covenant of God with Men, which was made by the Interposition of a Mediator.*   75

Sect. 28. *The Promulgation of this Covenant.*   76

Sect. 29. *The Religion resulting from this Covenant.*   78

Sect. 30. *The Particular Covenant of God with Abraham.*   80

Sect. 31. *The Covenant of God with the People of Israel made by the Mediation of Moses.*   82

Sect. 32. *The Conditions of that Covenant.*   83

Sect. 33. *The Sacrament of that Covenant.*   84

Sect. 34. *The Nature of the Jewish Religion.*   86

Sect. 35. *The Jewish Religion was interwoven with their Commonwealth.*   86

Sect. 36. *The Complement of the Adamitical Covenant,*   87

Sect. 37. *Which consists in an Agreement with God the Father, and the Son,*   87

Sect. 38. *And of the Saviour with Men.*   90

Sect. 39. *That Covenant presupposes the Mystery of the Sacred Trinity.*   90

Sect. 40. *Of the Mediator of the New Covenant.*   93

Sect. 41. *He is God.*   93

Sect. 42. *And Man.*   94

Sect. 43. *In One Person.*   95

Sect. 44. *The Nature of the Personal Union.*   96

Sect. 45. *The Consequence of that.*   97

Sect. 46. *What is become belonging to the Humane Nature by Vertue of this Union.*   97

Sect. 47. *This Covenant is less properly called a Testament.*   103

Sect. 48. *The Conditions of the Covenant on the Part of the Saviour.*   105

Sect. 49. *The Promulgation of this Covenant.*   106

Sect. 50. *The Sum of those Things which are to be performed by Men.*   107

Sect. 51. *By Faith we are engaged in this Covenant.*   108

Sect. 52. *Baptism is the Sacrament of Initiation.*   109

Sect. 53. *Regeneration attends the Entrance into the Covenant.*   111

Sect. 54. *Of Sanctification as a necessary Fruit of Justification and Regeneration.*   115

Sect. 55. *The chief Heads of Holiness are to abstain from Evil,*   118

Sect. 56. *And to do Good, and practice the Christian Virtues.*   120

Sect. 57. *Of the Holy Eucharist.*   122

Sect. 58. *Concerning the Invisible Matter of this Sacrament.*   124

Sect. 59. *The Union of those who come into this Covenant.*   126

Sect. 60. *What are Fundamental Articles.*   127

Sect. 61. *Of the Controversies among the Protestants.*   129

Sect. 62. *And indeed about the Person of Christ.*   132

Sect. 63. *About the Lord's Supper.*   134

Sect. 64. *The Controversies concerning Grace and Predestination.*   139

Sect. 65. *The Original of these Controversies.*   142

Sect. 66. *In these Controversies there are some things unsearchable by Men.*   144

Sect. 67. *The absolute Decree cannot be admitted.*   145

Sect. 68. *Of the Cause of Particularity.*   148

Sect. 69. *The Controversies of lesser Importance.*   152

Sect. 70. *Remarks upon the Consultation about making Peace among Protestants, by* Peter Jurieu.   157

Sect. 71. *Of the Legislatory and Decreetory Will of God.*   159

Sect. 72. *The Nature of the Divine Prescience.*   163

Sect. 73. *Concerning the calling of the Reprobate.*   165

Sect. 74. *Of the Conditional Will of God.*   167

Sect. 75. *Of Future Contingencies.*   169

Sect. 76. *Concerning the Universal Good Will of God.*   170

Sect. 77. *Concerning the manner of reconciling the Expressions which seem to contradict one another in this Matter.*   174

Sect. 78. *Concerning the Universal Redemption of Mankind by Jesus Christ; and the first Argument of* Jurieu *against this.*   182

Sect. 79. *The second Argument of* Jurieu.   190

Sect. 80. *The third Argument of* Jurieu.   191

Sect. 81. *The fourth Argument of* Jurieu, *taken from Vocation.*   192

Sect. 82. *The fifth Argument of* Jurieu.   194

Sect. 83. *The sixth and seventh Arguments of* Jurieu.   195

Sect. 84. *The Places of Scripture Vindicated.*   200

Sect. 85. *Concerning the Order of the Divine Decrees.*   202

Sect. 86. *Whether or no there be a Predestination without any Respect to Faith.*   206

Sect. 87. *Of Reprobation.*   211

Sect. 88. *Of Irresistible Grace.*   212

Sect. 89. *Why there is little Benefit of Disputing.*   214

Sect. 90. *Concerning the Abdicating of former Principles.*   215

Sect. 91. *Of the Strife about Words.*   217

Sect. 92. *Of Toleration.*   218

Sect. 93. *Of Silence.*   223

Sect. 94. *The Conclusion.*   225

The Divine Feudal Law
Represented

ೞ

§1. As I often consider the Condition of Humane Nature, it is especially The Wickedness of Mankind a Cause of many Calamities among them. grievous to me to observe, that besides the Evils and Inconveniencies which attend our Natural Frailty, Mankind do pull upon themselves a vast Heap of Calamities more, by their own perverse Will and wicked Lusts; which it were easie to them to be free from, if they would follow the Conduct of right Reason. How many, for instance, might, in the Enjoyment of a long Health, reach to a good old Age, if they did not destroy their natural Strength by Intemperance, and procure to themselves Troops of Diseases, a hasty Decay, and untimely Death? How many have it in their Power, by Vertue of a large Patrimony, to spend their Days in Wealth and Plenty, if they did not overthrow their own good Fortune by extravagant Luxury, and ill-digested Accounts? How many are there who might live at Ease, a quiet, pleasant, Life, if they knew how to set Bounds to Avarice and Ambition, and could forbear to strive, that they might get more, and rise higher, than fair and favourable Opportunity, the certain Indication of the Divine good Pleasure in the Case, invites them to do? What a numberless Multitude of Evils does the Wickedness of some Men bring upon others? All which might be prevented, if Men would rather perform the common Duties which they owe to one another, than obey enormous Lusts. What else is it that destroys whole Nations by Wars, in which one Word a mighty Inundation of Woes is included, but an ungovern'd Desire of Rule, and of extending Empire without Bounds? When as on the other side, both Princes and People might be happy, if every

Prince would live contented with his own, and not desire that which is another's; and rather study and endeavour to govern his own Country and People well, than to disturb and encroach upon his Neighbours. And when in the present Disorder Rulers are involv'd in a Multitude of Anxieties, and are forced to live amidst the perpetual Jealousies and Designs of their Neighbours, and to support themselves by a Thousand Arts and Deceits: If they would treat one another mutually as good Men should do, they might enjoy a much more flourishing State, and undisturb'd Tranquility.

Religion is abused to encrease the Miseries of Mankind.

§2. Nevertheless there is an evident Reason, tho' it be such as does not agree with the common Duties of Mankind to one another, why Men contend for Things which accommodate this present Life; and which being taken from one Man do make some Addition to the Portion of another. But this seems to be altogether without any Reason, that Men should be provok'd to do Mischief to one another by their Disagreement in Opinion only: Forasmuch as nothing is taken from one Man by another Man's differing in Opinion from him, nor is any thing added to him by the other's Agreement with him therein; and it were possible enough to reject and refuse a Man's Errors without any Hatred or Aversation to his Person. But this seems to arise from the unreasonable Pride of Mankind; by virtue of which, when all Men should allow to others their due Esteem, and not prefer themselves before all the World: On the contrary, they take it as their Prerogative, that the Opinion they have embrac'd should be consented to by all Men, and they become enrag'd if any refuse to do this, as thinking their just Authority therein despised; and at the same time 'tis no less manifest that other Men have the same Value and Esteem for their Opinion too. Hence it comes to pass that he who condemns another Man as in an Error, because he differs in Opinion from himself, he not only arrogates to himself an infallible Judgment, but thinks it his Right to punish those who refuse to submit to his Judgment; forasmuch as Aversation and Hatred is not the least of those Punishments which naturally attend and follow the Commission of what is accounted a Fault. And this Disorder of Humane Nature is the more absurd, because it no Way regards the Interest of another Man what Course I propose to my self to steer for the attaining my Salvation; provided that which I am in does not make me omit any of the Duties which I owe to others; and because neither does his Salvation depend on mine, or mine on his. From hence too the Hatred which arises from a Difference in Religion is peculiarly attended with a kind of Envy, it being accounted intolerable and unworthy that *God* should be any Ways favourable to those who think fit to serve him in a different Manner. And every Aversation and Hatred which arises from Dissention in Religion may be charg'd with this Absurdity, whatever Religion it is concern'd about. But that, which seems the most deplorable of all, is, that even Christian Religion, which teaches Love, Benignity and Mildness, which ought to unite all its Votaries as Brethren; (see *Gen.* 50:17.) which commands us to love even our Enemies, and pray to God for them, is by the Madness of Mankind brought to this pass, while they force into different Sences its Doctrines and Precepts, that even this, as so divided and torn, becomes the Occasion of many Calamities to the Christian World by the Abuse of idle and ill-minded Men: And tho' not of its own Nature and Tendency, yet by the ungovern'd Lusts of Men it provokes to a Multitude of very grievous Evils. This no one can be ignorant of, who considers the Hatreds which attend these Dissentions, and the cruel Persecutions and Wars which the Controversies about Religion have caused and given rise to, or else have fomented and maintained. And the Pretence made use of by some to justifie such Things is manifestly weak; who would have it be thought a meritorious Kindness to save Men, even against their Wills, and by any Means to rescue them from a damnable Errour; even as Men beside themselves are constrain'd by Force to take the Medicines which are proper for their Cure. But besides that, 'tis a Matter as yet undetermin'd whether or no they hold the true Opinion, who endeavour by Force to impose what is theirs upon other Men; 'tis also manifest that the Saviour of the World has chose a very different Way of propagating his Religion, as appears by the Sacred Writings, and the Practice of the Apostles. And as he has declar'd *his Kingdom is not of this World;* that is, it is of another Sort and Nature, than those which are set up among

Men; so there is no Order or Rule among the Laws of it to erect, preserve or propagate it by Force and Constraint. And his Disciples were sharply rebuk'd by him, who would have been for calling down Fire from Heaven upon those who refused to entertain our Saviour. (*Luke* 9:55.) *Ye know not* (said he) *what Spirit ye are of.*

How far it may be endeavoured to reconcile the Dissentions in Religion.

§3. I believe no one can doubt but it becomes all good Men to wish that this last Source of Calamities among Christians might be stopp'd up; and that every one is bound to contribute all that they have in their Power to do towards it, in as much as so doing they would be then number'd among the *Peacemakers,* whom our Saviour pronounces *Blessed,* and honours with the Title of *Children of God, Mat.* 5:9. And the Apostle's Admonition to this Purpose is very evident and considerable, *Phil.* 2:2, 3, 4. in these Words; *Fulfil ye my Joy, that ye be like-minded, having the same Love, being of one Accord, of one Mind. Let nothing be done through Strife or Vain-glory, but in Lowliness of Mind let such esteem other better than themselves. Look not every Man on his own Things, but every Man also on the Things of others.* Nor is this a Matter that we should despair to do any Good in, because many have labour'd in it in vain, and have been derided and insulted for their Pains. For those Things which are built upon good and true Foundations will find Acceptance with some at least, if not with all, and what is at this time rejected, will after a time, when the prevailing Prejudices are worn off, have its due Esteem; and without doubt Almighty God has his appointed Times for such Mutations; which as they ought to be expected with Patience, so every Man has Right to declare his good Intention towards the thing, when it will hurt no one, and may be of good Use, at least, to some. But if any Man thinks fit to bestow his Pains in this Design of reconciling Differences in Religion, he must, above all Things, take Care that he does nothing that may prejudice the Truth: For 'tis better to retain a Saving Truth, even amidst Contentions and Contradictions, than to enjoy a profound Quiet by a Falshood. And neither may such a Concord or Agreement be attempted as would contradict the Nature of Christian Religion, or produce more Calamities than those very Dissentions, not irritated or provok'd, are the Cause of. It is not fit to be thought of then, that all who bear the Name of Christians should lay aside all Concern for Truth, and all agree and join into one of the Dissenting Sects. Or that, renouncing their own Judgment in the making of their Choice, they should give up themselves to be determin'd by any one Person, or that they should by Force be brought to embrace the Opinions of any one Party. Such a thing does not agree either with right Reason, or the Genius of Christian Religion; nor is it indeed possible to be according to the State of Humane Affairs. So likewise it were a very preposterous Method of Concord, if any should propose that all the disagreeing Parties in Religion should be held in the same Rank, as if Eternal Salvation might as well be attain'd and secur'd in one as in another. For he who should think thus, must first suppose that no Party of Christians have any Error which subverts the Fundamentals of Religion, and this I believe is what no one will allow. And forasmuch as by the Nature of Things it cannot be that more than one of many differing Opinions should be true, he who equally esteems all the Differences, does truly esteem no one among them. That the Evils therefore which arise from Disagreements in Religion may be taken away, there do seem to be only these Two Methods remaining that can be made use of to this Purpose, and they are *Toleration* and *Reconciliation;* and these must be either *Universal,* or in the *Fundamentals* alone. But when we say this, we do not design to limit the Divine Wisdom and Power, to whom it is easie to find out Remedies for those Evils which no Humane Prudence can foresee.

§4. Toleration is of the Nature of a Truce in War, which suspends the Effects of it, and the actual Hostilities, while the State and Cause of the War do remain. By that in like manner the Controversies, and different Opinions upon the Articles of Faith, do still persist and continue, but so that the evil Effects of them cease, and they are not made matter of Hatred and Persecutions: And those that differ from one another, live together as if there were no Dissention among them; at least one Party does not hinder those of another from the publick Profession of their different Opinion, or from Worshipping God after

The Toleration of Dissenting Parties is either Political.

their own manner; nor does one Party any ways incommode or hurt the other upon any such Account. And such *Toleration* seems to be the readiest Remedy to Cure the Evils, which are wont to proceed from Diversities of Religion, since it is so difficult a Matter for Men to be brought to lay aside inveterate Opinions, and to Unite in a full Reconciliation. And that Method our Saviour himself seems to have recommended, while he forbad the pulling up of the Tares, lest at the same time the good Wheat should be pluck'd up with them: And he would have them let alone to grow together till the time of Harvest, *Mat.* 13:18, &c. In which Place by the time of Harvest it is not necessary that we must understand the End of the World; but it may perhaps mean that appointed Period which the Divine Providence has fix'd for every Sect. For manifest it is, that many Heresies are so perfectly vanish'd, that there is nothing remaining of them more than their Names in the History of the Church: Which if any Attempt had been unseasonably and violently made to have rooted them up, it might have given no small Trouble to the Orthodox. But this *Toleration* is Twofold, one is what may be call'd *Political,* the other *Ecclesiastical.* Concerning the former it is to be observ'd, that the Subjects of a Commonwealth who differ in their Religion, may have their Liberty to do so Two manner of Ways; either in their own Right, or by the Concession and Favour of those who have Possession of the Government. It may several Ways come to pass that Two or more different Religions may be admitted in the same Commonwealth. If in any one Nation a great Part of the People depart from their ancient Rites of Religion, and the rest continue in them as formerly, or if any People Universally forsake their ancient Religion, but in forming the new One do differ from one another, and these People mutually yeild to each other by Agreement to their different Ways of Religion, both Parties in this Case must be judg'd to have a Right to their Liberty. Thus in the *German* Empire, both the Protestants and the Catholicks do in their own Right enjoy the Liberty of their Religion. So when in any State where a certain Religion is publickly receiv'd, the Prince thinks fit to depart to another, or a Prince of a different Religion is receiv'd and acknowledg'd by the People, in this Case the Prince injoys the new, and the People their old Religion, and both with full Liberty, and in their own Right. So in *Germany*, by the Constitution of the Peace of *Osnabrug*, if a reform'd Principality should fall to a Prince of the Lutheran Profession, or a Lutheran Principality should come under a Prince of the reform'd Way, both People and Prince are to have Liberty of their Religion in their own Right. And in such a State, if the Prince or Ruler be of a different Religion from that of the People, or of the greater Part of them, yet the Religion of the Prince is not therefore to be accounted the ruling Religion, and that of the People precarious and obnoxious: Forasmuch as the Religion of the Ruler is one thing, and the ruling Religion is another. So when King *James* II. reconcil'd to the Romish Religion, came to the Kingdom of *England*, it must not be said that thereupon that became the ruling Religion there, but that Prerogative remain'd in the Possession of the Church of *England;* and when that King, led by evil Council, would needs go about to Impose the Roman Rites upon his People, it was without Injury that he lost his Kingdoms.[1] Which was the thing that formerly befel to *Sigismund* the King of *Sueden*.[2] But those who in this manner enjoy the Liberty

---

1. After succeeding his brother, Charles II, to the throne of England in 1685, James II (1633–1701) remained a staunch adherent to the Roman Catholic faith. When James openly opposed the Test Act of 1673, which barred all Catholics and Protestant Dissenters from holding administrative positions, by appointing Catholics to high positions, public opinion turned against him. In 1689 Parliament invited James's Protestant daughter, Mary, and her husband, William of Orange, to take the throne after an orchestrated invasion by the Dutchman the previous year. For a more detailed account of the Glorious Revolution, see Pufendorf's posthumous history of Frederic III of Brandenburg-Prussia, *De rebus gestis Friderici Tertii, Electoris Brandenburgici, post Primi Borussiae Regis Commentariorum Libri Tres, complectentes annos 1688–1690. Fragmentum posthumum ex autographo auctoris editum,* ed. E. F. de Hertzberg (Berlin, 1784). See the analysis by Michael J. Seidler, "'Turkish Judgment' and the English Revolution," in *Samuel Pufendorf und die europäische Frühaufklärung. Werk und Einfluss eines deutschen Bürgers der Gelehrtenrepublik nach 300 Jahren (1694–1994),* ed. Fiammetta Palladini and Gerald Hartung (Berlin: Akademie Verlag, 1996), 83–104.

2. In 1592 the Catholic king Sigismund III of Poland inherited the throne of Sweden from his father, John III. Lutheranism had been established as Sweden's

of their Religion, cannot properly be said to be tolerated; but they only are so who have their Liberty not in their own Right, but by the Concession of the Government. Which may come to pass, and is wont to do so when Strangers of a different Religion are receiv'd into any Nation. Who owe it to the Favour of the Government there, both that they are admitted into that Nation, and are admitted with a Religion different from that of the Nation which receives them. So also when a smaller Number of the People change and forsake their ancient Religion than are of any Importance to the Commonwealth, or than can by their Wealth obtain a Right to their Liberty, they must owe it to the Indulgence of the Government, that they are allow'd without Disturbance to Practice their new and different Way of Religion.

And that either Universal or Limited.

§5. Now the Political Toleration of Religion, which is yielded to such as have not a Right to it, consists in this. They are suffer'd, notwithstanding their difference in Religion, and while that remains, yet to live quietly in the Civil Society, and enjoy in common with others the benefit of the Laws, and Protection of the Government. And this Toleration is either *Universal* or *Limited.* The *Universal* one is when all of every Sort have equal Liberty for the publick Exercise of their Religion, and there is no difference made upon the account of Religion, but every one enjoys all the Rights and Priviledges of a Subject in that State. The *Limited* one is when the greater Part of the Nation indulges to the lesser the Exercise of their Religion, limited by certain Laws. As for instance, that it be in their Houses only, or with their Doors shut: And when they are excluded from some Benefits of the Subjects of that State, and from bearing Offices of Honour and Profit. This Political Toleration, where those Things are observ'd, which I have mention'd in *the Relation of Christian Religion to the Civil Life,* Sect. 51.[3] is found

---

state religion, which Sigismund was obliged to uphold as a condition for his coronation in 1594. His strong promotion of Catholicism, however, led to conflict; he was defeated by his successor, Charles IX, and deposed by the *Riksdag* in 1599.

3. *Of the Nature and Qualification of Religion in Reference to Civil Society* (1698), ed. Simone Zurbuchen (Indianapolis: Liberty Fund, 2002).

by Experience to produce a great Increase of People in a State; because a Multitude of Strangers will put themselves in there for the sake of that desir'd Liberty, which they could not elsewhere enjoy. And in such Places it is more necessary that the Ministers of the Church be well studied in Divinity, and very exemplary in their Life and Manners, that they may maintain their Esteem and Reputation, and be free from the Reproaches of the adverse Party, than where they have none to emulate them, in which Case they are more liable to fall into Sloth and ill Manners. And in such Places too it commonly comes to pass that they are wont with more Application and Endeavour to instruct and confirm their People in their Religion, as accounting it their Disparagement to have them drawn away to another Sect. But that which greatly concerns the Prince of such a People where different Religions are tolerated, is, that he do take care that the Liberty granted to all be strictly maintain'd, and that it be not either openly violated, or by any indirect Methods abridg'd. And he must not suffer that any one Party, where the Toleration is Universal, and much rather where all have the Liberty of Religion in their own Right, do by Factions, or secret Artifices, put by those who differ from them in Religion from bearing publick Offices, or withhold them from any of the common Benefits of Subjects, or be any otherwise troublesome to them. For indeed the Prince, if he does with Equity and Prudence manage this Matter, will find, that those of the Subjects who profess a different Religion from his own, will be more respectful and officious to him than those of his own Religion; because they will hold it a special Demonstration of his Goodness and Favour, if they find themselves not the less esteem'd and regarded by him for their different Opinion: When as they who profess the same Religion with him, will think all Things their right and due that he does for them, and hardly hold themselves at all oblig'd to him for it. But when we recommend a Toleration of those that differ in Religion, it must be understood that this is to be granted only where the tolerated Party has no Principles of Religion, which are contrary to the Peace and Safety of the State, nor such as are apt and tending in their own Nature to create Troubles and Commotions in the Commonwealth. As among the Roman Party, the Priests, especially, hold many Opinions which are greatly to the Prejudice of the Civil Magistrate. The Fountain and Source of which Opinions is this, that they feign the Church to be a peculiar and distinct State, altogether Independent, and no way Obnoxious to the civil Government. So that in the Toleration of those who are subject to that State, they must be tolerated, who will not account themselves the Subjects of the Government of their Nation, but of him who is the Head of their Church, that is, of a Foreign Prince. At least where the State cannot be freed altogether from the Men of that Party, there must be care taken that no Foreign Priests do make their Nests there, or such who are bound by peculiar Vow to the Bishop of *Rome.* Who are always acted by a boundless Zeal to promote his Dominion, and to ruin those of a different Religion. Moreover, it must be observ'd, that what we have said above concerning the Toleration of different Religions, concerns only those who live in the same Nation. And as for several Nations, as in all other Things, every one of them ought to injoy their Liberty without being Obnoxious to any other; so since Religion ought not to be propagated by Force, and the Sword, none of them is bound to be accountable for the Religion they entertain to any but Almighty God. Therefore every Nation does in its own Right, with respect to other Nations, practice the Religion which it likes best: And if upon that account it is Invaded by another, it may justly oppose Force to Force in this Case, as well as in Vindication of any other of its Rights. But if any Nation professes a Religion which obliges and drives them to the Oppression of all other Religions, the same Remedies are lawful to be made use of against them, which may be used against any others that seek to destroy in general the Liberties of their Neighbours. Nor do we believe that the Directions which we have in Scripture for Patience under Persecution, are to be extended further than so as to be reckon'd to oblige Subjects to the practice of it, when their Princes abuse their Authority and Power to impose upon them a Religion which they cannot in Conscience receive.

§6. That which we call the *Ecclesiastical* Toleration, is, when those who differ about some Points of Religion do notwithstanding this hold each other for Members of the same particular Church, and maintain Communion with one another, and especially come together to the Lord's Supper, which is wont to be accounted the principal Test of Concord among Christians. For as it is not every Errour in Religion that does directly, or by consequence, subvert the Foundation of the Faith; so it is not for every Errour that any Man should be cast out from the Communion of a particular Church, nor for every Errour in a Church has a Man sufficient Cause to withdraw and separate himself from it. It is evident that in the Primitive Church some of the Men, whose Writings still remain, did receive some Erroneous Opinions who yet were not, that we find, excluded for them from the Churches to which they belong'd. And certainly it was altogether an intemperate Zeal which drove from Communion those who would observe their *Easter* upon the 14th Day of the Month, forasmuch as that Matter did not concern any Article of Faith. And if we may profess the Truth, their Opinion who thought fit to do so was more agreeing to Reason, and the common receiv'd Custom of those who observe the Commemorations of any particular Transactions, than that which afterwards came to obtain in the Church. But also among the modern Parties of Christians we may observe, that they who do differ from others not in a few Things, and they who differ in Opinion not only from particular Persons, but from whole Congregations, are not for all this cast out from the Communion of their Churches, nor do they separate and divide themselves from such Communion.

§7. The Reconcilement of differences in Religion can by no means be so done, as to have it declar'd that both are Truth, forasmuch as it is necessary from the Nature of Things, that in a Contradiction between Two Propositions one or other of them must needs be false. But to effect a Reconcilement in this Case, one Opinion must of necessity be declar'd and approv'd for Truth, and the other be rejected as false. Nor further, is a Reconciliation to be made by bringing all Parties to account that all Religions are alike useful, and effectual towards the Salvation

Or Ecclesiastical.

Of the Reconciliation of differing Opinions.

of Men; or by a Declaration that this may be attain'd in any Religion which bears the Name of Christian. For this were to make the Christian Religion altogether Irrational, and a Discipline not rightly cohering with it self, but a Mass of Principles disagreeing with, and mutually destroying each other. Nor is it a fit Method of composing Differences to declare that the Opinions about which the Parties differ are only Problematical, and such as that it concerns not any Man's Salvation to which Part of the Contradiction he gives his assent. For although within the whole Body of Divinity there may be many Questions handled, which a Man without any damage might be Ignorant of, or such as that it matters not to which Part he gives his assent; and that because in the Sacred Writings themselves many Things are deliver'd, which are not precisely necessary to Salvation, or because the Professors of Divinity have with more niceness and subtilty handled some Points of Christian Religion than were necessary to the plainness and simplicity of a saving Faith; yet we must not think it an Arbitrary thing, or what depends upon the Will of Man, that a Question be declar'd Problematical and Indifferent: But every thing must be tried to the Foundation, that it may manifestly appear whether it does necessarily belong to the Essence of the Faith or not. That we may obtain a compleat Reconciliation of Differences in Religion, it is necessary therefore, that after the controverted Opinions are searched to the Foundation, and the truth of the one, and the falshood of the other, are plainly demonstrated from the genuine Books of holy Scripture; they who have heretofore held a false Opinion do Renounce this, and yield to, and embrace the Truth. But alas, a perfect Reconciliation of this sort, such as that they who have hitherto cherish'd and maintain'd erroneous Opinions, should abandon these, and agree with others in the Truth, considering the present State and Manners of Mankind, is a thing rather to be desir'd, than it can be hoped to be accomplish'd. Not for that 'tis impossible in the Nature of the thing, that the Truth should be established, or Errour discover'd and confuted: But by reason of the Obstinacy of Prejudices, which have taken possession of Mens Minds from their Childhood; and because of the Pride of Humane Nature, which disdains that others should seem wiser than ourselves, and will perti-

naciously retain Opinions once receiv'd, even out of hatred to those
that believe otherwise, especially if it be so that they who differ from
us may be safely despised. If therefore any one should attempt such a
Reconciliation of the Differences he would certainly bestow his Labour
in Vain, and expose himself to contempt. And if it shall ever please
God to heal the Breaches of the Church, and to Bless it with a perfect
Union, which is the thing many do suppose may be expected from
some Prophecies in the Sacred Writings, concerning a happy and flourishing State of the Church, which are not yet fulfill'd, he will certainly
put another sort of Disposition into the Minds of Men, and such as
will be fit to produce such an end, and that by some great Revolution
which shall altogether change the State of Humane Affairs. But there
is no appearance of any such thing at present, nor is it within the reach
of Humane Foresight; tho' 'tis very possible and easie to Almighty God
to make Way for it by very small and seemingly inconsiderable Things.
In my Opinion therefore for the present there is nothing else that
remains to be done in this Case, but to propose a *Reconcilement* mixed
with a *Toleration*. And that I think should be thus order'd, that in the
first Place on both sides there should be an Agreement in a solid,
sufficient, and adequate, Foundation of Faith, or that those Articles of
Faith should be clearly defin'd and agreed upon which are so necessary
to Salvation, as that they ought neither to be unknown to any Man,
or deny'd by any one, nor wrested and drawn into a diverse Sense and
Meaning. And that with relation to other Opinions, which do not
come within the compass of the Foundation of the Faith, and in which
if a Man does err, his Errour would not so much as indirectly destroy
the Foundation, in these a Toleration should be granted; and for the
sake of them no Man should be cast out from the Communion of any
Church, or withdraw and separate himself from it, nor should any
form a distinct and separate Communion for the sake of them. For it
may so come to pass that an Errour which is not in its own Nature
prejudicial to Salvation, may yet be so by some other Way. As for
instance, if a Man should obstinately deny any Point whatever, which
is manifestly contain'd in the Sacred Writings, and upon that account
charge those Writings with falshood, and deny their Authority, by

which he would subvert the very Foundation of the Christian Faith, which is built and depends upon the infallible Truth of those Writings. But it is another, and a very different thing from this, to deny a Doctrine deliver'd in the Sacred Writings, as believing that another Sence ought to be put upon those Places from whence it is said to be deriv'd. For in this Case the Authority of the Scriptures remains untouch'd, and only the true Sence of this or that Passage in them is disputed. On the other Hand, if a true Faith about the Fundamental Articles, other Requisites being added, is sufficient to Salvation, and to render a Man a true Member of Jesus Christ, why may not the same thing suffice among Men to make them exercise a brotherly Charity to each other, and live together in the same Communion? Provided there be nothing in a Man's outward Appearance, and which the Sences can observe, that should hinder them from receiving him into external Communion, who cannot see into his Heart, nor know the Faith which he has there. See 1 *Cor.* 3:11, 12, 13, 14, 15. And what has been commented upon that Text by *Georgius Calixtus* in his literal Exposition upon that Epistle.[4]

The Dissention is either about Principles or Emoluments.

§8. But in this Affair it must be well observ'd, whether or no the Dissention is concern'd about meer Opinions or Principles, or whether the disagreeing Parties have no other Cause of their Disagreement but this, that they differently explain certain Places of Holy Scripture, and are not willing to depart from the Opinion they have espoused, or that they are govern'd entirely by the desire of defending the Truth: Or, because they fear a Diminution of their Authority and Esteem, if they should seem to have hitherto maintain'd an Errour, or do out of Envy or Pride disdain to embrace the Opinion of another; or else, if there be not a Contention really about some worldly Advantages, while different Principles are pretended to; such as are for Instance, Rule, and

4. Pufendorf refers here and in other sections of this work to the Commentary on the Epistles of the Apostle St. Paul (*In Acta Apostolorum Expositio Litteralis...*), which the Lutheran theologian Georgius Calixtus (1586–1656) published in 1654. Calixtus is well known for his efforts to unite the Protestant and Roman Catholic Churches.

Authority, and Riches. And so it must be consider'd, whether or no the Principles that are contended for may not be defended as serviceable to those Advantages, and the contrary Opinions may not be such as tend to overthrow them. The Controversies of the former Sort, which are about meer Principles, tho' they also cannot, but with difficulty, be ended, by reason of the Pride and Obstinacy of Humane Nature, and the Aversation to the Disparagement of being thought to have been in an Errour; which Vice is found especially in many of the Priests, and Men of the School, and such as have not had their Minds subdued to the Management of Business and Affairs of the World; yet are they not so insuperable as those wherein any considerable Advantages are con-cern'd, and in which the Contention is for the *God, their Belly*. And it is manifest by Experience, that the Controversies of the former Kind are in process of Time gradually mitigated and allay'd, and at length do entirely vanish. So long as the first Authors of those Controversies survive, or those who value themselves highly upon the Defence of them, these Men for the most part will stiffly contend to maintain the Opinions which they have once advanced, nor will they admit of any thing that should lessen their Authority. But when these Men are gone off the Stage, those that come after, tho' they continue in the same Sect or Party, yet they do not so eagerly contend for their Opinion, nor with so much Prejudice reject the Reasons of the Adverse Party, unless by chance any of them should propose to make themselves em-inent and considerable in that Contention. And that Fervour is the rather lessen'd in Process of Time, because fresh Contentions for the most Part are carried on with the greatest Vehemency, old ones of themselves grow out of use: When Men disdain to employ themselves about those Matters which have been so long and so fully examin'd, as that there is nothing more to be done in them, by which they can hope to make themselves famous or considerable.

§9. Further, the Controversies of this sort, and all others, so far as they only concern Opinions, we suppose may be so throughly examin'd, that they who are not overcome with Prejudice may clearly discern on which Side the Truth lyes, and who do by meer Obstinacy defend themselves with Sophistry, as not being asham'd to retain those Prin-

The Contro-versies about meer Princi-ples may be entirely decided.

ciples which have over and over been prov'd false. For when there is an infallible Rule from which a Judgment may be made, such as the Holy Scripture is in Controversies of Divinity, it must needs be that the Controversies relating to that may at length find an end. And no less possible is it that the Genuine Sense of Scripture be perfectly found out, from whence the Decision of Controversies must proceed, if due Means and Helps of interpreting them be made use of. But if there be any Question which cannot have its Decision from Holy Scripture, that may justly be look'd upon as Problematical, and as not belonging to the Foundation of the Faith, and as what may be assented to on either Side, without any Prejudice to Salvation. Tho' it were certainly much better if all such superfluous Questions, which are fit only to create Disputes and Contentions, were altogether banish'd from the Body of Divinity. Nevertheless it is a thing which we have clearly observ'd, both in the Histories of ancient and latter Times, that there is but little Success to be expected towards the reconciling of Differences in Religion from appointed Conferences between the Divines of different Perswasions. Not only because when they grow warm with Dispute, they do often inconsiderately utter some things which cherish the Strife, and give new Occasions of exasperating one another. But also because the Result of such Conferences commonly follows a Flood of Eloquence, the Volubility of the Tongue, the Craft of Disputing, and a ready Sharpness of Wit; by which Arts they oftentimes prevail, who yet have not the Truth on their Side. Which Inconvenience does also attend Councils, in which Factions oftentimes, and ill Arts, have an Influence, and Votes prevail rather by Number commonly than by Weight. But if any thing worth while of this sort were to be done, it seems to me that it could no Ways be more likely to have a good Success than if there were an Assembly constituted of such a Form, as is often agreed upon between several Princes: That is, that if any Debate arises among them, there should be Commissioners of an equal Number, chosen out of both the Parties, who after a mature Consideration of the Matter committed to them, may consent into a Conclusion, form'd rather after the Manner of an Agreement, than of a Decree of a Majority of Votes. And this Assembly ought to consist not only of Priests or Professors of Divinity, but there ought to be join'd with them some other Men, eminent for Piety and Prudence, who are also well furnish'd with a solid Knowledge of Divinity, and who are moderate Men, and skilful in the Management of Affairs. And this not only because such may be necessary to allay and temper the Fervour and Zeal with which the others are apt to manage such Matters; but also because by Divine Right, and by the Nature of the Kingdom of Christ, the Judgment in Matters of Faith does not belong to the Ministry alone, but to the whole Church; which would betray its own Right, if it should relinquish the Exercise of it to one Order alone, and would her self give Occasion to the Abuses which would certainly follow from thence. Therefore to such an Assembly there ought to be added not only some of the Ministers, and Counsellors of State, but also some chosen out of the third Order, who should represent their Persons, and maintain their Rights. If some of the most learned Divines, chosen out of both Sides, were set to debate in writing before such an Assembly one Point of the Controversie after another, order'd in a clear and well-digested Method, as is wont to be done in Judiciary Proceedings, and the Assembly were to moderate and govern the whole Process of the Dispute, that it might not wander from the true and right Subject of it, but be kept close to a right State of the Controversie, the Fruit of this would certainly be, that the Reproaches and false Accusations made by the Parties against each other before, would be condemn'd and remov'd. And thus it would be manifest in what Things the differing Parties do truly agree, and in what the Difference between them does still remain. *Lastly,* If a Controversie were in this manner manag'd, it is not possible but they who have any Measure of the Knowledge of Divinity, and who are not biass'd by Affection and Prejudice, must needs see which Side has the better in the Dispute. And altho' it should so happen, that they who came thus to be Convinced, and put to Silence, should by Obstinacy of Mind shut their Eyes against the Light, yet would not such a Dispute be altogether without Fruit, and they notwithstanding would be held convicted of Errour. So *Mat.* 22:34. 'tis said our Saviour *put the Sadducees to Silence,* tho' 'tis not said that they had the Grace to acknowledge the Truth that was shown them.

The Contro-
versies which
concern
Emoluments
seem to be
irreconcileable.

§10. But where there are some valued Advantages of this World annexed to the controverted Points of Religion, or where any Principles
are invented or fitted to preserve Power, or acquire Wealth, it is not to
be imagin'd they can be ended by Disputes or Reasonings: Especially
among those whose Interests are peculiarly concern'd; unless some singular Mutation of the State of Things should come to pass, which
should by meer Force and Violence put an end to them. No one can
be ignorant how obstinately Men will contend to gain, or to preserve,
Dominion and Rule, for which they account it glorious to do so, even
to the Death. And in Truth, the Belly is a thing that has no Ears, and
it were manifestly in vain to go about to pacifie that with Subtil Reasons
and Flowers of Eloquence. That rich young Man therefore whom our
Saviour order'd to sell all that he had, and give to the Poor, and come
and follow him, went away sad, as unwilling to embrace Poverty, that
he might become a Disciple of Christ. From whence our Saviour took
occasion to pronounce this as a Maxim generally true, that 'tis *easier
for a Camel to go through the Eye of a Needle, than for a rich Man to
enter into the Kingdom of God, Mat.* 19:21, 22, 24. But since the Points
in Controversie between the Protestants and Papists do chiefly concern
the Establishment and Support of the Authority, Power and Revenues,
of the Hierarchy or Pontifical Monarchy, it is manifest that it would
be utterly in vain, and but ridiculous, to go about the determining of
them by Disputation. Indeed, to demonstrate solidly and plainly the
Falshood of the Popish Principles may be of use to establish and confirm those of the Protestant Party, and to keep them from returning
again to those Errours. And sometimes a particular Person may be
dispos'd thereby to renounce the Roman Religion, and join himself to
the Protestants. But there is no reason to hope that a Considerable,
much less an Universal, Reconcilement can that Way be accomplisht.
For the Attempt would be like that of endeavouring in any Kingdom
to perswade by Eloquence, and Philosophick Reasonings, those who
are in Possession of the Government to lay aside their Authority, and
cast away the Wealth which helps to support it, and all the State and
Pomp which gives it Reverence and Awe among the Vulgar, and to put
themselves into a private Condition, and be contented to associate

themselves with the meanest of the People in a Democratical Equality; as in *Tacitus* it is mention'd as a Jest of *Tiberius,* when he made a Motion concerning restoring the Commonwealth.[5] On the contrary, if such a Debate as this should be set on foot, the Protestants would have nothing else to do, but to throw away the Liberty they have gain'd, and again to put their Necks under the Yoke of the See of *Rome.* For between him who pretends to a Dominion over others, and them who have withdrawn themselves from Subjection to him, there is no way left of Reconciliation, but either he must renounce his Pretences to a Right of Dominion over them, or they must again come under their former Yoke. For the obtaining of which certainly no sufficient Reasons can ever be found out which can generally prevail, or bring all Men to consent to, and embrace again, those Opinions which have been serviceable to establish and enrich that Sacerdotal Dominion. Tho' for the gaining some particular Persons there may not be wanting some Arguments from their Profit: As for instance, if a Man has Hopes, by uniting himself to that Party, to come to have a Share in the Advantages of the Hierarchy, or to get some Ecclesiastical Dignities, or Fat Benefices, or to obtain with a Popish Prince such Honours and Offices as a Protestant one has not to bestow; which Arguments however can be of Force but only with the younger Sons of Princes, or those who are thrust out of their Dominions, or with private Persons. For 'tis so much the Interest of Princes, who are in Possession of Dominion and Rule, to retain the Liberty gotten, by withdrawing from a Subjection to the Hierarchy, that those who are not beside themselves can never be so foolish as to throw away a Prerogative of that importance for nothing; nor unless they can hope by such a Change of Religion to gain a Dominion of more Worth and Value than that which they are already possess'd of. As *Henry* the IV. did so to gain the Kingdom of *France,*[6]

---

5. The reign of Tiberius is described in P. Cornelius Tacitus, *The Annals,* book 1.

6. Henry IV (1553–1610), King of France and Navarre, was the leader of the Huguenots during the religious wars of the sixteenth century. To establish himself on the French throne, Henry renounced his Calvinism for Catholicism in 1593, saying, according to legend, "Paris vaut bien une messe." In 1598 he issued the Edict

and *Sigismund* King of *Sueden* reconcil'd himself to the Romish Religion, that he might possess the Kingdom of *Poland,* together with that of *Sueden,* tho' he for this Reason lost his Hereditary Kingdom.[7] Humane Reason therefore can conceive no other Way of destroying that Dominion of the Priests, and to take away the Opinions on which it is founded, but that the Princes, and other Soveraign Powers, who have that Hierarchy mixed with their Dominion, to the manifest Prejudice of it, do resolve to shake off that Yoke, and claim the Rights which are withheld from them by it; and that they put an End to those Methods of raising the Revenues of the Hierarchy, by which their State is reduced even to the Condition of Tributary. This being done, that vast Machine which is built upon Props that are utterly repugnant to sound Reason, and true Politicks, would fall of it self; and the huge Beast, when its Nourishment were taken away, would grow lean, and die. For where Princes and Free States are possess'd of a solid Knowledge of the true and genuine Doctrines of Christianity, there is nothing more easie for them, if they will, than to despise the King of that Religion, and withdraw themselves from his Dominion. Which is a thing that the last Age has given illustrious Proofs and Presidents of. See *Rev.* 17:16, 17. To which Place I cannot forbear to add the Discourse which Ishmael Bullialdus[8] held with my Brother Esaias Pufendorf, in the Year 1669, at *Paris,* at the time when the Pope suppress'd some Orders that the Venetians might make use of their Revenues in the Turkish War.[9] *The*

---

of Nantes, granting toleration to the Huguenots. In 1685 Louis XIV revoked the edict.

7. See note 2.

8. Ismael Boulliau (1605–94).

9. In 1668 Pope Clement IX issued a bull by which he suppressed the fourteenth-century orders of the Jesuats and of the Hieronymites and placed their possessions at the disposal of the Holy See. It is most likely that the pope wished to use the financial means in support of Venice. Venice was at war (1645–99) with the Turks for Candia, on the island of Crete, which had been in the possession of Venice for centuries. Pufendorf provided a new edition of the bull, which he published together with his commentary. He used the bull to legitimize Protestant demands to secularize possessions of the Church. For more details, see the introduction to Pufendorf's commentary on the bull in Samuel von Pufendorf, *Kleine Vorträge und*

Venetians, said he, have raised M. CCM. Crowns from the Revenues of
Three Orders of Canons Regulars, who were suppress'd by the Pope. The
greatest of which Revenues fell into the Hands of Secular Persons against
the Pope's Will. For the Venetians judg'd it useful to the strengthening of
the State that these Revenues should come into Secular Hands; because the
Ecclesiasticks, while they possess'd them, contributed nothing towards the
Preservation of the Commonwealth. The Council of Milan *did better yet*
than the Venetians; and because their Dukes had in former Times endow'd
those Orders, they thought fit, when the Foundations were taken away by
the Pope, that the Revenues of them should of right return to the Desmeans
of the Duke. This was therefore a thing very imprudently done of the Pope,
and gave a very bad Example; for Princes might hereby be induced to
attempt the same thing, and to spoil the Church of all its Revenues; which
being taken away, Christianity it self would be in the greatest Danger. For
as Things now stand, the Temporalities of the Pope cannot be taken away,
but the Spiritualities will fall too; for as much as it has pleased the Bishops
to join an Earthly Government to a Spiritual Jurisdiction, which whether
it were well done or not, he would not dispute. But however, he believ'd
that all the Authority of the Pope at this time does depend upon the Tem-
poral Power; of which he can be no sooner depriv'd, but he will be the
Contempt of every Prince, and Kings themselves within their own Domin-
ions will exercise the Offices of the Pope. Thus did he then discourse; and
if we would express the whole State of the Case, in a Word, it must
be said of the Popish Clergy, that their *Belly is their God, Phil.* 3:19.
But that the Belly wants Ears is a known Proverb, and for that Reason
'tis very superfluous and vain to use Arguments against it.

§11. There is moreover another thing to be observ'd concerning the
Diversities of Religion: Which is, that many of them are satisfied with
the discharging of several External Rites and Performances, which may
be done without any inward Amendment and Sanctity of Mind; but
this nevertheless is that which God chiefly requires in the true Worship

Of solid and superficial Religion.

Schriften. Texte zu Geschichte, Pädagogik, Philosophie, Kirche und Völkerrecht, ed.
Detlef Döring (Frankfurt/Main: Vittorio Klostermann, 1995), 218–33.

of him. And that we may judge to have come to pass by this Means. They to whom God has reveal'd the true Religion, suffering themselves to be overcome with Sloth and Lukewarmness, have come to think it a Task too hard for them to refrain their Lusts, and conquer their Vices, and so at length have fallen to acquiesce in External Rites, and to devise such a Religion as would give them Leave to indulge their wicked Inclinations, and to think themselves at the same time in Favour with God. And all those who have invented a Religion for themselves, have agreed in this to reduce all Religion almost to some External Actions and Performances, and such as may be most exactly done by the most wicked Men. As it is indeed an impossible thing that Humane Wit, without Divine Revelation, should frame a Religion that would purifie the Mind. We may therefore in general divide Religion into that which is *Solid,* and that which is *Superficial* or Theatrical. Certainly if all the invented Religions, both Ancient and Modern, be examin'd, it would appear they may be referr'd to the Superficial sort, which for the most part are comprehended in certain Rites: And if there be some Sprinklings of Morality join'd with them, they are not enough to purge the Mind of Man from its inward Wickedness. But he who peruses the Sacred Writings shall easily see that 'tis the perpetual Endeavour and Design of the Divine Spirit to root out of the Minds of Men that Opinion, that any External Actions whatsoever are a sufficient Worship of God, unless there be join'd with them an inward Purity of Mind. And altho' the Divine Wisdome thought fit to bind the Israelitish Nation to a laborious Yoke of Ceremonies, and especially to possess their Minds by their Sacrifices with the future expiation of the World to be perform'd by the Messiah: Yet when they stopp'd at the meer External Rites of Religion, and growing forgetful of the Messiah, thought to expiate their Guilt by their Sacrifices, and that the lives of them should serve instead of, and excuse their own, and so had turn'd the whole Levitical Worship into a Form of superficial Religion; God frequently reprov'd this Errour by his Prophets and let them know, that they must not think the Observance of any External Rites would satisfie for the Neglects of the Moral Law. See 1 *Sam.* 15:22. *Psal.* 50:8, &c. *Isa.* 1:11. &c. 9:13. *Jer.* 6:20. *Amos.* 5:21, &c. *Micah* 6:6, 7, 8. and many other Places. So also our Saviour had the greatest Contention with the Jews of his time upon this Ground; who had turn'd the Religion deliver'd to them from God almost into a meer superficial one. See *Mat.* 5:20, &c. 6:1, 18. 15:1, 20. 23:3, 28. *Mark* 7:1, 23. *Luke* 11:38, 47. 14:23. 17:20, 21. From this superficial Religion the Papists have deriv'd and borrow'd many Things: Who have dress'd up the Simplicity of Genuine Christian Religion with an infinite Multitude of Ceremonies, which engage the Senses, but have no Efficacy towards purifying of the Heart. It shall suffice, for instance, to mention only the vain Repetitions of Prayers, which for the most part are not understood, and come only from the Lips; a thing expressly forbidden by our Saviour, *Mat.* 6:7. Which Prayers it is their manner to number by the Beads of their *Rosary.* For which Purpose, as a late French Writer says,[10] the Women of Quality in *Spain* carry *Rosaries,* or their String of Beads, reaching almost to the Ground, by which they recite their Prayers without end, as they walk in the Streets, as they play at Cards, as they are in Discourse with others, even while they are carrying on their Amours, are telling any manner of Lies, and are traducing their Neighbours. In whatever Companies they are, you shall observe them continually muttering something with the dropping of their Beads. To the same Rank we may place all the Intercessions, and the Merits of those alive or dead (the Merits of our Saviour only excepted) which are said to be applied to others for the Expiation of their Sins. And also that by a Confession of Sins made to a Priest, and the Penance enjoin'd by him, this Remission may be obtain'd. For 'tis thought a light Matter with a great many, that by the Shame of Confession, and the Burden of a Satisfaction impos'd by the Priest, they can atone for the Liberty of sinning as they desire. And the whole Matter of Indulgences belongs to this superficial Religion, by vertue of which sometimes very easie and light Works can obtain the Remission of Sins for many Ages. Especially is that horrid Abuse of numerous Masses to be reckon'd a

---

10. Marie-Catherine Le Jumel de Berneville, comtesse d'Aulnoy (c. 1650–1705), French author of historical fiction. The reference here is presumably to *Mémoires de la cour d'Espagne* (1690) or *Relation du voyage en Espagne* (1690).

principal Instrument of a superficial Religion, which has proceeded so far, that if a Man has thro' his whole Life wallowed in all manner of Wickedness, yet he may after his Death be purg'd of all, and gain the Eternal Happiness, which is the Reward of good living, by vertue of Masses said for his Soul. This is indeed the Golden Harvest of the Priests. Concerning these I cannot forbear to add what a late French Writer relates in his Itinerary in *Spain*. A certain Person (*says he*) of great Birth, but of a shatter'd Fortune, would not omit, upon the Approach of his Death, notwithstanding the Disadvantages of his Estate, to order that there should be 15000 Masses said for his Soul. And this his last Will was so punctually executed, that till the Money requisite for so many Masses was rais'd, none of his Creditors could be paid any of the Debts he ow'd them, tho' they were never so fairly prov'd. Whence 'tis, as a Proverb said of such in *Spain*, That he or she have made their Soul their Heir; which is said of them who leave their Estate to the Church to be pray'd for when they are dead. The Will of *Philip* IV. King of *Spain*, is very remarkable, by which he order'd that 100000 Masses should be said on his Account; but so, that if so many should not be necessary to himself, then they should redound to the Advantage of his Father and Mother; but if they were in Heaven already, they should be applied to the Souls of those who should die in the Spanish Wars. I must add further, the vile marketing of these Masses, which was practised by a certain Man at *Vienna*, at the Time when the Nobility of *Hungary* were put to Death for their Rebellion against the Emperor *Leopold*;[11] their Estates being sold, it was as a Specimen of Clemency granted, that out of what they yielded, a sufficient Sum should be given for the Purchase of many Thousand Masses for their Souls; but because a single Mass at *Vienna* is wont to cost almost Half a Crown, the Man whom I have mention'd, whose

---

11. Under Leopold I (1640–1705; emperor from 1658, a fierce anti-Protestant) the German empire had prolonged wars with the Ottoman Empire (Turkey) in the east and King Louis XIV's France in the west. A revolt in Hungary against Hapsburg rule was supported by the Ottomans, who besieged Vienna in 1683 but were thrown back by Leopold.

Name was Triangle, dealt with those who had the Execution of this Order committed to them, that they should resign the Care of providing these Masses to him, which he would procure to be said in *Italy*, where for the Eighth Part of a Crown a Mass may be purchas'd; for the Efficacy of them would be the force in what Part of the Earth soever they should be said. So the Executors themselves made some Gain of the Bargain; but the greatest Advantage remain'd to him that form'd the Affair, who got an Hundred Thousand Crowns to his Share, and so is said to have obtain'd the Title of a Baron; so I suppose for his great Merits of the Commonwealth, and because he has given great Light to that Text, *Rev.* 18:15. and has shewn us who may be understood by them who make Merchandize of the Souls of Men. We know well enough that they pretend to teach, that who so would be benefited by a Mass said for him, he must depart this Life in Grace and Penance. But that Doctrine is restrain'd by so many Limitations and Exceptions, that there is hardly any thing requir'd to that Penance but one or other small Ceremony, which conduces nothing to the Cleansing and Reformation of the Mind. But all these Things, and many more to the same Purpose, will abundantly appear to any one that considers with a little Care the whole Frame of the Romish Religion.

§12. From these Things it is easie to collect, that those who have busied themselves about reconciling the Differences in Religion, by reason that they did not observe the Difference between meer Principles, and the Emoluments of the Hierarchy, and between the Things Solid and Superficial, have not taken a reasonable Course, nor have been able to do any thing that was worth their Labour. And thus have all these lost their Labour, and such are still likely to do so, who have endeavour'd a compounding of Matters between the Protestants and Papists, so as that something being yeilded on both Sides, the Protestants should again come into the Communion of the Papists. For he that considers well the Frame of the Popish Religion will easily see that the Papists can yeild nothing, at least for this Reason, because they cannot do it without acknowledging they have been in an Errour. Forasmuch as the Infallibility of the Pope and of the Church is a chief

It is vain to attempt a Reconcilement between the Protestants and Papists.

Corner-stone upon which their State depends, and this being away, the whole Building will fall to the Ground. And if all those Doctrines of the Roman Church, which belong to the Superficial Religion, and are invented for the raising of Revenues should be taken away, in a little time the greatest part of the numerous Clergy of that Church would be famish'd. But neither can it be expedient to the Papal Kingdom to be reconcil'd with the Protestants upon this Condition, that the Protestants shall have their Churches distinct, and no Ways depending upon the See of *Rome,* and that there shall be Friendship maintain'd between them without Subjection. For in this Way the great Secret of State in the Roman Dominion would be betray'd by themselves: Which is, that only the Roman Communion, which acknowledges the Pope for the Head of it, is the true Church; and thus they must be brought to acknowledge that there are other true Churches which are not subordinate to that of *Rome.* Since therefore there is no way left of making a Reconciliation between these Two Parties, unless the Protestants would again submit themselves to the See of *Rome,* and retract all that they have said hitherto against such Submission, which they cannot do either in Conscience, or according to the State which they are now in, it must be concluded, that an Ecclesiastical Concord between the Protestants and Papists is morally impossible, and so, that *Rome* is altogether irreconcileable. And if any of the Papal Party should propose, in order to a Reconcilement, that there should be nothing said about restoring the Revenues of the Church to those who return to the Roman Religion, we ought to beware of them, and to believe, that nothing but meer Shows and Snares are intended in such Proposals, and they are made to bring again under the Yoke such whom they can catch in their Net. And it is also very manifest that those Divines do not well consult the Interests of the Princes of *Germany,* who diminish and alleviate the Controversies with the Papists, as if they were such as might without any great Difficulty be compos'd. For when some of those Princes would wish there could be a Way open'd, by which their numerous Offspring might share the Dignities and Benefices of the Church, which is quite obstructed by the Protestant

Religion, they might be very apt to entertain a Desire of returning to the Roman Religion, if they were perswaded that there is no great Difference between that of the Protestants and it. And tho' the Heads of the Families should account it Foolish to lose Part of their Dominion to become again the Slaves of the Priests, yet if the Younger Sons should change their Religion, when in process of Time these might succeed to the Dominion by the Extinction of the Elder Family, their Provinces must come under the same Danger.

§13. For the better Illustration and Proof of these Things, I shall not unwillingly examine a certain Form in Manuscript, of *a Method to restore an Ecclesiastical Union between the Romanists and the Protestants, written by the special command of the most Serene Prince and Lord N. N. by Two of his Highness's Divines,*[12] which I shall here produce, with Observations here and there upon it, but not with any design to detract from them, or to condemn their Intention, which I suppose not to have been Evil, but only with a desire of serving the Truth.

An Examen of a certain Form of a Reconciliation between the Protestants and Papists.

(§1.) *The Protestants freely acknowledge and confess that an Ecclesiastical Union and Peace between the Romanists and them is among those Things which are possible, and is what in some respect ought to be, and so is a matter of Precept. Tho' they do not determine that it is simply a Precept, so as that we are absolutely oblig'd to make or keep such a Peace but upon Condition that it may be, and as far as in us lyes. This appears by those Words of the Apostle, if it be possible, as much as in you lyes live peaceably with all Men,* Rom. 12:18. *If this cannot be accomplish'd unless against our Consciences, we will call Darkness Light, then that other Expression of the Apostle must take Place, What Communion has Light with Darkness?* 2 Cor. 6:14. *Then a disagreement which is risen for the sake of Piety is better than a vitious Concord. They are the Words of* Greg. Nazianz. Orat. 1. d. Pace.[13]

12. See section IV of the Introduction.

13. *Oration* 1 on peace by Gregory of Nazianzus (c. 325–89). This Doctor of the Church is recognized as one of the foremost orators of the ancient church. In 380

We on the contrary believe this Ecclesiastical Peace of the Protestants with the Romanists, to be no ways due, but rather to be forbidden; since at least the far greater Part of the Protestants do believe the Papal Empire to be that Apocalyptical Beast, whose Tiranny by the great Favour of God they have thrown off, and from which they with the People also, that are yet oppress'd by it, would free themselves. And there is no Man but must acknowledge it a thing morally Impossible who will consider what we have lately said, and the very Nature of the Papal Monarchy. The Expression of the Apostle concerns a Civil Peace, which we may justly Maintain with them; and we may readily yield all the good Offices of a Civil Friendship to those who are still addicted to the Romish Religion: And a Civil Toleration may be indulg'd to the Exercise of that Religion, where according to Covenant, or for other weighty Considerations, it cannot be remov'd.

(§2.) *And as the Protestants in the* Augustan *Confession it self, offer'd to* Caesar, *did profess that they were forward and ready for a Peace and Union with the Church of* Rome, *so far as this might be pleasing to God, and agreeing with a good Conscience:*[14] *So also to this Day they offer themselves to do all those Things towards it which can be done by them holding still the Faith, and a good Conscience.*

But this Condition is Morally impossible: For it must be requir'd, that the Romanists do approve the Doctrines in which the Protestants have differ'd from them, and that they do profess the same Principles: And also, that the Pope do not pretend to exercise his Dominion over their Churches, nor endeavour to impose the Abuses of the Church of *Rome* upon them. Without this Condition no Man of the Protestants can think an Union with the Papists may be embrac'd, unless he can

---

Gregory was appointed bishop of Constantinople, where he held the oration about peace. The following year he presided at the Council of Constantinople, which confirmed the orthodox Trinitarian position of the earlier Council of Nicea against the Arians.

14. The "Augustan," or Augsburg, Confession of faith (1530) was designed to be relatively open to the Roman Catholic Church and to other reformed but non-Lutheran parties. It failed in that design but has remained the Lutheran confession of faith.

think fit to approve of Samaritanism. But to think that the Pope will ever consent to any such Condition is directly foolish.

(§3.) *Altho' between those who adore one God the Father, Son and Holy Ghost, and one Redeemer, Saviour and Mediatour between God and Man, the only begotten Son of the Eternal Father, and do acknowledge him to be the Man Jesus Christ, and worship him, and so do agree in the Mystery of Three Persons in the One Divine Essence, and of the Son of God incarnate, and believe that he suffer'd to expiate our Sins, that he died and rose again from the dead, and was carried up into Heaven; who agree to believe the Creation of the World, the Resurrection of the dead, the last Judgment; and that the Sacrament of Baptism ought, without neglect, to be afforded to Infants; and that a new Obedience to the Divine Law must be perform'd by those that are Born again. Tho' I say, between such, in whatever visible Communion they live, there is a vertual, if not an actual, Communion, which lyes in the serious Desire, and affectionate Wish, and Endeavour, of restoring and frequenting one and the same Communion; because in the mean time they are hindred from this by several great Obstacles that lye in the Way, they ought to endeavour with all their might that those grievous Obstacles, which have hitherto caused or maintain'd the Schism, may be remov'd.*

The Articles here recited, tho' they take in no small Part of Christian Religion, yet they may, by the Addition of some others to them which are Erroneous, be so wrested, as that their saving Effects may be intercepted. Just as the best Food in it self may be so corrupted, being mixed with an absurd Sauce, or nastily order'd, that it may be no longer grateful or wholesome. And as in a Commonwealth which has degenerated from a lawful Government into a Tiranny, there may remain several Footsteps of the old Institutions, and Words and Terms may be in use which did belong to them, tho' the Genius and Nature of the Dominion be deprav'd: So in the Roman Church, which is degenerated from its Primitive Purity, by unobserv'd Degrees, into a most pestilent Sink of Superstitions, yet there must be retain'd many Articles of Christian Religion; for otherwise there could not an Ecclesiastical Dominion ever have had Place in it; that is, such as should exert its Influence under the colour and presence of Christianity. But yet we

ought not to have at all the less Aversion to the Pontifical Dominion
for the sake of those Articles; which, as no Man is bound to put himself
under, so neither can he be bound to have it in his Wish or Inclination
that he may ever be united to that Church; nor therefore, that the
Protestant Churches, which have separated themselves from it, should
again associate with it as before, and concur to constitute one Body
with the Roman Church under the Dominion of the Pope of *Rome.*
Therefore is that vertual Union mention'd an empty Fiction; forasmuch as we ought to Wish that they who are yet under the oppression
of the Papal Dominion would come over to us, and the great Obstacles
of Union might be remov'd; which do not lye in a meer Dissention
upon some Points of belief, but that which is to be accounted a Principal one among them is that Dominion brought into the Church, and
supported with so many Superstitions, and false Opinions, and which
is indeed intolerable, and deserving the detestation of all Christians;
certainly where the Dissention is about Rule and Liberty, there cannot,
on either side, be any other Wish but that one Part might be brought
under the Dominion of the other, since none could ever bear con-
tentedly the Diminution or Division of Empire. For the Foundation
of the Papal Kingdom is the Infallibility of the Pope and Church of
Rome, which being taken away, the whole Kingdom tumbles. But if
the Protestants acknowledge this, they at one Blow destroy their own
Cause, and have nothing to say why they should not return to their
former Slavery.

(§4.) *But since it is of no small Importance that both Parties do simply
and ingenuously Profess that which is their Opinion, and do not endeavour
to impose upon each other by obscure or ambiguous Expressions; the Protestants must propose the Sence of their Minds about this pacifick Affair
sincerely, and without any disguise, as determining that it is not only
expedient, but necessary, that they do propose all the Fundamental Truths
to the Dissenting Party very clearly. And it must be desir'd of that Party
that they do put away all those Errours, which are repugnant thereto very
expressly, and that they would profess with the Mouth unto Salvation that
heavenly Truth which they embrace with their Hearts, and that they own
this not only in Words, but also in Actions of Religion. The former of which*

may be call'd the Formal, and the latter the Material, Confession of the Faith.

As for what concerns an ingenuous, clear and simple Profession of their Principles, the Protestants were never yet wanting in that Matter; who have also solidly prov'd their Principles by clear Testimonies of Holy Scripture. But to how little purpose they have done this, and how little Inclination the Papists have to acknowledge or correct any Errour and Abuse which they have receiv'd, appears sufficiently by the Actions of the Council of *Trent:*[15] And in that after so long a time they have amended nothing of any Importance that is condemn'd by the Protestants, but have rather with the greatest Obstinacy vindicated the Errours which have been shown them. And they who have taken upon them to soften Matters have only fram'd Disguises to impose upon the simple. From which Things 'tis easie enough to see what is to be expected.

(§5.) *As for the Obstacles and Impediments of an Ecclesiastical Peace and Union between the Protestants and Romanists, 'tis Certain, and without Controversie, that they are some of them of greater, and some of less, Weight and Importance.*

(§6.) *The Impediments of the former Sort are those, which tho' they do not directly overthrow any Fundamental Article, yet they advance what will but ill agree with such an Article: And those which as they directly and immediately relate to Practice, they do disturb the Concord, and take away actual Union and Communion. Such are for instance the Things held concerning the Communion under one kind, the Masses without Communicants, the Justification of a Sinner before God, the Celibacy of the Clergy, the Ordinations of the Pastors and Teachers of the Protestant Churches, the Episcopal Rights transferr'd by the Treaty of* Passau[16] *upon*

---

15. The Council of Trent (1545–63) aimed at a definitive statement of the doctrines of the Catholic Church in response to the Reformation. It also sought reform of the inner life of the Church.

16. The Treaty of Passau (1552) gave legal recognition to Protestantism in the German empire.

the Protestant Princes and States, and some other Questions which we shall take notice of below, in Sect. 18. n. 4.[17]

Here is no Determination of the Number of the Fundamental Articles, nor any Mark or Character given by which they are to be clearly distinguish'd from those that are not Fundamental; which is what I must needs think to be of principal Concern in this Affair, and that which ought to be first rightly setled, or else all endeavour in it must come to nothing. Moreover, he must have very slightly consider'd the Mysteries of the Pontifical Kingdom, who believes that these Articles contain the chief Matter of difference between us, or that this Dissention turns entirely upon a difference about Principles. Certainly it is the least Part of the controverted Points, and of the Interests of the Hierarchy, which is here touch'd; and therefore the Work must be accounted very maim'd and imperfect.

(§7.) *The Controversies of less Importance are about such Things, as that we may affirm either of the opposite Opinions, and neither of them would have any influence upon our necessary Practice, or establish, or overthrow, any necessary Principle.*

But among the Principles of less Importance then, you must not include those which are advanced for the procuring of Wealth, or retaining the People under the Yoke of the Priests. For all such Things, since they nearly touch the Interests of this Hierarchy, are deservedly to be accounted of great Importance.

(§8.) *The greatest Endeavour ought to be applied about taking away the Impediments, which are of greatest Importance: For those being remov'd, the Union, and actual Communion, will at length be renewed.* What may be said to this is already observ'd upon § 6.

(§9.) *Among the Obstacles of Peace, and Ecclesiastick Union, which are of greater Importance, we have set in the first Place the Controversies about the Holy Sacrament of the Eucharist. For as to partake of that one Bread, or to be Partakers of the Table of the Lord, and to drink of the Cup of the Lord together, is a Symbol of the perfect Christian Union: So the*

17. Here (§14).

Controversies concerning the Eucharist do chiefly disturb that participation of the Table of the Lord, which Christians ought to have common among them, and by consequence do chiefly trouble and interrupt their actual Union.

It favours of no small Ignorance in the Controversies between the Protestants and Papists, to put the Controversies about the Eucharist in the first and chief Place, when as the main and chief Dispute is about the Power of a Vicar of Christ, the Infallibility of the Pope, and the Authority of the Church. And to this purpose *Bellarmin* himself speaks in the Preface to his Books concerning the chief Bishop.[18] *For what is it* (says he) *which is treated on when we treat upon the Primacy of the Pope? I will say in short it is concerning the Sum of Christianity. For the thing question'd on that Head is whether or no the Church ought any longer to subsist, or it must be dissolv'd, and fall to Ruin?* The participation of the Table of the Lord is no otherwise a Symbol of perfect Union among Christians, than as it may be a Token of their Agreement in the rest of the Fundamental Articles. Therefore if the Papists would abjure Transubstantiation, and agree with us in restoring the Communion in both kinds, yet unless they would part with their other Errours, it must be judg'd that there would be but little advance made towards an Agreement. But when in the last Age it would have been thought worth while if the Papists would have restor'd the Communion in both kinds, tho' there is no pretence to deny, but that this is conformable to our Saviour's Institution, and the practice of many Ages in the Church; they must be thought to have been under a Sort of Madness for defending the Communion in one kind with so much obstinacy as they did this, if this Consideration had not hindred them from yielding in this Point, that if they should once admit that the Pope and Church of *Rome* had err'd in one Point, they must have been forc'd to acknowledge that they might also happen to be Erroneous in

18. Robert Francis Romulus Bellarmine, *De Potestate summi pontificis in rebus temporalibus adversus G. Barclay* (On the Power of the Pope in Worldly Affairs) (Rome, 1610). Bellarmine (1542–1621), Jesuit theologian and cardinal, was an important political theorist of the Catholic Church.

more. For it is a very thin Disguise in this Matter, which Bossuet the Bishop of Meaux[19] makes use of, as the rest of his are such for the most Part, when he says, The Church might for certain Reasons forbid the use of the Cup by the Laity, which it might also restore if it thought fit to do so. For he ought to have produced those weighty Reasons which constrain'd them to depart from the Institution of Christ, and the Practice receiv'd in the Church through so many Ages, and what Causes there are beside that which I have mention'd why they should not return to the ancient Custom.

(§10.) *The Protestants teach and believe concerning the Sacrament of the Eucharist, that while the consecrated Bread is therein eaten, and we drink of the consecrated Cup, we also eat the Body of Christ, and drink his Blood, according to his express and plain Assertion. 2. As the Holy Sacrament of the Eucharist is instituted under both kinds, so by virtue of this Divine Institution, which has the force of a command, it ought to be distributed to those who have right to come to this Sacred Feast, and to be receiv'd by them under both Kinds, or both the consecrated Symbols. 3. The presence of the Body and Blood of Christ is annexed to the receiving.*

I know not to what purpose this Confession is inserted here, since the Romanists well enough know what is our Opinion on this Point.

(§11.) *They also teach, that an Adult Person, who is desirous to partake of the Divine Favour, of the Remission of his Sins, and Eternal Salvation, he must confess his Sins, and sincerely grieve for them, and rely not upon any Merits of his own, but only upon the Death and Merit of Christ, with Trust and Hope to obtain thereby the Remission of his Sins, and Eternal Life; and for the future he must abstain from Sin, and follow after Holiness, without which no Man can see God.*

Perhaps the Romanists will not deny this Article as it lyes, especially a *Bossuet,* or such Vender of false and disguis'd Wares. And yet there may be Interpretations and Additaments tack'd to the Article of Jus-

---

19. Jacques Bénigne Bossuet (1627–1704), the most important French theologian of the time, took the lead in discussions about union of the churches.

tification which may be serviceable to encrease the Treasury, by which the Pontifical State and Grandeur is maintain'd.

(§12.) *It must be permitted the Clergy of the Protestants to marry once and again, till this Matter shall be decided by a general Council; and their Marriages, if there be nothing else to forbid it, must be held legitimate.*

But we must needs admire in what Respect the Point of the Marriage of the Clergy comes to be reckon'd among the chief Articles of the Faith, and to have the next place to the Doctrine of Justification, when it is a thing, certainly, that has nothing in it which comes within the Compass of the Christian Faith. For if the Celibacy of such were of Use to the Commonwealth, and the Clergy could live in due Chastity without Matrimony, no Man can imagine that such a Celibacy would diminish any thing from the Sanctity of the Christian Religion. For in Truth that Principle of the Celibacy of the Clergy is among the Mysteries of the Pontifical Kingdom; but I have much doubt whether or no the Clergy of the Protestants would approve of this Position, which pronounces so timerously and ambiguously concerning their Marriages, as what are only to be permitted, and not so much as simply approv'd, till a general Council can be held. And there the Question of its Lawfulness must be fully decided; which Decision may fall as well upon the Negative as upon the Affirmative Part. In the mean time they shall be held for legitimate. Let such Reconcilers look to themselves against the Married Presbyters.

(§13.) *In like manner let the Ordination made by Presbyters of Pastors and Teachers in the Protestant Churches by Prayer, and the Imposition of Hands, be held legitimate, and conform'd to the Apostolick Practice, and those who are in this manner ordain'd and admitted to the Sacred Office be accounted to have Power both of Order and Jurisdiction.*

This Principle indeed is of greatest Importance. For as the State of the Protestant Churches depends, as External, upon the Ordination, and it is by this that they must deserve to be accounted Legitimate Bodies; so the Proposal obliquely overthrows the whole Pontifical State, as it is altogether Repugnant to that to allow any for Lawful Pastors that do not depend upon that. And it is well known with what Fervour, and also upon what Counsels, those who were chiefly addicted to the Court of *Rome* in the Council of *Trent*,[20] opposed the defining that the Residence of Bishops is of Divine Right. For the Pope, saving his Dignity, cannot treat with others of the Clergy, as Independent upon him, as Princes treat with one another: But whoever of them will not be subject is an Enemy; or as Christ speaks, *Luke* 11:23. *He that is not with me, is against me.* And the Pope, if he be not Universal Bishop and Vicar of Christ, is no more but the Bishop of *Rome:* So that to him may be applied that Saying of the Duke of *Valence*,[21] *Either* Caesar, *or nothing; either Universal Bishop, or nothing.*

(§14.) *Lastly, It is notorious enough, not to need any Proof, that in the Treaty of Passau,*[22] *and the Peace of Religion which attended it, the Power and Jurisdiction of the Bishops was transferr'd by Consent of the whole Empire upon the Princes and States of the Protestants. That we may not meddle at present with any other Controversie.*

This Thesis has nothing of Divinity in it, and declares nothing but this: That a Political Toleration of the Protestant Religion has been establish'd in *Germany* by a Publick Convention. But such Agreements as have been brought to pass by Arms and War may conduce to the Peace of Commonwealths, when they can contribute nothing towards reconciling controverted Principles: For the doing of which it must be defin'd which part of the Contradiction between them agrees with the Truth reveal'd in Holy Scripture, and which contradicts it.

(§15.) *These Things being thus expounded, and, together with those which follow, being by the Principal Doctors of the Protestant Church* (it should have been added, and the Princes, and States, and whole Churches; for that the Right of managing such Affairs does not lye only in the Hands of the Doctors) *agreed upon, and calmly approv'd,* (which is a thing will never come to pass with this End, unless perhaps

---

20. See note 15.

21. Cesare Borgia (1476–1507), Italian soldier, politician, churchman, prince, and illegitimate younger son of Pope Alexander VI, traditionally seen as the model for Machiavelli's *The Prince.*

22. See note 16.

they should all become delirious) *the Pope is to be tried,* (1.) *Whether or no he be willing to hold those Protestants who are ready, upon equal Conditions, to submit themselves to a lawful Council, and the Ecclesiastical Hierarchy, for true Members of the Christian Church, notwithstanding that they are perswaded that the Communion in both Kinds, or in the Symbols of Bread and Wine, is commanded by Christ, and so that it ought to be always receiv'd in this manner by the People.* That is as much as to say, it should depend upon the Declaration of the Pope whether or no the whole Christian World, for more than 12 Ages, are to be accounted true Members of the Christian Church, who have put this Matter out of Doubt. *And that he should not impose upon the Churches of the Protestants Masses without Communicants, or at least that he should not forbid them their Practice of not celebrating the Sacrament without some present, to whom, after Consecration of the Bread and Wine, they may be distributed, when the Eucharist is so, and no otherwise celebrated than as it was instituted by our Lord, and as it is describ'd in the Gospel.* That is to say, We must precariously obtain from the Pope, that it may be allow'd us to use the Mystical Supper no otherwise than as Christ himself did celebrate it at its first Institution. But they whose Necks do not itch to be in the Roman Yoke, will maintain, even tho' the Pope be never so unwilling, that this is a Right which is Divine, and is join'd too with Obligation. But to lay aside the Masses without Communions, is to stop the main Spring of the Revenues of the Pontifical Kingdom; for these are the things which plentifully furnish the Kitchens of the Priests, and are not unfitly call'd the Priests Porridge-Pots. (3.) *That the Doctrine of the Justification of a Sinner before God, which has been expounded before, be left to the mention'd Churches.* But this is a thing that cannot be with Safety to the Revenues of the Papal Kingdom. (4.) *To permit to the Pastors of the Protestants their Marriages in the manner aforesaid, and to declare them legitimate.* By this Thesis the greatest Prejudice that can be is done to the Protestant Cause. Inasmuch as it is submitted to the Pleasure of the Pope to permit the Marriages of their Presbyters, or declare them legitimate which is to give him a Supream jurisdiction in the Church. (5.) *That he would confirm and ratifie the Ordinations or Admittances to the Sacred Office, which have been hitherto made by the Protestants in such a manner as may be acceptable to both Sides, and can prejudice neither, and can render the People, as far as he can do it, satisfied concerning the Sacraments.* Besides what has been said to the foregoing Thesis, this may be added, that the Romanists cannot with any Safety to their State consent to any acceptable manner of doing the thing here proposed. (6.) *That the Protestant Princes and States of the Empire be so dealt with upon the Point of that Right and Authority, which they have, or pretend to, over the Clergy, and Sacred Things, by vertue of the Treaty of* Passau, *as that they may not oppose these Religious Endeavours for Peace, but may be willingly induced to contribute what they can towards promoting so happy a Work.* These Things are obscure and ambiguous: But if I guess aright at the Meaning of them, it must be this; the Protestant Princes must be allur'd by the Pope to put themselves under his Dominion, by his yielding them the Ecclesiastical Revenues, and a Jurisdiction over the Priests, or by admitting them to the Benefices of other Ecclesiastical Jurisdictions, which they are not yet possess'd of. But so soon as the Protestants have upon this Condition acknowledg'd the Divine Authority of the Pope, he will find Means, by creating Scruples in their Consciences about the Matter, to bring them off at length, for their Ease and Quiet, and to put an end to Importunity and Trouble, to part with these Revenues again.

(§16.) *These Things, if the Pope shall condescend to do,* (observe the Phrase) *the Doctors of the Protestants on their Side shall promise to him,* (1.) *That as the Bishop of Rome possesses the chief Place among all the Bishops of the Christian World, and so has in the Universal Church a Primacy of Order and Dignity, but in the Western or Latin Church he has a Primacy and Patriarchal Rights only by Positive Ecclesiastical Right, (but if he pretends to have more Power belonging to him by Divine Right, he must prove this from the Holy Scriptures in a Council to which he refer that Matter) so they will account him as such, and reverence him as the Supream Patriarch, or Prime Bishop, of the whole Church, and yeild to him due Obedience in Spiritual Matters.*

It manifestly implies a Contradiction to assert that a Patriarchal Dignity belongs to the Pope by a Positive Humane Right, and yet that there is due to him from hence a Reverence and Obedience in Spiritual Matters. And besides, those Patriarchal Rights, which are said to belong to the Bishop of *Rome*, should be first distinctly stated before we may acknowledge them, which is a thing that ought not to be blindly done; tho' without doubt the Pope would give them but little Thanks who should go about such a Business. But the Protestants Churches too have Reason to detest it as an unparallell'd Boldness and Presumption, that Offers of so great Importance should be made by Two Divines to the old Tyrant, whose Yoke they have with much ado made a Shift to shake off. Besides, it is the greatest Imprudence to grant such Things before a Council is held, to which the final composing of the Differences is to be referr'd, as by which the Liberty of the Protestants is prejudg'd, and before it does appear that the Pope will admit of reasonable Terms in a Council. *Heretofore our Ancestors have gone so far, as to profess it might be yeilded by us to the Roman Bishop to have a Superiority over other Bishops, which he has otherwise by Humane Right, for the Peace and common Tranquility of those Christians, who at present are, or hereafter may be, under him, with whom it becomes other Christians, laying aside all Hatreds and Animosities, to maintain Peace: If he will allow of the Gospel, that is, if he will suffer us to believe that our Lord Jesus Christ died for our Salvation, and that no Man can be sav'd by his own Merits, or by any other way but by the Merit of his Passion. In a Word, if he would impose upon us no Sacrament, nor Principle of Faith, but what is taught in Holy Scripture, and was receiv'd by the ancient Church, as recommended by the Gospel.* Our Ancestors offer'd something liberally enough through Fear; and because while they had not yet searched to the Bottom the Nature of the Papal Dominion, they had hopes, that in a Council to be call'd such gross Errours and Abuses would be amended. Which hopes are now, since the holding of the Council of *Trent*, utterly cut off. But there was also a Condition added, which the Pope could not possibly perform, unless he would suffer his Servants to be famish'd by the withdrawing of the Revenues. (2.) *That they will not account those of the Romanists, who without Scruple of Conscience chuse to continue the Communion in one kind alone to be Hereticks, or erroneous in the Fundamentals, or as committing a Sin worthy of Eter-*

nal Damnation. I would willingly know how this maiming of the Sacrament can, without Scruple of Conscience, be endur'd; unless among those whose Minds are so blinded with the Antichristian Darkness, as to judge that the Commandments of Men may take place, and be preferr'd, before the Precept of Christ. (3.) *That the Presbyters will be subject to their Bishops, the Bishops to Archbishops, and so on according to the Hierarchy receiv'd.* This Subordination may very well be granted as a Humane Constitution; which is also in Use in some Protestant Churches.

(§17.) *Both sides having sincerely promis'd and engag'd to each other, the Princes of* Germany *of both Religions* (who while they profess the Romish Religion do account it a Wickedness for them to meddle in such Matters) *shall be solicited by our Invincible* Caesar, *that each of them do send a Doctor or Two, Men eminent for Moderation, no less than for Learning, to the Convention, who shall give their Counsel about restoring an Ecclesiastical Union and Peace between the Romanists, and the Protestants. But the Case it self speaks that none ought to be sent by them, but such as have agreed to the manner of transacting the Affair, which must till then be kept Secret, or who are of like Sentiments with them who have agreed to this.* But in my Opinion such an Assembly will never be brought together, and if it should be, it could have no good Effect.

(§18.) *In this Assembly or Conference these Questions shall be examin'd (excepting those before excepted, which are suppos'd to be already agreed upon) which the differing Parties do, as yet, manifestly disagree, or not fully agree in; and it will appear that those are not of the same Kind, nor of the same Importance. For some of them depend upon the different Acceptation of their Terms; as for Instance, whether or no the Eucharist be a Sacrifice properly or improperly so call'd; and whether Matrimony be a Sacrament or no.*

It must needs be that those Men have never but carelesly consider'd the Frame of the Pontifical Kingdom, if they believe that those Controversies depend entirely upon a different Acceptation of the Terms: When the former Question concerns a great Part of the Revenues, the other of the Authority and Jurisdiction of the Papacy. For on the former Question an infinite Trade of Masses, and that a very gainful one, does depend. And because Matrimony is accounted a Sacrament, all Matrimonial Cases, even of the greatest Importance, are by vertue of that Pretence drawn into the Ecclesiastical Court. *Other Questions are so form'd, as that for the Love of Peace, the milder Sentence of the same Church may be embraced.* The Love of Peace ought to be so govern'd, as that our Salvation and Liberty may not be thereby betray'd. It is better to have an open Contention and War, than be under a heavy Yoke, and enjoy a miserable Peace. *For Instance, that the Bishop of* Rome *is not Antichrist.* That this might be granted 'tis necessary to blot out of the Sacred Writings that Expression of our Saviour, *My Kingdom is not of this World,* and also many Expressions of St. *Paul,* and the whole Apocalypse of St. *John. That a good Work is meritorious, which is perform'd by a justified Person through the Grace of the Holy Spirit; and tho' it has no Intrinsick Dignity and Proportion to the Reward or Eternal Glory, yet there is in Mercy promised to it a Degree of Glory, and that does truly and properly follow well doing,* &c. This Concession does not at all favour the Pope, with whom the meritorious Vertue of good Works is urg'd to enrich the Treasury of the Papal Kingdom. *Other Questions are so form'd that they cannot possibly be decided.* St. *Aug.* l. 3. against *Julian,* c. 3.[23] says well, *There are some Things about which the most Learned and best Defenders of the Catholick Rule cannot agree among themselves with Safety to the Connexion of the Faith.* There will be no Difficulty about these Questions, provided there be no Gain depending upon them. *Other Articles are in Truth controverted. As for Instance, Of Transubstantiation, and the keeping, carrying about, and Adoration of the Host, which depend on that; the Enumeration of Sins in private Confession: Of Purgatory, Prayers for the Dead, the Worship of Relicks, and the Image and Sign of the Cross: Of the Saints, the Number of the Books of Holy Scripture; the Compleatness, Reading, Plainness of Holy Scriptures: Of Traditions; of the Judge and Determiner of Controversies of Faith; of the Papal Power, or the Roman Bishop; of the Church of* Rome, *of the Immaculate Conception of the Blessed Virgin, Festival Days, several Cere-*

---

23. Augustine, *Against Julian of Eclanum,* chap. 3.

monies, the Choice of Meats; and lastly, of Indulgences; which have given Occasion to the Reformation, as well as the Schism, in these Western Parts of the Church, &c.

(§19.) *The Determination of these and other Articles, especially such as cannot remain undecided, without the Scandal of one Part or other, or without which a constant and lasting Ecclesiastical Union cannot be obtain'd, must be committed to some chosen Judges on both Sides who are eminent in Learning, Judgment, Piety and Moderation.* Tho' we should grant that such Men may be found, who besides that they have the foremention'd Dispositions, may be able to manage such an Affair without any Prejudice or Partiality, yet will the Pope never be brought to refer any of those Matters to an Arbitration. Besides, it must be known that Controversies about Matters of Faith are not of that Nature, as that they may be committed to the Decision of Arbitrators. *As after the exhibiting of the Augustan Confession,*[24] *and the contrary one of the Romanists, in the 30th Year of the foregoing Age,*[25] *this Method of Transaction was begun to be entred upon, at which Time there was a great Appearance of an Agreement about not a few of the Controversies, and those not of the smallest Moment. Insomuch that* David Chytraeus *in his* Chronicle *of* Saxony, *l.* 13.[26] *writes, That from the beginning of these Controversies in* Germany *the Parties differing in Religion never before came nearer to one another, nor do they seem likely, even to the last Day of the World, to come nearer together. For of* 21 *Articles of the Augustan Confession, Fifteen were in a little time reconciled; Three were suspended to a general Council, and in Three only it was that a manifest Dissention still remain'd.*

But if there were an Agreement then made at *Auspurg* of any Sort, it were Folly to believe that the Pope would suffer a Hair's Breadth to be diminish'd of his Dominion, or of the receiv'd Principles; or that

---

24. See note 14.
25. The Council of Trent. See note 15.
26. David Chytraeus, *Chronicon Saxonicae et vicinarum aliquot gentium: ab anno Christi 1500 usque ad 1593* (Chronicle of the Saxons and some neighboring peoples from 1500 to 1593) (Leipzig, 1593), book 1, chap. 13.

any thing would be done to secure the Protestants, unless they would altogether return to their ancient Yoke. For in all Cases, if any have withdrawn themselves from any Sort of Dominion, it is never safe for them to have any Confidence or Trust in their former Lord, but they must put themselves into a separate State, and so confirm themselves, as that they may be able to sustain and repel his Force with theirs. *Or lastly, the Determination of the aforesaid Articles may be referr'd to a Council.*

(§20.) *But that Council ought to be* (1.) *Lawfully gather'd, and as general as the State of the Times will allow.* (2.) *That Council must not appeal to the Decrees of that of* Trent,[27] *or of any other, in which the Principles of the Protestants have been condemned.* (3.) *Neither may that Council be assembled till the Agreements are made, and all Things are fulfill'd which in this Writing it is suppos'd ought to be done, fulfill'd, and agreed. But before all Things, for satisfying the Minds of the People about the Sacraments, the Ordinations must, as hath been said above, be confirm'd: Yea, to accomplish an Universal Uniformity, and for the Preservation of Union with the Churches of the Roman Communion, the Pope must set up or confirm as Bishops in all the chief Cities of the Protestant Kingdoms and Provinces, those among the chief of the Protestant Superintendents, who shall be assign'd to this by the Kings, Princes or States, of the Protestants. But because according to the Canons 'tis not lawful for any but a Bishop to give his Vote in Councils, all the foremention'd Bishops of the Protestants united, as is abovesaid with the Romanists, must be call'd to this Council, and ought to be accounted, and to sit there as Judges, together with the Romanists, not to be cited as the Part to be judg'd.*

Such Things as these may come together in a pleasing Dream, but can never be brought to pass in Effect. But if they could be effected, they would be the certain Ruin of the Protestant Churches.

(§21.) *Such a Council must have the Holy Canonical Scripture both of the Old and New Testament for its Foundation and Rule of proceeding. For among the Things manifestly contain'd in Holy Scripture will be found*

27. See note 14.

all those Matters which belong to the Faith, or the Rule of good Living, as
Augustine *speaks,* l. 2. *Of the Christian Doctrine,* c. 9.[28] *And the same*
Holy Father does so prefer the Scripture before all the Epistles of later
Bishops, as that it cannot be doubted or disputed concerning any thing
which is agreed to be written in them, whether or no it be right and true.
L. 2. *Of Baptism, against the Donatists,* c. 3.[29]

Thus indeed it ought to be. But the Romanists have given plain
Specimens of what Esteem that Rule is with them in the Council of
Trent, and other later Writings.

(§22.) *The Words of Holy Scripture are to be understood in the first*
Place as the Mind of Man does naturally take them; the Scholastick Doctors
would say as they lye, and as they sound; St. Hillary *says, as the Force of*
the Expression requires. He is the best Reader of Scripture, says he, l. de
Trin.[30] *who expects to receive the Meaning or right Understanding of what*
is said there from the Expressions, rather than he does impose it upon them;
and who fetches it from thence, rather than carries it thither. Further, the
Protestants are willing to receive among the Means of interpreting Scrip-
ture, the Sence or Consent of the Ancient Church, and of the present
Patriarchal Sees, so far as that Sence can be obtain'd, notwithstanding the
Tyranny of the Turk, under which some of them live. For in the Interpre-
tation of the Scriptures we may and ought to use with a grateful Mind the
Labours of the Ancient and Modern Doctors of the Church.

Lawyers are wont to protest that they will not be oblig'd to a superfluous Proof; but our Reconcilers voluntarily charge themselves with
a most operose and infinite Proof, the Consent of the Ancient Church,
and that which they add of their own Heads, the Consent of the present
Patriarchal Sees. Amongst which, since the See of *Rome* possesses the
first Place, they herein give a great Authority to the Testimony of the
Adverse Party, and do very plainly yield to the Pope the judging in his

---

28. Augustine, *De Doctrina Christiana* (On Christian Doctrine), book 2, chap. 9.
29. Augustine, *De baptismo contra Donatistas* (On Baptism against the Donatists), book 2, chap. 3.
30. Hilary of Poitiers, *De Trinitate* (On Trinity), book 1.

own Cause. And in general it must be said, we allow not the Sentence of any Church or See as infallible in defining the Sence of Scripture; but the Sence of Scripture being well establish'd from Scripture it self, we readily yield it may be illustrated by such a Consent.

(§23.) *To these Means of interpreting Scripture there may be added a Lawful, Sedate, Learned, Disputation, and such as is entirely devoted to the finding of Truth. When a thing is rightly understood, and in the same Sence by both Parties (lest one should impose upon the other by Equivocation or Ambiguity) they must be commanded to prove by Canonical Scripture, and the Unanimous, Constant, Consent of the Antient Church. If the Affair be carried on after this manner, those that are not Pertinacious and Obstinate, but Pious, Prudent, Considerate, and well Dispos'd,* (add also, and not possess'd with Prejudice, and whose Dignity, Power and Revenues, are not concern'd in the Dispute) *will easily observe on which Side of the Controversie the Truth is placed, what may be prov'd, and what may not. The Words of St.* Aug. *(Cont. Epist. Fundament. c. 1.)*[31] *must be well observ'd; On both Sides let all Arrogance be laid aside. Let no Man say he has already found the Truth, if that be sought for as on both Sides unknown. For so it may be Diligently and with Concord sought, if none by a rash Presumption believe that it is already found and known.* But the Protestants are in a miserable Condition if the Truth is at length to be sought for by such a Council.

(§24.) *What might be propos'd here concerning the manner of holding such dispute, as whether it were best to be held in Council, or to be manag'd by Writings between them, this, with many other Things, are reserv'd for another Opportunity. Whatever is just and equal the Protestants will not be unready to allow, that they may in fact declare for themselves, that they are and will be most free from the guilt of Schism.* But it is to me a Matter of great Doubt, whether or no the greatest Part of the Protestants would approve of these Things, and much rather whether the Romanists will ever admit of them. *May the Great and Good God preserve us in Truth by the Holy Spirit, and make those of us acknowledge this who have not*

---

31. Augustine, *Contra epistolam Manichaei quam vocant fundamenti* (Against the letter of Manichaeus called fundamental), chap. 1. This letter dates from 397.

yet done so; and may He favourably Pardon those that are in Errour or Ignorance, for the sake of his only begotten Son, our Lord Jesus Christ, Amen. *Written by Command,* &c. *the 30th Day of* March, An. 1683. *saving in all Things the Judgment of the more learned,* G. A. L. H. B. E. A. H. What is to be thought of this writing does sufficiently appear by what has been said, if indeed the Authors were serious in the thing. But if the same was conceiv'd to oppose and silence the importunate and ensnaring Sollicitations of some Popish Reconciler, then it may be taken a subtil Piece of Mockery. I shall here willingly insert the Opinion of *Joachim Hildebrand,* Superintendent of *Cell,*[32] concerning this Debate, and the Things that are to be observ'd with Relation to it. *When I consider how much Blood the Evangelical Liberty has cost us, I can never consent to an actual Communion with the Popish Church, unless she would Renounce the Errours of the Council of* Trent, *and the immense Authority of the Pope, that is, unless she would cease to be Popish. And therefore I look upon the Bishops meditated Pacification as a meer Delusion, by which it is endeavour'd to bring our Church under the Papal Yoke, and so under that of Antichrist, under pretence of giving us a temporal Liberty of Doctrine: And he allures us with the vain hope of Bishopricks, Canonicates, and Ecclesiastical Benefices, and I know not what Honours and Riches, who has none of these in his Power, as Satan tempted Christ,* Mat. 4. *I fear too, that the Princes will not be brought to submit their Necks to the Tyranny of the Pope, which was so intolerable to their Ancestors; or that they will not resign and yield the Episcopal Rights into the Hands of the Clergy, that the Pope, a Foreign Lord, may set up a new and distinct State within theirs, since 'tis manifest how tenacious of the Rights of Superiority in their several Territories Princes commonly are, the One or Two might at first reap some Advantage from thence.* Freyheit vom Pabst und Pabst-hum halt ich vor das beste und Sicherste; *Freedom from the Pope and Popery, I held for what is best and securest. To this may be applied the Words in* John 21. *When thou hadst Power over thy self, thou didst gird thy self, but when subject to the Pope, another shall gird thee, and carry*

---

32. Joachim Hildebrand (1623–97), Lutheran theologian. It remains unclear to which of his numerous theological writings Pufendorf refers here.

thee whither thou wouldst not. Justly do the Footsteps of the Pope, and of our Ancestors, terrifie us. God grant you may be fill'd with Abhorrence of the Pope, was the wish of Luther. *The Papists do not value a vertual Communion, and an actual one is at least morally Impossible without the Destruction of one Church or the other.*

§14. But among those whom meerly difference in Principles does divide, without the Intervention of any Emolument, some dissent in the whole System of their Divinity, and notoriously Deny even Fundamental Articles of the Faith. Others again dissent in some Points of Faith, but so that the Divinity of both may be deduced from the same Principles, and brought into one and the same System; to the former Rank we refer the Socinians, and those who come nearest to them: And the most of the Tribes of Anabaptists, the Quakers, and those that deserve the Name of Phanaticks, who deny or wrest those Articles which the Protestants hold as Principal ones, and expound them so as to take away the Kernel, and leave nothing of them but a meer Shell. So that the System of Theology which they have form'd, departs manifestly from ours; and there is hardly any Agreement among them about any thing else, but what may be known by the Light of Natural Reason, and what belongs to the Regulation of Mens Manners. I think it altogether unprofitable, and next to Madness, to go about the reconciling them with us, so long as they will hold to their own Hypotheses. And that which is rather to be endeavour'd with respect to them, is that the Gangrene of their Errours be withheld from spreading by a solid Confutation of them. Especially when 'tis very pleasing and agreeable to profane Men to teach, that nothing should be propos'd to our belief, but what our Reason can easily comprehend; and nothing more should be requir'd of Men, than what is requisite and necessary to our living peaceably and quietly in Societies. From whence it also follows, that they have mightily forsaken their Reason who have attempted a Reconciliation of these Sects also, which have been mention'd with the Protestants; and who to that end have propos'd either the Apostles Creed, or some other loose Form; as if it might suffice to an Ecclesiastical Concord to consent in those Things, and have left it indifferent

Some differ in the whole System.

what every one should believe concerning any Articles not contain'd within that Form, and determin'd that such dissent shall not be any prejudice to the Peace. For if a Form of Concord or Agreement should be compos'd so loosely, as that it might please every one of the Sects mention'd, it would produce a Divinity very jejune and maim'd and which would retain little of true and solid Christianity, all Things being plainly thrown out of it which do contain in them any thing of Mystery.

Some differ only upon a few Articles. §15. But there are others again whose Doctrine does not seem to differ in the whole Frame or System of it, but who agree in a great Part of the Articles of Religion, and there remain only some Questions or Differences about a few particular Articles. And this I think is what all Parties do acknowledge, that every erroneous Opinion is not damnable, but only such as overturn the Foundation of a saving Faith. For after that there was a departure from the simplicity of the Christian Faith, it became the Affection of many to turn the Mysteries of it, which ought to be ador'd with a most profound Adoration, into Matter of exercise for their Wit and Subtilty, and to enquire nicely into the manner in which the Divine Wisdom and Power was pleas'd to exert it self. And then whatever accounts of these great Things they thought most agreeing to their Wit and Reason, these they would needs impose upon others as principal Points of Faith, and would condemn as Heterodox all that dissented from them. Therefore since the Theological Discipline has encreas'd to so vast a Bulk; and is come to abound with such a Multitude of needless Questions debated in it, 'tis now become the grand Question of all, what Questions concern the Foundation of Faith? And what do not? For this before all Things ought to be determin'd, if one would endeavour to any purpose to reconcile the disagreeing Parties. For as it is vain to attempt the making an Ecclesiastical Peace with those who err in the Foundation, so long as they will obstinately defend that Errour: So if any have their Opinion right concerning the Foundation, and their dissent reaches only to some innocent Questions, it is repugnant to that Charity so much recommended to Christians, to exclude them for this Cause from Communion and Brotherhood. This also is what every sober Person will readily acknowledge: That ambiguous and obscure Forms, and such as leave room for secret Exceptions, and particular Explications, are of no Advantage towards a Concord. But to restore Peace, we must deal candidly and sincerely with one another, our Opinions must be expounded clearly, and without any thing that is ensnaring: And if we do use all of us the same Forms of Speaking, we must all design to use them in the same Sence. And because the greatest Difficulty that is to be determin'd lyes in this, whether a controverted Question belongs to the Fundamentals of Faith or not, because some extend the Fundamentals further, and some bring them within straiter Bounds, nor do all in the same manner deduce them; I judge it would avail very much towards the abolishing the Controversies, if some Person would take those Principles about which there is an Agreement on both Sides, and endeavour to compose of them a full and compleat System of Theology, which should not be any ways maim'd or incoherent, but should hold together, in a well connected Series of those Principles, from End to End. For I cannot see any thing to hinder, but that they whose Principles may all be reduced into the same Frame or System of Divinity, might also themselves Unite into one particular Church, provided they would but put off those evil Dispositions which are unworthy of the Christian Profession. And if some controverted Questions remain among them, since however they may be left out of that Method, they are to be reckon'd not reaching the Foundation of the Faith, and therefore they should not be sufficient to break Communion and Concord, or to maintain the breach of it. And if those Questions can no ways be compos'd, it were better to leave them, and to banish them altogether from Divinity, as superfluous and unprofitable, and as moreover Mischievous, and yielding Occasion of Strife and Contention. But that which we are now speaking of is a just System, or Body of Divinity, and such as shall contain all that it is requisite a compleat Christian should know, and which therefore should include all the Articles which would make up the whole due Chain of the Faith. For it is another thing to enquire what Articles may suffice for Salvation to a Catechumen, or a Child, or one of the most untaught vulgar, since such as they may innocently enough be ignorant of many Things, provided they put their Trust in the Saviour of the World, and do hold no positive Errour which is a Contradiction to such Trust. So the Thief on the Cross, and many plain Persons, and formerly those who profess'd themselves Christians, at the sight of the constancy of the Martyrs, and were immediately with them dragg'd to Execution, we must believe obtain'd their Salvation, tho' no Man can think they understood the whole Oeconomy of the Faith or Method of Salvation. Whence we also believe that many may be sav'd, even from amidst the corruptest Sects of the Christians, who do not understand the Depths of Satan; meaning too those of them that are deceiv'd, not the Deceivers: If they have but a simple Faith and Trust in the Saviour of the World, which is the principal Head of Religion. But many more Things are requisite to a full System—which must contain a compleat Body of Christian Doctrine.

A Specimen of a System of Divinity, in which it seems that all Protestants may agree.

§16. Let us make trial then whether such a System of Divinity may not be compos'd, as in which the Two Parties of Protestants which have commonly gone under the Names of *Lutherans* and *Reform'd,* may consent and agree. Upon which the Decision of that grand Question seems to depend, namely, whether they agree in the Foundation of the Faith, or in the Fundamental Articles or not. Which hitherto the most of the *Lutherans* have denied, and on the contrary the *Reform'd* have affirm'd. Which debate comes to this, what are Fundamental Articles, and what are not. For the determining of which Articles there does not seem to be any more expeditious Way than this: That a System of Divinity be fram'd of Points which are yielded on both Sides first, and then that the Controversies which remain be examin'd, to see whether or no they are of so great Concernment as to justifie a Difference between these Two Parties, and the maintaining it with so much Animosity and Bitterness against each other, to the Prejudice of the common Cause, and the great Advantage of the Enemy who seeks by this means to ruin both.

§17. We will premise some Things to be suppos'd and granted, that   Things pre-
we may find the better entrance into that Scheme, which Things are   suppos'd to it.
easily admitted by both Parties without a laborious Proof. Among
which we may set in the first Place this; that the natural Knowledge
of God is not sufficient to the due Worship and Acknowledgment of
him, whereby he may become propitious and favourable to us. 'Tis
true, Mankind, assisted by the meer Light of his own Reason, may
attain to understand the Existence of some superiour Power from
whom all Things in this World proceed, and all the Motions which
are observ'd in it. Forasmuch as these Things cannot have come to
pass of themselves, nor could Motion give it self its Original, and the
force it has, and the constant Laws which it acts by. And by the Exercise
of Reason this also may be learnt and understood, that this Supream
Power is not Brutal and Irrational, or such as hath nothing but meer
Force and Power of Acting. But it is an Intelligent One, and so knows
what it self does, and determines it self to Act, and to the manner of
its Acting. Nor is it difficult upon a serious Consideration of the State
of the World to conclude from thence the Excellency and Greatness
of the Author of it. And when Man contemplates himself, he not only
understands that he is not of himself, and that he owes his Original to
that Supream Power. But also he may see his Condition so dispos'd as
that with a due Exercise of his Reason, he may understand that it is
much better than that of other Things which he sees about him in the
World. From whence he can deservedly conclude that Mankind are
the particular Concern and Care of that Supream Power, whom we
call God, and are held by him among the chief of his Works which are
upon Earth. And then, if from the Works of this Supream Power he
raises his Contemplation to his Nature, he will see Reason to acknowledge him Good, and in the highest manner Perfect and Eminent, and
so to be worthy of his Veneration and Love: So as that if he should be
otherwise affected towards him, he must needs understand that he
should act contrary to Reason, himself being Judge. But however, from
these Speculations alone, if no further Light be added to them, Mankind cannot gather what Acknowledgment and Veneration God requires from him, nor in what Signs and Actions it ought to consist,

that it may be such as he will approve with this Effect that for it he will bestow on Man any peculiar Good beyond what the common course of Nature can afford. See: *Isa.* 44:9, &c. *Col.* 2:22. Tho' on the contrary God has permitted those who did not use their Natural Knowledge of him, as they might, to degenerate into the absurdest Lusts, *Rom.* 1:21, &c. And this moreover cannot be clearly and firmly deduced from Reason alone, whether or no any thing of good or evil remains to Mankind after this Life, or what that is; and what Course he must take to attain the one, or avoid the other, 1 *Cor.* 1:19, 20, 21. and 1 *Cor.* 2:6, 7, 11, 12, 13, 14.

It is agreeable to Reason that there should be a Reveal'd Religion. §18. But because Man rightly concludes from this that he has a Mind capable of Religion; that it is not inconvenient to him to be Religious; he also apprehends it agreeable to Reason to believe that God may approve the Worship of himself perform'd by Man; and that he has it in his Power to advance him to a greater Felicity than what he now enjoys: But it is altogether agreeing to the Wisdom and Goodness of God, having made Man a Creature that understands Divine Worship, to give him also due Instruction concerning the right Performance of it. And it seems repugnant to Reason that there should be a Being worthy of Divine Honours and Acknowledgments, and such Beings also as are capable of paying them, and as have besides abundant Reason and Cause to pay such to that excellent Being, and yet that no Intimation or Instruction should be given them for the right Performance of that Acknowledgment and Honour.

There are no good Reasons to call in Question the Divine Revelations. §19. That Revelation concerning Divine Worship came with such Indications of its solidity and certainty to those whom it was immediately made to, as left them no Suspicion, or so much as a probable Fear, that they were deceiv'd. And among those to whom it was brought by Tradition from Hand to Hand in the first Ages of the World, and to whom it has been afterwards deliver'd by Writing, besides the Nature of the Things therein contain'd, and many other Marks of Truth attending it, there is this moreover that may justly give it due Credit: That altho' the Revelations were not all at once made to one particular

Man, but they were given to several Men, and not at the same time, nor in the same place, and were given by Parts, yet there is such a Harmony and Uniformity among them, as that it is impossible so many Persons, in so distant Times and Places, should Conspire in a Fiction; it is impossible also to find such a Harmony and Agreement among the Imaginations which proceed from Melancholy, since that is wont to offer to the Fancy a Thousand disagreeing and incoherent Forms of Things. And it may be added, that in those Revelations there are many Predictions made of Things long before they came to pass in the Event, and while there was as yet no appearing Disposition towards them to give Ground for conjecture that such Things might come to pass, and which yet did so exactly according to the Prediction. Which are Things that can certainly be referr'd to no other Cause but that which has the Government of the Universe, and to whose Knowledge all Things past, present, and future, are expos'd. See *Isa.* 41:22, 23, 26. and 42:9. and 44:7, 28. and 45:1. and 46:10. But to the End and Design of such Revelation it is necessary that it be so clear, as that the Will of God, as far as is sufficient to that end, may be plainly and manifestly known by it; and so that it do manifestly represent this so far as may suffice to teach Men what that Worship is which will be approv'd of God. The Treasury of these Revelations is the Holy Scriptures, about the Divine Original of which, and their Authority, and other Attributes, there is no Controversie between the Protestants; excepting that which relates to the unequal Efficacy of Scripture upon the Minds of Men, upon Supposition of an absolute Decree, which those call'd the Reform'd have rais'd.

§20. Since therefore it is confess'd among all Christians, that Religion and the Worship of God is not a Humane Invention, and that it does not depend upon the Will of Man after what manner we are to worship God; but that it has been reveal'd by God himself to Men what worship he will have them give him, and what Effects shall follow, as Men rightly perform or neglect this. From hence it may be understood, that in true Religion there is a Covenant between God and Men. See *Deut.* 4:2, 12, 32. *Isa.* 8:20. For a Covenant is the Union, Consent and Agree-

In true Religion there is included a Covenant.

ment of Two Wills about the same Thing. When therefore God discovers how he will be worshipp'd by Man, and Man takes it upon him to perform that Worship, then there is a Consent of the Divine Will, and the Will of Man, and Man is said to have Faith in God and Religion, which before that Consent he had not. For altho' God by a bare Command might enjoin Man to worship him, and Man is bound to this by God's creating him; yet it has pleas'd the Divine Wisdom and Goodness rather to appoint this in the Way of a Covenant, and with the Proposal of a Reward, so as that the Consent and Acceptation of Mankind may be added to the Proposal made by God, and from thence there may arise, as it were, a mutual Obligation, and the stricter Friendship and Union between God and Man. By which, nevertheless, there is nothing taken from the Dominion of God over Men which he has obtain'd by Creation; nor does it follow from thence that it is of Right at the Pleasure and Will of Man whether or no he will enter into this Covenant with God, or that he should not be liable to Punishment if he disdains to do it, and chuses to live without any Religion. For indeed we are under Indispensible Obligation to comply with the Covenant offered by God, insomuch that to refuse it deserves the heaviest Punishment, *Mat.* 10:14, 15. *Mat.* 22:7. *Luke* 14:21, 24. And there arises from that Covenant a stricter Obligation than from a naked Precept; forasmuch as a Precept may be enjoin'd upon him that is unwilling to obey it, but a Covenant is voluntarily undertaken; so that if this be not observ'd there can no Excuse be made for it. Hence it is that in *Exod.* 24:8. it is said of the Covenant, that God made it; and in *Heb.* 9:2. 'tis said of the same thing, that God enjoin'd or commanded it. The Meaning of this Method of proceeding with Men is this: It pleases God in his Infinite Wisdom not to impose upon Men his Worship or Religion with all the Force and Efficacy of his Dominion over them, which he uses in his Disposal of the Creatures destitute of Reason, *Psal.* 148:5, 6, 7, 8. But he has determin'd to govern Men by Motives and Inducements, that they may willingly consent to his Religion, and take it upon them or themselves. He is therefore said to have some time winked at the Times of Ignorance, *Acts* 17:30. For since God requires a Worship and Veneration which does include the Love

and Inclination of the Heart, such an one is more fitly drawn from us
by pleasing Motives, than extorted as a rigid Command. And the Punishment which is due to the Condemners of Religion does not immediately, and by a manifest Execution, take Place, as is wont to be
done for the Violation of Humane Laws: But it is commonly put off
to the future, and deferr'd in the greatest Part of it to the end of this
present Life. Accordingly God does not deal with us in the Matter of
Religion, nor in the whole Business of our Salvation, with the utmost
Exercise of his Power; but as he is a free Being, he does exert his Power
with a certain Temperament and Order, and within such Limits as he
has been pleas'd to set to himself. So that in this Matter it is not to be
enquir'd what God can do by the Force of his Omnipotence, but what
he will do according to the Disposition of his Counsel. From whence
it appears that all Religion were taken away, and turn'd into a naked,
natural, Motion, if any should account the whole Man to be but a
meer Machine, and mov'd only by the External Impulse of another
Being. Tho' he does indeed depend on God, not only in his Original,
but he also has need of a continual Divine Influx to preserve his Existence, and that he may perform his Operations. For if any thing may
be imputed to Man, as what he has done or omitted, and is bound to
give an Account for, it must needs be that this must have been within
the Reach of his Will and Choice, and that which he could of his own
Motion do without being forced to it by any Necessity from without;
so as that if he cannot by his own Force and Instinct move himself to
any sort of Action, yet at least he can reject the Power offer'd him from
without to do this; and when he has receiv'd, he may neglect this, and
throw it away again. Otherwise his Actions or Omissions could no
more be imputed to a Man than the Errours of a Clock can be to that
which has in Truth no Liberty in any of its Motions; but they only
proceed from the Determination of the Artificer that made it. Every
Predestination therefore, or Predetermination, which does not leave to
Man at least that Negative Liberty, or the Faculty of rejecting and
resisting, makes of him a meer Engine or Machine, and utterly overthrows all Religion and Morality. For whatever Signs of Religion and
Worship do proceed from such an one, they could no more be ac-

counted true Religion or Worship, than if a Statue were so contriv'd by an Artificer as to bend it self to those that approach it; this were to be accounted an Expression of Respect. And that the Prescience of God, which cannot be denied, lays no Necessity upon the voluntary Actions of Men, which are foreseen, comes to pass thus. That in God there is no Succession of Time, but all Things are present to him, by reason of his Infinite Essence, which is without beginning or end, and are understood to be beheld by that present Intuition, and so the Providence and Direction of God does, as it were, accompany the Motion of the Creatures. But the Succession of Motions and Times belongs to the Creatures only; and the finite, created, Mind of Man being suited to finite and created Things, conceives of them as past, present, and future. Therefore the Attribute of Prescience, when 'tis given to God, must be purg'd from that Imperfection.

The peculiar Nature of Covenants between God and Man. §21. But the Covenants between God and Men have this among other Things peculiar to them: That towards the making of them there is not requisite such a Combination of Wills, as that there must be a Motion to them alike on both Sides, but the Invitation and Declaration on the Part of God may a great while precede, and persist unmov'd, till the Acceptance follows on the Part of Men, tho' this be a long time after it. Which Acceptance on Man's part being added, then there is an Union of Wills between God and Men, and so a compleat Covenant is made, John 15:16. Further, the Covenants made between Man and Man commonly are such as contain some Advantage and Profit on both Sides, tho' it may be sometimes an unequal one. For such is the Nature of Man, that no Man is willing to bring himself under any Obligation, unless he can expect some Benefit and Advantage from it. But in the Covenants of God with Men the Things perform'd on our Part bear no Proportion in worth to those which are afforded on the Part of God. But 'tis agreeable to the Divine Majesty and Perfection that all the Benefits of those Covenants should redound to Mankind alone, who are the weaker Part, and that he do reserve only the Glory of his Benignity to himself, Rom. 9:35. Hence the Things which Man expects to obtain by such Covenant he can in no wise attribute to his own Merit, but what God is pleas'd to do according to his Covenant is nevertheless owing to the Divine Grace, *Apoc.* 5:12.

§22. To him that searches the Holy Scriptures it will appear that several Covenants, at Times, have been made by God with Mankind. Among these may that deservedly be first consider'd which was made when God placed Man, being now newly created, in the Paradice which he had planted for him, *Gen.* 2:16, 17. and 3:2, 3. For understanding the Nature of which there are to be consider'd the Condition of the Covenanters, and the Heads of the Covenant it self. God therefore, as the Primary Covenanter, after he had made and set in Order the Heavens, the Earth, and other Animals, created Man; in whom he was pleas'd to give a glorious Specimen of his Wisdom and Goodness, and by whom it was his Pleasure to be acknowledg'd and worshipp'd. It is therefore said that God created Man after his own Image and Likeness, *Gen.* 1:27. Which as the Emphasis of the Words do signifie, that it was something very eminent, so, however in what Perfections it did consist is not distinctly express'd in this Place, but it may be gathered by Consequence from other Places of Scripture. He had created the whole System of the World, and every sort of Animal; but these being all but Corporeal Machines, they could not have any Similitude of God as Incorporeal. But there is in Man something which is not to be found in other Animals, which is a Mind of a Nature Spiritual and Immortal, and endow'd with a Faculty of Understanding, and of Willing; and this, as a Table, is that on which the Image of God was inscrib'd, which Image did properly consist in the eminent Light of the Understanding, and the Rectitude of the Will, *Col.* 3:10. *Eph.* 4:24. Therefore the Image of God being lost by the Fall, there remain'd indeed the rational Soul, endow'd with an Understanding and Will, but depriv'd of those Perfections. As for the Light of his Understanding, it is not to be doubted but it was much clearer, and more perfect than that which now remains to Man, even after it is improv'd to the utmost by the most diligent Study. And therefore what we now know of God and his Attributes by natural Light, and of the Way in which it is fit we should acknowledge and worship him, was far more perfectly understood by the first Man:

The Original Covenant of God with Man.

Yet the Things belonging to a Federal Religion, or covenanted Worship, or what it pleas'd God to add to natural Religion, 'tis most certain *Adam* himself must have deriv'd the Knowledge of, not by the Light of Reason, but from Divine Revelation: Otherwise there had been no Place at all for the false Reasonings of Satan, in order to seduce him from his Duty; which Reasonings might immediately have been eluded by contrary Reasonings of his own. So also in what Order the Frame of this World was made up by God he could not know by his own Inspection, because he was not in Being while it was doing, nor could he gather this by Reason: But that Knowledge also he deriv'd from Revelation, and transmitted it to his Posterity by Tradition. From which Tradition *Moses,* the Compiler of the Sacred History, seems to have learnt those Things which relate to the Originals of the World, having also the Assistance of the Divine Illumination and Inspiration, which can neither deceive, nor be deceiv'd. I doubt not too but the first Man understood the Things which are said, *Psal.* 33:6. and *Joh.* 1:1. concerning the Word and Spirit of God; and so that the Mystery of the Trinity was then reveal'd to him; and that God is Three in One. That he had a ready and exquisite Knowledge of natural Things, so far as was useful to Humane Life, which arose from the first Sight of them, may, as it seems, be concluded from that which the Scripture tells us of his giving Names to all Living Creatures. Nor is it to be question'd but *Adam* would have been well acquainted with his Duty towards other Men, who were to be in the World at least when they should have come to be, *Gen.* 2:23. In a Word, we may say, that he perfectly understood what we call Physicks, and the common Ethicks. Nor do I doubt but in the Application of his Mind to them any Mathematical Truths had been very evident and clear to him; but yet so, that Experience and Meditation might have rendred his Knowledge larger, and more perfect.

The Will of the first Man. §23. The Will of the first Man was from the beginning upright, and void of all Fault and Sin, and so it shin'd with Righteousness and Holiness, *Eph.* 4:24. Which Affections of his Will, according to the State he was then in, may be reckon'd natural, because accompanying the Nature of Man, as it was made by God: But which now, after the

Depravation that was contracted, must be reckon'd among the super-natural Goods. And in Truth, that the Will of the first Pair of Mankind was not so liable, and enclin'd to Evil from the beginning, may from thence be manifestly gather'd, that in the present Condition of Men, tho' we would exclude from the Rank of Sins the first Motions of Concupiscence, and Concupiscence it self, and the Proclivity of Nature to what is Evil, (which cannot, and ought not, to be done) at least it is morally impossible, even to him that does most carefully observe his own Mind, not to fall sometimes into a Sin. But if from the beginning God had fram'd the Nature of Men so dispos'd, it does not appear how he could consistently with his Justice have appointed Punishment promiscuously to all Sorts of Wickedness, since 'tis an easie Step to go from those Faults which are almost Involuntary to more grievous Trans-gressions. But altho' the Will was enclin'd to Good, and averse to Evil, as left to it self, yet it was capable of being drawn into Evil by the Seducement of Temptation from without, as the sad Event demon-strates.

§24. With Man therefore thus prepar'd and dispos'd, it pleas'd God from the beginning to enter into a Covenant concerning Religion, or the Worship of himself. But we cannot particularly and certainly de-termine what were the Heads of that Covenant, because the History of the Paradice State is finish'd in a few Words in Holy Scripture. The Reason of which may be, that the time was very short during which the first Pair of Mankind continued in that State; and because there being as yet no use of Letters, and Writing, all Remembrance of Things must have been preserv'd by Tradition, which in time wears out, and is lost. Tho' it be also very probable that our first Parents, through shame for their Fall, and to avoid as much as might be the upbraidings of their Posterity, whom together with themselves they had brought into a miserable Condition by their Sin, would very sparingly deliver any thing to them concerning their first State, and the Felicity which attended it; as every one will study to bury in Silence his own Dispar-agement. But perhaps we might rather say, that by the Fall it self they lost much of the Knowledge of their former Condition, and being now prone to Evil, they did no longer remember the former State and

The Heads of the first Cov-enant of God with Man.

Disposition of their Minds. But that there was in Being even then, a Covenant of God with *Adam,* may be easily concluded from hence, that in general there can be no Religion which can be acceptable to God, but that which he proposes to Man, and which Man takes upon him to perform. For tho' that place of Scripture, *Hos.* 6:7. which otherwise would express this Matter very clearly, is not taken by all as speaking of *Adam* as the Transgressor of a Covenant, but the Word *Adam* there is by some taken for an Appellative; yet is this Matter clearly evinced from *Rom.* 5:14, &c. where the single Sin of *Adam* is spoken of as distinct from the Sins of all other Men, because there was in it the Violation of a Covenant, which he was engag'd in with God for himself and his Posterity, and so for all Mankind; which thing also is shown by the Opposition made there between *Adam* and Christ. For as the Righteousness of Christ does by Covenant serve to the Salvation of Mankind, so the Sin of *Adam,* because it was the Breach of a Covenant, involves all Mankind in Sin and Misery. For without such a Federal Nature in the thing, neither the Righteousness of one could any way redound to the Advantage of others, nor the Sin of one be any Prejudice to another. But the Heads of that Covenant in the greatest part of them may be reduced to these Two Things; That there was requir'd on Man's Part an Engagement to pay to God a Supream Reverence and Love, and that he would in general love his Neighbour: Tho' the former of these might result from the Contemplation of the Divine Benefits bestow'd on Man, the other from his Social Nature. Certainly it cannot be understood that there can be any Religion without the Veneration and Love of God, and a Fear of him temper'd by them. But the Love of his Neighbour may be gather'd from that Joy which is said to have possess'd him when he first saw his Partner and Companion, whom God brought to him. And where any of Mankind are suppos'd to be happy together, there must of Necessity be supposed a mutual Love to be between them, since the Affections contrary to this are apt to produce nothing but Troubles, Contention and Unhappiness. Again, there was promised on the Part of God to Man, upon his observing the Laws of this Covenant, the Continuance of his present most happy State, and a Freedom from Death, or the Destruction of the Body, join'd with Pain, and also Eternal Life. The first of these Things may be collected from this; that Man, after the Violation of this Covenant, was cast out of the Garden of Felicity, and condemn'd to a laborious kind of Life: The other from the Divine threatning, *Gen.* 2:17. and from his being excluded from the Tree of Life, *Gen.* 3:22, 24. Add what is said by the Son of *Sirach, Eccls.* 15:14, 15, 16, 17, 21. and 17:10. For since the Frame of the Humane Body was compos'd of Matter that was by Nature frail, it was impossible that it should not by little and little be worn by the Motion and Succession of Particles, so that the Destruction of it must needs, at length, follow of it self. For since we see that the Nature and State of Things at present is such, as that Corporeal Parts, frequently striking against each other, must in time be worn, and lose their former Form, and so the Frame compounded of them must be disposed towards a Dissolution, there does not any good Reason appear to perswade us that this Law of Nature and Motion was not in Being from the beginning of the Creation, or that it took Place only upon the Fall of Man; and the Bodies that shall not be liable to such Alteration, are to have Being only in the other Life, which are therefore call'd Spiritual Bodies, 1 *Cor.* 15:44, 45. But if any one will chuse to say, that the Habitation of a Soul possess'd of the Image of God, as yet uncorrupted, must needs have been such as to excel in many Respects the Bodies which we now dwell in, we shall not oppose this; especially since it may also be said, that against that Attrition and Decay, which other Bodies by the Motion of Life must be liable to, Man had a Remedy given him by God in the Tree of Life, the Use of which might be able to supply that Attrition, and to prevent that Destruction. And no Man can deny but it was in the Power of God to provide such a Remedy. See *Rev.* 22:2. but that Condition may be reckon'd free from Death, in which, by a Remedy at Hand, it may be kept off, and prevented from ever actually invading a Man; even as that is call'd a perpetual Fire, which has perpetual Nourishment afforded it. But the Translation of Men from this Life to another, an Eternal one, after a long Space spent here, would have been made not in the Likeness of a Death, but of a pleasing Passage from hence. And that it is said in the Book of *Wisdom,* Ch. 2. V. 23. that God created

Man for an eternal Life, does not deny but that a Covenant was order'd
to intervene as the Means or Method by which he was to obtain it.
For when God might have requir'd his Worship of Man by bare Command, without the Proposal of a Reward, it is a necessary Consequent
from his instituting a Covenant that Eternal Life must follow Man's
Obedience.

Of the
Forbidden
Tree.

§25. But that a great and singular Sacrament, and something more
august than is commonly believ'd, was contain'd in the Prohibition of
eating the Fruit of the Tree of Knowledge of Good and Evil, may
certainly be gather'd from the Severity and Importance of the Sanction
annex'd to that Prohibition; which does not seem to have been establish'd for a meer Abstinence from so small a thing as an Apple. For in
that Abstinence was plac'd the grand Condition of the Covenant,
which being violated, the whole Covenant was broken, just as it is
among Men in Feudal Covenants: The Right to the Benefit is perhaps
made to depend upon a certain Point of Time, or some other Condition which is in it self of small Moment; which however, if it be
neglected, that Right is forfeited, and the thing held by that Tenure
falls to him to whom it is committed. Therefore the Sin of *Adam* is
not to be measur'd after the manner of Crimes committed simply
against the Precepts of a Law, where some Proportion is wont to be
observ'd between the Matter of the Crime, and the Severity of the
Punishment; for such Proportion is not wont to be observ'd in Feudal
Covenants. Certainly if we did more distinctly understand the Nature
of the first Covenant, and of the Religion built upon it, no one would
have any Scruple in his Mind concerning the unjust Proportion between the Matter of the Prohibition, and the Punishment that was to
follow the Neglect of it. But tho' by Man's Violation of that Covenant
it was thus far broken, that he forfeited all those Benefits which otherwise he might have expected from it, and fell under the Evils and
Inconveniences which are contrary to them; yet was not Man discharg'd from all Obligation to Almighty God, but still he remain'd
bound to observe exactly the natural Law of God; forasmuch as the
Obligation of this Law follow'd from the natural Condition of Man,

and from the Right of Dominion over him, which God had by creating him. Which Obligation, tho' God might have requir'd him to have answer'd without the Promise of a Reward to it, and with the Threatning of a Punishment if he should neglect to do it, yet he was pleas'd to insert it as a Condition in the first Covenant, and that it should be reckon'd a Worship of him, and be follow'd with a Reward.

§26. Thus therefore did Man, after the Violation of that Covenant, fall from the Benefits that were annexed to it, and contracted a Soil or Pollution, whereby his Understanding was corrupted, especially with Relation to Divine Matters, and his Will became enclin'd to Evil. Which Pollution cannot properly be said to be the Punishment of that Violation of the Covenant; for that it seems hardly consistent with the Justice of God to appoint another Sin directly for the Punishment of Sin, or such a Condition as puts Mankind under a Necessity of Sinning: But it was as it were a natural Consequent of the Fall, and a Corruption of the Mind, which proceeded from that first Sin: By which Sin the Original Sanctity and Integrity was destroyed, and the Divine Grace which accompanied it was also expell'd. For even now we know that one heinous Sin leaves after it a proneness to more; and he who once has lost his shame in consenting to Lust, will with the more proneness rush into any Filthiness: And as the Historian says, A Woman that has lost her Modesty will hardly refuse any thing. Nor is it to be believ'd that there was in the Sin of our first Parents but a slight and small Disorder when they fell into the Breach of this Covenant. For instead of a Reverence for God, there came upon them a Contempt of him, while the Suggestions and Perswasions of the Serpent prevail'd against a Covenant guarded by the threatning of so severe a Penalty. And in the Room of a filial Love, they entertain'd a Contempt, join'd with Hatred, affecting an equal Condition with God himself. For he who affects to be equal with his Superior, it is not possible but he must despise and hate him. As when after the Knowledge of their Crime began to grow upon them, the first Parents attempted to hide themselves, which was a sign of Folly, and a corrupted Understanding, in that they went about to deceive and conceal them-

Of the State of Man after the Fall, and of Original Sin.

selves from the Omniscient God; and also of Hatred, and the Disdain of Subjection and Obedience, as if they would hereafter live entirely to themselves, and have nothing to do with him. And the excuse which they afterwards made for themselves signified nothing of Submission, but rather much of Fierceness, and a Tacit blaming of God himself. But since the preserving of *Adam* in his present State, in which God had created him, was a Condition of the Covenant which could not take place, or be fulfill'd, the Covenant being broken, God was not bound, as we may say, or engaged, to restore him to his Original State: Therefore he left Man to the Corruption which he had contracted by his own Fault, by which he is drawn after the Allurements of External Objects, even in Contradiction to the Divine Law. And that Corruption was moreover propagated to his Posterity, because in the New Covenant God has not promised the restoring of the Primitive Perfection, but to find out another Mean for the obtaining of our Salvation. He therefore has suffer'd the Corruption introduced upon the Humane Nature to remain; which it is no more repugnant to Nature that it should be propagated by natural Generation, than it is (as we see) that the Inclination of the Parents to particular Vices, or their Disposition towards particular Distempers of the Body do pass to their Off-spring, *Job* 14:4. *Joh.* 3:14. 1 *Cor.* 5:48. And that Corruption contracted by the Fall of *Adam* is what is wont to be call'd by the Name of *Original Sin*. The chief Place of Scripture which concerns this Matter is *Rom.* 5:12, &c. to which may be join'd 1 *Cor.* 5:22. where, by the Opposition of Christ and *Adam,* it is manifest, that as the Imputation of the Righteousness of Christ is by Covenant, so the Sin of *Adam* was the Violation of a Federal Condition, which *Adam* was bound to have perform'd in the Name of all Mankind; and which being violated by him, all Mankind became Obnoxious to the penal Sanction of that Covenant, tho' they had not sinned actually after the Similitude of *Adam's* Transgression. From thence Death invaded us, and the Things that prepare the Way to it, and the loss of the primitive Sanctity, and their most happy Habitation; but so as that the Obligation to the having of that Sanctity was not extinguish'd with the Fall, for that God gave it to be kept and retain'd under a Federal Condition, or as it were a

Feudal one, and as Obnoxious to a Commissory Law, *Rom.* 1:18, &c. 2:9. The Condition of Man thus far fallen was so much the more miserable, for that his Understanding knew no Way of appeasing God, and his Will, prone to Evil, could not but be averse to him, whose Anger he was afraid of, and from whom he could expect nothing Propitious or Favourable, without some new Pledge of Favour receiv'd from him.

§27. But when this Original Covenant was broken, it did not please God to withhold altogether his Mercy from Mankind, nor to suffer that the Generations of Men should go on without any Divine Worship, or Covenant between God and them, or that they should so be utterly excluded from Everlasting Happiness. But it was agreeable to his Goodness to establish a new Covenant with Man by the Interposition of a Mediator. For indeed after that *Adam* had in so ill and unhappy a manner borne the Person of all Mankind, and had overthrown the Happiness of all his Posterity by his Fault, it did not seem fitting to Almighty God to Covenant immediately with him, as he had done before, nor without the Intervention of an Umpire or Sponsor, who would expiate the Crime of Mankind, and who should dispence the Divine Favour to Mankind from thenceforth, since they were become unworthy and uncapable by Sin, of an immediate and familiar Intercourse and Correspondence with Almighty God. And because he was not pleas'd to put it upon *Adam* any more to bear the Person of all Mankind, there was also for this Reason a need of a Mediator; because for the giving Being to the Obligation, it was necessary that the consent of both Parties covenanting should concur at the same Time. But forasmuch as the Humane Race could not be all in Being at once, but the Persons of whom it consists must come successively into Being; and those who come first cannot engage for the Rest, nor those that come after be bound by the Engagement of the Former: Therefore that this Covenant might include or comprehend all Men in whatever Age they should come into the World, it was to be constituted in the Person of the Mediator; so that by his Interposition particular Men might at any time come into it. For here we must

The Covenant of God with Men, which was made by the Interposition of a Mediator.

observe, that in this Covenant Mankind were not consider'd as a Society so gather'd and join'd, as that there could be no proceeding in it but by the consent of them all, or of the greatest Part, or so as that the Whole were to be reckon'd to stand for One, or One to stand for all the Rest: But they are consider'd as particulars, who have every one of them right by himself, and without any respect to others, or what they do to enter into this Covenant. Which is quite otherwise than as is wont to be among those who are bound and join'd into one Society; in which Case 'tis not lawful for any one to enter into a Covenant to the Acknowledgement of any Sovereignty, unless the whole, or a major part representing the whole, do consent to it. From which State of the Case this also follows now, that every one forsakes this Covenant, or breaks it only for himself, or at his own Peril, which is otherwise than as the Case was with *Adam* in the first Covenant.

The Promul-
gation of this
Covenant.

§28. The notice of this Covenant was given by God to Man immediately after the Fall, as we have it, *Gen.* 3:15. *The Seed of the Woman shall break the Serpent's Head, who on the other side shall bruise his Heel.* By which Allegorical Way of speaking it is intimated that of Woman, who had been drawn into the Fall by the Devil, under the Form of a Serpent, (*add* 2 *Cor.* 11:3.) he should be Born, who should bruise his Head, or crush his Strength, which exerts it self through the Sin of Man, but he himself should upon that account undergo Death. Compare *Gen.* 22:18. *Gal.* 3:16. and 4:4. And 'tis absurd and ridiculous to think that all which is meant here is the Natural Aversion that Mankind have to Serpents. Yet neither is it to be doubted but that God did expound that Fundamental Principle of Religion in clear and simple Expressions, that he should be Born of a Woman, who should destroy the Power of the Devil, and Sin, the consequent of it, in whom Mankind should repose their Trust for this purpose, and whom they were with a devout Hope to live in the Expectation of. But I would not positively affirm that the first Ages of Mankind were so distinctly acquainted, as afterwards the World was with the Person, Office, and Benefits, of the Saviour; it being suitable enough to the Divine Wisdom to feed Men with Milk, before strong Meat. This is certain, that as the World grew in Age, we find more Light in this Matter to have been afforded it, while the following Prophecies give more distinct Notices of it than the former ones. That Covenant also we must understand belongs in its Nature to all Men, there being no appearance in it of the Exception of any. Nor does it seem Congruous to the Justice of God, while he propos'd to heal the Pollution which was common to all Men, to offer a new Covenant only to a few of them, and to leave the rest, without any particular Fault of theirs, destitute of any Remedy of their Misery. As also the first Promulgation of this Covenant was universal, for it was made to them who were then the whole of Mankind in Being, from whom their Posterity might easily derive the notice of it. Yet afterwards the greatest Part of Mankind did, in the dispersion of Nations about the Earth, through Negligence, or a wicked Contempt of this Covenant, fall by little and little into a forgetfulness of it: So as that Times of *Ignorance* and *Darkness* thence ensued, which it pleased God to *wink* at till the coming of the Saviour thus far, that in all that Space there was not made an Universal Promulgation of this Covenant, *Acts* 17:30. And in this respect it is, *Eph.* 2:12. that the Nations in that time are said to have been without Christ, and to have had no Knowledge of a Messiah that had come, or that was to come for the Redemption of Mankind: They were also *Aliens from the Commonwealth of* Israel; not only from the Communion of Believers, *Gal.* 6:16. but of the People of *Israel,* to whom God had made a peculiar Revelation of his Will, *Psal.* 147:19, 20. They were *Strangers to the Covenant of Promise;* because, tho' it had been publish'd first to *Adam,* and then to *Noah,* and so to all Mankind without exception or difference, being publish'd and offer'd to the common Parents of all; yet there was after this a particular Repetition of this Covenant made to *Abraham,* and his Posterity alone, when other Nations, the Posterity of *Cham* and *Japhet,* had by little and little separated themselves from the Doctrine and Communion of the Patriarchs, and falling to the Worship of Idols, rendred themselves Strangers to the Covenant. Therefore they came in that Way to want the Participation of those good Things which were promised them in that Covenant; and were *without God in the World,* or without a Knowledge of God sufficient to Salvation, and without a true and right Worship of him. Add *Eph.* 3:5, 6, 9.

The Religion resulting from this Covenant.

§29. From this Covenant, the Heads of which we shall hereafter more fully unfold, there arose a new Religion, which in its primitive Simplicity consisted in the observance of the Law of Nature, both towards God, and towards Man, *Gen.* 4:26. and 6:9. and 12:8. and 13:8. and 14:23, 24. and 17:1. And that part of Primitive Religion remain'd as of perpetual Obligation, because it arises from the very Nature given to Man by his Creator. But because through the Corruption of our Nature the observance of the natural Law must needs be very imperfect, and sullied with many Transgressions, therefore by the new Covenant there was added Faith or Trust, and Hope in a Saviour of the World, who was to come, as one by whom God would be render'd Propitious to Men, and forgive them their Sins. And without this that former Part could not be esteem'd for a truly Divine Worship; for the Worship cannot be acceptable to God unless the Worshiper be so; but Men defil'd with Sin are not accepted with God, unless with respect to a Saviour. Nor could Man entertain the Love of God, unless he knew him to be Propitious; but God is not Propitious or Favourable to Men, but by the Saviour. But because it did not please God to send this Saviour in the beginning of the World, but rather about the middle of its Duration, therefore he order'd that the Efficacy of the Death which he was to undergo should exert it self backwards to the Believers of all the foregoing Ages. Whence he is call'd the *Lamb slain from the Foundation of the World,* Rev. 13:8. to which that of St. *Paul* belongs; Rom. 3:25. *Whom God hath set forth to be a Propitiation through Faith in his Blood to declare his Righteousness for the Remission of Sins that are past:* For otherwise those Sins which had preceded the Satisfaction of Christ might seem to have been wink'd at, and past by in that *forbearance of God* which he speaks of. Add *Gal.* 3:8, 9. *Acts* 4:12. and 15:11. *Heb.* 13:8. But we judge this Expiation of our Saviour to have had a Symbol or Sacrament through the foregoing Ages, and this was the bloody Sacrifices then used, or the Sacrificing of living and clean Animals. For there does not any Reason appear why it should please God to receive into his Worship from the beginning such a sort of cruel Performance, unless it were to represent that Sacrifice which the Saviour of the World was to exhibit in his own Body. *Col.* 2:14, 17. *Heb.* 10:1. And we may believe it to have been at least a principal Cause, if not the only one, why God despised the Sacrifice of *Cain.* That this did not consist of an Animal, as God had appointed it should be, and such as could represent the Death of the Saviour, but he brought his sacrifice of the Fruits of the Ground. And these he chose for his Sacrifice, either out of Pride, as disdaining to Obey, and do as directed and order'd, or out of Emulation against his Brother, lest he should seem to have chosen a less noble Kind of Life than his Brother. It is therefore intimated, *Heb.* 11:4. that he offer'd his Sacrifice *without Faith;* for Faith presupposes both a Divine Precept and Promise. But afterwards the Fruits of the Ground were by Divine Order receiv'd into their Sacrifices, and then they also from thenceforth might be offer'd in Faith. And this is a manifest Indication that God is not to be pleas'd with a Religion of Humane Invention, especially about positive Rites, which derive all their Sanctity from a Divine Command; and so we must be assur'd that he is not pleas'd that any of his Federal Laws should be wrested, eluded or chang'd, by any Arbitrary Interpretations of Men. From thence also it is that before the Institution of the Levitical Worship, *to build an Altar to the Lord* was the same thing with setting up the publick Worship of God; because indeed the chief and primary Part of the Federal Worship was the Death of the Saviour of the World, which the Sacrifices did then represent. So that 'tis wonderful that the ancient Jews, forgetting almost the Sacrifice of the *Messias,* should come to believe that the guilt of a Man was transferr'd to the Soul of his Victim, and that his Crimes were directly expiated by the Death of that. The Occasion of which Errour seems to have been the perverse Interpretation of *Levit.* 17:11. *The Life of the Flesh is in the Blood, and I have given it to you upon the Altar, to make an Atonement for your Souls; for it is the Blood that maketh an Atonement for the Soul.* Whence *Isaac*

Abarbenel in his Preface upon the Book of *Leviticus*[33] writes thus, *It was just and due that the Blood of the Sacrificer should be shed, and his Body be burn'd for his Sin, were it not that the Divine Benignity would accept from him in the Way of Commutation or Expiation that Sacrifice, that so Life might go for Life, and Blood for Blood. So* Bechai, *because the Sinner deserves that his Blood should be poured out like as the Blood of a Victim, and that his Body should be burn'd as that is; but the Blessed God accepts of a Victim from him, as a certain Commutation and Ransom; behold how great and glorious is the Benignity of God to him! In that through his Mercy and Indulgence he admits the Soul of the Beast, for the Soul of the Sacrificer, and the Expiation is made by that.* Which Errour however might have been sufficiently confuted from *Psal.* 49:7, 8. and 50:8, 9, 13, 14. and 51:16, 17, 19. *Hos.* 6:6. *Mic.* 6:6, 7. and the same is expresly refuted, *Heb.* 9. and *Heb.* 10.

The Particular Covenant of God with Abraham.

§30. But lest the Knowledge of this Covenant, and of a Saviour to come into the World, should in process of time be utterly lost from among the Nations dispers'd upon the Face of the Earth, it pleased God to continue the Memorial of it by some particular Covenants; by Virtue of which, the Race of which, according to the Flesh, the *Messias* was to come, was confin'd to a certain Nation and Family, and afterwards also the Place and Time of his Nativity was assign'd by the Prophets, that Men might be led as it were by the Hand to the Knowledge of him. The Covenant which God made with *Noah* after the Flood, that he would no more bring a Flood upon the Earth, does not belong at all to this, as being a thing out of the Compass of Religion, *Gen.* 9:9, &c. Therefore we Assign the first Place in this Matter to the Covenant which God made with *Abraham*, by Virtue of which he was bound to depart from his Father's House and Country, that he might live separate from a Company of Idolaters, lest his Posterity being mingled with them might be infected with that Pollution, *Gen.* 12:1, &c. and 13, 14, 15, 16. The Conditions of that Covenant on the Part

---

33. Isaacus Abarbeneles, i.e., Yshac Abravanels (147?–1509), Jewish scholar, author of biblical commentaries.

of God were, that he assign'd him the Land of *Canaan* for an Habitation to his Posterity, who were to be very Numerous, *Gen.* 15:18. and 28:3, 4, 13, 14, 15. and 35:11, 12. *Exod.* 2:24. and 6:4, &c. *Deut.* 4:31. And that the Saviour of the World should be Born of his Off-spring, from whom should come a Blessing upon all People, *Gen.* 18:18, 19. and 22:18. and 26:4. *Gal.* 3:8, 16. And a peculiar Favour of God, and as it were a Friendship with him, was to be afforded them, *Gen.* 18:17. On the Part of *Abraham* the Condition of the Covenant was the retaining the Doctrine of a Saviour to come, *Gen.* 12:8. Or the Preaching and Proclaiming the Name of God, *Gen.* 13:18. and 14:19, 20, 22. And indeed since Faith in a Saviour that was to come, was that which was requir'd by the Universal Covenant, it was incumbent upon *Abraham,* by the particular Covenant that he should publickly profess, and own, and endeavour to propagate, that Doctrine, *Gen.* 18:19. *Rom.* 4:13. And when his Faith of that was beginning to waver, by reason of the Barrenness of his Wife, God repeated that Promise, and renew'd the Covenant, *Gen.* 15:4, 5, 6, 18. Where we read that Sacrifices were applied to the Establishment of that Covenant, *V.* 9, 10. And there was added also to this Covenant that which is the general Condition of every Covenant with God, an earnest Endeavour after Piety, *Gen.* 17:1, 17, 18, 19. God instituted for a Monument and Sacrament of this Covenant the Rite of Circumcision, *Gen.* 17:10, &c. by which as a Mark and Character, also the Posterity of *Abraham,* from which the Saviour of the World was to spring, was distinguisht from all other People, and Salvation, and Righteousness, to be obtain'd by the Saviour was seal'd, *Rev.* 4:11. For it was without any Consideration of a Covenant that Circumcision was used among some other Nations, and as it is believ'd, because of the length of Foreskin; and perhaps those Nations were of the Posterity of *Kethurah,* or of *Esau,* who retain'd the Rite, altho' this Covenant did not belong to them. This Covenant was to continue till the time of the Saviour's coming into the World, by whose presence the force of it died of it self: Because in the Exhibition of him, and in his visible presence among Men, did consist the completion of this Covenant on the Part of God. Whence St. *Paul* says, *Gal.* 5:2. *If ye be still circumcised, Christ shall profit you nothing;* for Circumcision respects

Christ as to come. Therefore if any would after this make use of that Sacrament, he would therein deny that the Christ was already come: And so a Christian that should observe Circumcision would maintain an Opinion repugnant to his Profession as such. And therefore tho' Circumcision might contribute something of Sanctity and Prerogative to that People before, 1 *Sam.* 17:26. yet after the coming of the Saviour *there is no more Circumcision or Uncircumcision, no more Jew or Greek,* Gal. 5:6. And the end and design of that Rite being accomplish'd and attain'd, it was also grown out of Use; nor is there any longer any Prerogative or Difference among the Nations upon the Account of that.

The Covenant of God with the People of Israel made by the Mediation of Moses.

§31. Further, as by this Covenant God confin'd the Nativity of the Saviour to a certain Nation, which was afterwards restrain'd by his peculiar Promise to the Tribe of *Judah,* Gen. 19:10. and after that to the Family of *David,* 2 Sam. 23:5. So, that the Hope of Mankind might be the more assur'd, and the Knowledge of the Covenant might in the more Illustrious manner be preserv'd even till it Should be fulfil'd God for that purpose erected a peculiar Commonwealth. For lest the notice of this, if it should remain the Care only of the Heads of particular Families to continue it, should fail through their neglect, or by the oppression of them, if the Posterity of *Jacob* should live mingled with other Nations, or being brought into Subjection to more Potent ones, should be compell'd to Conform to their Manners and Religion, he brought that People out of *Egypt* in a miraculous Manner, and furnished them with Laws of greatest Wisdom both relating to Sacred and Civil Affairs and he also enjoin'd them Rites and usages different from all other Nations; and gave them a peculiar Tract of Country flourishing with all manner of Plenty, whereas a Light set in a Conspicuous Place there might shine to, and enlighten, their Neighbours; and this People he took into his particular Protection, *Deut.* 7:6, 7, 8. And for this end he made a particular Covenant with this People, using *Moses* as the Umpire or Mediator of it. Which Covenant however did neither take away the new Covenant which had been made with *Adam,* nor that particular Covenant which had been made with *Abraham,* but included both of these also, and made many Additions to them both, *Gal.* 3:17, &c.

§32. The Conditions of this Covenant strictly taken on the Part of God were a particular Protection, and the Supream Government over that People: So that God was pleased to call himself a God to the People of *Israel,* and that People his Peculiar; and also that he would bring them into the Land of *Canaan.* See *Exod.* 25. *seq. Deut.* 27:9, 10, 28: throughout; 29:1, 9, 12, 13, 14, 15, *seq.* 30: throughout; 31:9, 10, 11, 12, 13, 32:10. 1 *Sam.* 8:7. 12:22. 1 *Kin.* 8:9, 21, 51, 53. 9:6, &c. 2 *Kin.* 11:37. 17:7, &c. 15, &c. 23:3. 1 *Chron.* 18:21, 22. *Psal.* 44:17, &c. 80:18, 19. 105:8, 9, 10, 11. *Jer.* 11:3, &c. 16:11. Son of *Sirach* 17:15. And this Land he would maintain them in Possession of till the end of the Covenant was fulfill'd and compleated. The Conditions of this Covenant on the Part of the People were a peculiar Sanctity of Life and Manners, by which they might be distinguish'd from the Impurity of other Nations: See *Exod.* 19:5, 6, 8. 1 *Pet.* 2:9. *Exod.* 24:3, 7, 8. *Lev.* 20:22, &c. 26: throughout; *Num.* 23:9. *Deut.* 3:23, 40. 5:33. 6:21, &c. 11:22, &c. 26:16, &c. *Jos.* 24: throughout. To this Purpose he propos'd the Primitive Law reduced into Ten Heads to their Observation, with a particular Recommendation of the Precept concerning the Sabbath. See *Exod.* 31, &c. But not that they should obtain Eternal Life by the Observance of that, but that by forming their Lives according to that Rule they might testifie and declare that they were engag'd in the perpetual Covenant of God, and were ready and desirous, as far as the present State of Nature would permit, to perform and fulfil the Obligation which they were under to Almighty God as Creator, and that they might invite others by their Example to seek their Salvation in the same way with them. Whence the Punishment of Treason was appointed for those who should endeavour to seduce any of that People to a false Religion, as being a Crime against the whole State of the Nation, and tending to the Dissolution of it, *Deut.* 13: throughout; 17:2, &c. add 18, 19. Tho' in Process of Time a false Perswasion took Possession of that People, as if an External and Superficial Observance of that Law would

The Conditions of that Covenant.

suffice them to the obtaining of their Salvation, *Mat.* 19:20. And this was among the Things which made the later Jews dream that they should have a Messiah; who being great himself in an earthly Authority and Power, would make them Partakers in the Glory and Greatness of his Dominion; and to forget, and take no manner of notice of, the Expiation of Sins, which was to be made by him. Against which Errour both our Saviour himself, and St. *Paul,* in his Epistles to the *Romans, Galatians* and *Hebrews,* sharply disputes. But especially was it enjoin'd to the Jews as a Federal Condition that they should exercise the Religion and Worship prescrib'd them by God, which was very laborious, and consisted of a Multitude of Ceremonies, was Uniform and Immutable, and different from the Rites and Religions of all other Nations. By which Rites of Worship, as by Types and Figures, the Office and Benefits of the Saviour were represented. To all which there was added a Law, that the People should not return into *Egypt,* but inhabit the Land assign'd them, and keep themselves separate from any Mixture with other People, and should in their Commonwealth govern themselves by the Laws which God had given them. And if that People had broken this Covenant by any enormous Violation of it we find that they sometimes renewed it, by a solemn swearing to it, 2 *Chron.* 15:12, &c. 23:16. 29:10. 30:6, &c. 34:31. *Ezra* 10:3. *Neh.* 9:38. *Jer.* 50:5.

The Sacrament of that Covenant.

§33. For a Symbol of this Covenant, and that the Memory of it might be continued, God appointed the Paschal Lamb about the Time when the Israelites were to be brought out of Subjection to another People, and to become free, and a distinct People and Commonwealth by themselves. So was that Lamb a Federal Sacrifice, which the particular Masters or Heads of Families did offer in Confirmation of that Covenant, by which God claim'd the Supream Government over that People, and so made them peculiarly his, and brought them into a full Liberty, having deliver'd them from Subjection to another People; they again on their part binding themselves to acknowledge the Dominion and Government of God. About which Affair there is this in particular to be observ'd; that immediately upon God's asserting his Claim to that People, he made a Difference between them and the Egyptians, to whose Dominion they had been hitherto subject, so that the Plagues which afflicted the Egyptians touched not them. And when the Angel slew all the First-born throughout *Egypt,* he pass'd by the Doors of the Israelites which were mark'd with the Federal Blood. It pleased God also, that from the Month in which the People gain'd their Liberty, they should take the beginning of their Year for a Memorial of their Liberty then gain'd. And that Sacrifice God was pleased to order should be eaten by those who offer'd it, and entirely consum'd as treating therein his new People or Subjects with a Feast, and this for a Remembrance of the Thing was to be repeated every Year. And besides, there was a mystical Reason in this Thing, by vertue of which that Lamb did represent another Lamb of God which has taken away the Sins of the World; by the Merit of whose Sacrifice of himself, we being deliver'd from the Dominion of the Devil, are brought into the happy Liberty of the Sons of God. The Paschal Lamb had also this in common with all other Sacraments, that it could confer Spiritual Grace, and seal it to these who rightly made use of it. And there was so grievous a Punishment appointed for the Neglect of the Paschal Lamb, because it contain'd a Denial of God's Dominion over the People of *Israel;* and because he who should despise that Sacrament was reckon'd therein to refuse to be a Subject of God. In which thing also, according to the Apprehension of those Times, all the whole Federal Religion was renounced, when as there was not so strict an Obligation in the other private Sacrifices. Further, because Laws are the principal Bond of a Commonwealth there was also a Federal Sacrifice celebrated; but which was not to be repeated when those Laws were afterwards publish'd in the Wilderness, and the People bound themselves to observe them, *Exod.* 24. Also because that Commonwealth was erected by God for the sake of Religion, the Tabernacle was, not without Reason, set up on the first Day of the first Month, *Exod.* 40:2. So also the Temple built by *Solomon,* as the Seat of their Religion, was consecrated by a magnificent Sacrifice, 1 *Kin.* 8:62, &*c.*

The Nature of the Jewish Religion.

§34. As therefore the peculiar Covenant which God made with *Abraham*, and with the People of *Israel*, by the Mediation of *Moses*, did in no wise take away that Universal Covenant which God made with Mankind after the Fall, but those later ones were superadded to the other: So also the Jewish Religion included all that Worship or Religion which resulted from these Three Covenants, insomuch indeed that every one of these Covenants retain'd its Nature, its Effects and Conditions. From whence the Salvation of Souls among the Jews was to be obtain'd only by the Covenant made with *Adam*, and so by a Trust in the Saviour of the World that was to come: Not by those Rites which had been introduced by the Covenant with *Abraham*, and that made by *Moses*, both of which were temporary, and regarded a certain temporary Prerogative. Whence also the Promises of these later Covenants, or the Things which God engag'd on his Part to perform, did consist almost wholly of Temporal Goods; but from whence it cannot but very ill be concluded, that there were before Christ no Promises given of Eternal Life to them that should believe; forasmuch as such Promises were included in the Adamitical Covenant: So also by the Law of *Moses*, as such, and as it was distinguish'd from the Adamitical Covenant, none ought to expect the Salvation of Souls, as it could not be thereby obtain'd.

The Jewish Religion was interwoven with their Commonwealth.

§35. But it must be well observ'd that the Publick Liberty of the People of *Israel*, and their Religion, were so mingled together, and interwoven, as it were, with one another; that immediately, when the Israelites departed from the Divine Covenant in the Matter of Religion and betook themselves to feigned and strange Religions, God suffer'd a Part of their publick Liberty to be taken away, as may be seen abundantly in the Books of the *Judges*, and of the *Kings*. And when at length they would set no Bounds, nor put an End, to their Idolatry, he suffer'd them to be carried captive to *Babylon*, and to be detain'd so for many Years, that so at length their inclination to strange Religions might be cured. And the Jews were so corrected by that Chastisement, that we never read of their falling again into Idolatry after their Return from Captivity to the promised Land. Afterwards that Covenant being fulfill'd or compleated by the coming of the Messias, died of it self, *Acts* 15. *Gal.* 5:2, 3, 4. *Eph.* 2:13, 14, 15. *Col.* 2:20. And so when God was no longer bound on his Part to maintain them in the promised Land, and to preserve their Commonwealth, this was utterly destroy'd, and they were dispers'd. From whence the obstinate Blindness of the Jews is manifest; forasmuch as when from the time of the Babylonish Captivity, and the Destruction of *Jerusalem,* they addicted themselves no more to the Sin of Idolatry; notwithstanding this he has not for so many Ages restor'd their Temple and Religion, which he were indeed bound to do if the Covenant with that People did still continue, *Deut.* 30, throughout. Therefore no other Reason can be assign'd of their so long Banishment, and most miserable State, under which that Nation have been for so many Ages oppress'd, but that they with the highest degree of Wickedness, refused and rejected the Saviour promised by the Covenant, when he was, according to it, sent to them from God.

§36. But when the Saviour, who is the Umpire of the Covenant made with *Adam,* after his Fall appear'd in this World, and finish'd that which he had undertaken to do, that Covenant receiv'd its Execution and Perfection, and exerted its Force with great Glory, and a greater Abundance of Grace through the whole World, the Abrahamitical Covenant, and the Mosaic one, as Temporary being taken out of the Way. (See *Deut.* 18:15, &*c.*) And this Covenant from that time, with Respect to the Jewish People, was call'd a new one, because the former one made with that People being Temporary, was antiquated. — *The Complement of the Adamitical Covenant.*

§37. But that Covenant, as we have intimated above, consists of a double Agreement; *the one of God the Father with the Son, the other of the Son, as Mediator, and Saviour with Men.* By the former Agreement the Son interpos'd himself, as Mediator for Mankind, and substituted himself by the Father's Consent into the Place and Person of Mankind, to satisfie the Divine Justice for their Guilt contracted by the Fall, and all the Sins which spring from thence, and to expiate that, and procure to us the Favour of God, a Righteousness approv'd by him, and eternal Salvation. Also he undertook to publish this Benefit to Mankind, and — *Which consists in an Agreement between God the Father, and the Son.*

to join them to himself by a particular Bond, who should embrace it; and that he would exercise a Dominion over them to the end of the World. We have everywhere Intimation concerning that Covenant, and the Heads whereof it does consist in the Holy Scripture. *Isa.* 42:1, 6, 7. he is said to be *chosen of God, whom he had given for a Covenant to the People, that he might teach the Right to be truly observ'd by the Nations.* 49:6, 8. 55:3, 4, 5. 59:21. *Ezek.* 34:23, 24. 37:24, &c. *Isa.* 53. 'tis said, *God laid on him the Iniquities of us all;* v. 4. he is said to have *borne* them, or *to have taken them upon himself. Mal.* 3:1, 2, 3. *Jer.* 31:34. *Isa.* 54:9, 10. 55:3. *Gal.* 4:4. God is said to have *sent forth his Son, made of a Woman.* And *Heb.* 1:6 to have brought *his first begotten Son into the World.* And the Son himself, *Heb.* 2:14, 16. is said to be made *Partaker of Flesh and Blood,* and to have taken *the Seed of* Abraham. So *Rom.* 4:25. Christ is said *to be deliver'd for our Sins;* and *Rom.* 8:32. God is said *not to have spared his own Son, but to have given him up for us all.* And yet elsewhere the Son is said to have deliver'd or given up himself *an Offering and Sacrifice for us,* Eph. 5:2. Joh. 10:17, 18. *The Father loveth me, because I lay down my Life, that I may take it again: No Man taketh it from me, but I lay it down of my self.* All which Things do manifestly show an Agreement between God the Father, and the Son. So also, that the Son did substitute himself in the Place of Mankind, it is intimated, 1 *Cor.* 3:23. *Ye are Christ's but Christ is God's.* 1 Cor. 8. *We have one God the Father, of whom are all Things, and we for him; and one Lord Jesus Christ, by whom are all Things, and we by him.* 1 Cor. 11:3. *The Head of Christ is God.* Joh. 10:29. *The Father hath given me my sheep.* Luk. 1:32, 33. *God hath given to the Son the Throne of his Father* David, *and he shall reign over the House of* Jacob *for ever, and of his Kingdom there shall be no End.* Add 2 *Cor.* 5:18, 19. The Foundation of that Kingdom is express'd, *Joh.* 11:51. because *Jesus should die for the Nation.* Concerning the Promulgation of that Agreement it is said, *Joh.* 12:44, &c. *He that believeth on me, believeth not on me, but on him that sent me. And he that seeth me seeth him that sent me. I am come a Light into the World, that whosoever believeth in me should not abide in Darkness. I have not spoken of my self, but the Father which hath sent me he gave me Commandment what I should say, and what I should speak.* Joh.

13:3. *Jesus knowing that the Father had given all Things into his Hand, and that he was come from God, and went to God.* Joh. 14:2. *I go to prepare a Place for you* in the House of my Father. V. 6. *I am the Way, the Truth, and the Life, no Man cometh to the Father but by me.* Add V. 9, 10, 11, 20, 31. 15:1, &c. 16:15, 28. 17:2, 3, &c. 21, &c. Acts 2:26. *God hath made him Lord and Christ whom ye have crucified.* 4:28. *Pilate and the People of* Israel *agreed to do whatsoever thy Hand and thy Counsel determin'd before to be done.* Acts 17:31. *God shall judge the World in Righteousness by the Man whom he hath ordain'd, whereof he hath given Assurance to all Men, in that he hath raised him from the Dead.* Rom. 5:1. *Being justified by Faith, we have Peace with God through our Lord Jesus Christ.* 1 Cor. 1:30. *Christ Jesus is made to us of God Wisdom, Righteousness, Sanctification and Redemption.* 2 Cor. 5:17, 19. *If any Man be in Christ, he is a new Creature: God was in Christ reconciling the World unto himself, not imputing their Sins unto them. God made him to be Sin for us who knew no Sin, that we might be made the Righteousness of God by him.* Gal. 1:4. *Christ gave himself for our Sins, that he might redeem us from this present evil World, according to the Will of God, and our Father.* That is, that he might deliver us from the World that lyes in Wickedness, 1 *Joh.* 5:19. and is for its Wickedness obnoxious to the Wrath of God, and everlasting Damnation; and also that he might deliver us from the Servitude of worldly Lusts, that *Sin might not reign in our mortal Bodies, that we should fulfil the Lusts thereof,* Rom. 6:11. Gal. 3:13. *Christ hath redeem'd us from the Curse of the Law, being made a Curse for us.* Add 4:4, 5, 7. *Eph.* 1:5, 6, 7, 9, 10, 11, 12, 20, &c. 2:12, 13, 14, &c. *Col.* 1:12, 13, 14, &c. 2:10, &c. *Phil.* 2:7, &c. 1 *Tim.* 1:2. And everywhere God is said to be our *Father*, for creating us; Jesus Christ our *Lord*, because of that Kingdom or Dominion over us. Because our Ransom being paid, he has freed us from the most cruel Servitude, *that we might serve him without Fear in Holiness and Righteousness,* and might change the most cruel Yoke for the most gentle one of Christ, *Mat.* 11:29. *Luke* 1:68. Sol. 12. Sect. 7. D. *de Capt. & posth.*[34] 'tis said.

---

34. *Digest,* XLIX, XV, 12, 7.

If any Man redeems a Slave in Captivity from his Enemies; he becomes his who has redeem'd him. And Grotius de Jure Belli & Pa. L. 13. C. 9. S. 11.[35] *It was first order'd by the Attick Laws, and after by the Roman, that he who was redeem'd from his Enemies should serve his Redeemer till he had paid the Price of his Redemption.*

And of the Saviour with Men.

§38. The Agreement between the Saviour and Men on his Part consists in this; that he offers the Benefit of his Engagement to all; bestowing at the same time the Power necessary to their Acceptance of it, and their complying with it; by which the Favour of God, or Reconciliation with him, and a Righteousness which is acceptable to him, and Eternal Salvation is gain'd, and the Right of a Subject in his Kingdom, or Admission into it, and Union with him, is obtain'd. All which Things are abundantly demonstrated by the Things which have been produced from the Holy Scriptures. And on the Part of Men it is required in this Covenant, that they embrace this Benefit with a sincere and firm Faith and Trust: With which Faith there is join'd by an inseparable Connexion a serious and earnest Desire and Endeavour after Holiness and Piety; forasmuch as the Son of God was manifested to destroy the Works of the Devil, the chief of which is Sin, 1 *Joh.* 3:8. and to restore the Primitive Holiness, *Isa.* 44:5. *Luke* 1:74, 75. *Col.* 1:27. Which Covenant it pleased the Saviour to adorn with Two Sacred Rites or Sacraments.

That Covenant presupposes the Mystery of the Sacred Trinity.

§39. To the more intimate Understanding of the Nature of this Covenant, it is necessary that One or Two Things presupposed to it be distinctly explain'd, without which it cannot possibly be understood, as well as also the Conditions of the Covenant it self on both Parts. To the former Head belongs the Article of the most sacred Trinity, or that there are Three Persons existing in one Divine Essence. For altho' it may be thought that even our first Parents in their State of Innocence had some Knowledge of this, as we have intimated before; yet it was

---

35. Hugo Grotius, *De jure belli ac pacis* (The Law of War and Peace), 1625, def. edition 1631, book III, chap. 9, no. 3.

necessary to make this known, to give us a right Understanding of the Nature of the new Covenant, inasmuch as without this that Covenant could not have been. For since the Saviour is by the Holy Scripture pronounced to be true God, and yet 'tis said God entred into Covenant with the Saviour about the reconciling Mankind to himself, it is necessary that there must be more than One Person to whom the Name, and Thing, or Essence, of true Deity or Godhead must belong. But because whatever Knowledge we have of more Persons than One in the Divine Essence is deriv'd entirely from the Holy Scriptures, therefore it is not lawful to those who call themselves Christians to oppose the wild Reasonings of Men to that Doctrine. And it ought to suffice to a sober and pious Christian, that divers personal Characters, and divers Actions, are attributed to the Persons who are honour'd with the Name of God, and such as cannot possibly meet in one Person; as for instance, to beget and to be begotten, to send and to be sent, to bear Testimony the one of the other. Altho' moreover the Works of Providence and Power are wont to be attributed by Appropriation to the Father, the Works of Counsel and Wisdom to the Son, and those of Love to Mankind; such as are Illumination and Sanctification are appropriated to the Holy Spirit. But the Holy Scriptures confine the Number of Persons in the Divine Essence precisely to Three, and the Sacrament of Initiation, whereby Christians are admitted into the number of the Subjects of Christ's Kingdom is expresly order'd to be administred in the Name of the Father, and of the Son, and of the Holy Ghost; which Form were certainly absurd, if the Holy Spirit were only an Affection or Vertue of the Divine Essence, not a true and distinct Person together with the Father and the Son. And that very thing, the Command to initiate in that Form, implies the Necessity of our believing this Article, and that it is laid as the Foundation to the Christian Religion; which if we deny, we overthrow the whole. As does also that which is said, *Joh.* 5:23. *He that honoureth not the Son, honoureth not the Father which hath sent him.* To the Holy Ghost also may be applied, *Rom.* 8:9. *If any Man have not the Spirit of Christ, he is none of his;* 1 Joh. 2. *Whosoever denies the Son, hath not the Father.* Add 1 *Joh.* 5:7, &c. But if any would fancy that the Son and the Holy Spirit are unequal and inferiour to the Father, he would therein utterly deny the Simplicity of the Divine Essence, and would make it compounded of Parts of an unlike Nature, and unequal Excellency, and so would indeed overthrow the whole Divine Essence. And to feign the Son of God to be among the Number of the Creatures, and to be taken by Adoption into a Communion and Fellowship of Godhead, is no less beyond Reason than to believe him to be of the same Essence with the Father. And therefore that we may comply with the Weakness of Humane Reason, which cannot reach these Incomprehensible Things, it is not necessary that we should much concern our selves with prying into the Mystery of the Sacred Trinity, or about the Equality of the Persons therein. But this we must take great Heed to, that we do not destroy that Mystery, or look upon the Three Persons but as Three distinct Names given to the Deity, with respect to certain Benefits bestow'd by God on Mankind. Under which Pretence some of the soberest of the Heathens excused the Multitude of their false Gods. Neither are the Persons of the Trinity by any Means to be conceiv'd of after the manner of moral Persons, which result from the State or Office, and of which 'tis certain several may fall together upon one Man. As *Cicero (de Oratore)* says,[36] *I alone sustain Three Persons; the one of my self, the other of my Adversary, the other of my Judge.* For tho' by that Way of explaining this Mystery there would remain no more Difficulty in it, yet 'tis plain this Sence cannot take place here. For 'tis not possible that one and the same Person can be Father and Son, with respect to himself, or that one and the same can be a Father and Son to himself, or can be he that sends, and him that is sent, or him from whom one proceeds, and also he that proceeds from him. As also it is incongruous that one should make a Covenant with himself. For where *Job* says, 31:1. *I have made a Covenant with mine Eyes,* there is nothing else meant by that Metaphorical Expression, but that he had made a holy and firm Resolution and Purpose not to abuse his Eyes in the Service of Sin. So then, he who denies the Trinity, does therein take away all that is Mysterious, and August, or Venerable, in Christian Religion; and he

36. Marcus Tullius Cicero, *De oratore* (On the Orator), II, XXIV, 102.

also rejects the chief Person upon whom our Salvation does depend, and does therein overthrow the whole Covenant.

§40. Further, it is especially necessary to our understanding this Covenant, to be well instructed concerning the Mediator of it; who extreamly differs from the Reconcilers and Umpires in other Covenants, and from *Moses* himself, who was the Minister of the Jewish Covenant. For the meer or common Umpires in these Cases do only communicate from one to another the Will of those that are entring into Covenant; and oftentimes it is their Business to remove Difficulties, and to dispose the Parties to a mutual Consent; and sometimes they come under an Engagement to concern themselves for the Performance of the Covenant on both Sides. So *Moses* did not covenant with God in the Name of the People of *Israel,* nor bear their Person in that Transaction with God; but had only the part of a meer Interpreter of the Divine Will, which he receiv'd from God, and deliver'd to the People; and the People on the other Hand did not oblige themselves to *Moses,* but to God; and when they violated the Laws of the Covenant, they broke their Faith with God, not with *Moses.* But the Saviour of the World is a Mediator of a much higher Nature; he entred into Covenant with God himself to expiate Mankind, and to take upon himself in that Respect to bear the Person, and stand in the Stead of all Men. And from thence, when he publishes his Doctrine, he commands Men to put their trust in him, that so we may become Partakers of the Divine Covenant, when with Faith we embrace the Saviour, and by this are united with him. From whence also we and our Works are no otherwise accepted with God, but in the Saviour; and whosoever believes not in him, he continues out of a State of Salvation, and out of Covenant with God, and, as the Scripture speaks, without God in the World.

Of the Mediator of the New Covenant.

§41. We must know and believe of this Mediator that he is true God, and the second Person in the Sacred Trinity; and that he is also true Man, and that the same, who is both God and Man, is yet but one Person. The Places of Scripture are numberless, which prove that the Mediator of the new Covenant is God, which give to him that Name in the proper Sence of it, and ascribe to him such Works as can be

He is God.

ascrib'd to none but God. And this indeed is what the very Nature of
the Covenant requir'd; forasmuch as no Creature whatever could be
of so great Dignity, as to be worthy and fit to bear the Person of all
Mankind, with an Effect so great, as even to equal the Creation of
them, *Psal.* 49:8, 9. And it must be a great Mistake, to imagine this
Person less or inferiour, in Respect of Essence, than God the Father,
who by Consent of all is acknowledg'd to be true God. As also it is
impossible and contradictory, that any thing which began to exist later
in time than the true God, should be advanced by Creation, Adoption,
or any other Way into the Essence and Nature of the true God. As for
those Expressions in Scripture which seem to give to the Son a Condition inferiour to that of the Father, they must be understood of, and
applied to, that Condition, to which he was pleas'd to submit himself,
by vertue of his Covenant with the Father on our Behalf, and in taking
upon him the Office of Mediator between God and Man. So for instance, he to whom a Charge is given is accounted less than he that
gives the Charge, with Respect to the Contract that is between them,
so far as he undertakes the Execution of that which is their common
Pleasure and Will; tho' otherwise, and without the Consideration of
that Contract between them, he may be of an equal Condition with
the other.

And Man. §42. But that this Saviour was also true Man very few formerly have
denied, and at present none that are willing to be accounted Christians.
For indeed it behov'd him to be also Man who was to stand in the
Stead of the whole Humane Nature, and to satisfie for it to the Divine
Justice; which he did, by yielding an expiatory Sacrifice in his own
Body, in the Sight of a famous City. Who also, while he dwelt among
Men, did himself publish this Mystery, that so that Covenant might
be manifested to all. And it does not call in Question the Truth of his
Humane Nature at all, that he was Conceiv'd in a Virgin without the
Help of a Man, as perhaps might be demonstrated from Physical Prin-
ciples relating to the Generation of Men. Certainly nothing can be
more easie to the Creator, who establish'd the present Order of Generation, than to supply the Concurrence of a Man, by exciting an

extraordinary Motion in the Blood of a Virgin. But the Saviour was in all Things like to other Men, Sin only excepted, with the Effects which follow that. For he underwent Death, which is call'd the Wages of Sin; not as that which came upon him by virtue of his own Sin inherent in him, but as a covenanted Performance for expiating Mankind: As also that Death came not upon him from any Intrinsick Destruction of the Humane Nature, but by External Violence, which he voluntarily submitted to. *Joh.* 10:18. *No Man taketh my Life from me, but I lay it down of my self.* This also was eminent in the Saviour beyond all Men besides; that as Man he never existed by a Peculiar Subsistence distinct from the Subsistence of the Word, but he always made up one and the same Person with the Second Person of the Trinity.

§43. And the manner in which the Divine and Humane Nature in the Saviour are join'd, is call'd the *Personal Union:* So that God the Son, and that Holy Thing which was Born of the Virgin *Mary,* was one and the same Person. And so it is not one Saviour who is God, and another who is Man, but the Saviour is God and Man in one Person. *Col.* 2:9. But because God the Son existed a perfect Person in the Divine Essence before the Virgin *Mary* brought forth the Man that was personally united to him, therefore God is said to have assum'd the Humane Nature, or that the Word was made Flesh; but it is not said on the other Hand that the Humane Nature assum'd God the Son, or that the Flesh was made the Word. But as this Mystery, the Incarnation of the Son of God, far exceeds all Reach of Humane Reason; so it is not fitting that we should dare to plunge our Curiosity further into it, than so far as the Sacred Scripture leads us, and as may suffice to understand the Office of the Saviour. For since that Union of the Son of God with the Humane Nature was made for the Performance of the Office of Mediator, and that the Office of a Saviour might be discharg'd by a Person who was both God and Man: From thence it follows, that for a right Understanding and Interpretation of the Effects and Consequences of the Personal Union we must always have regard to the final Cause of it. And as for those Things which have no Concern in that, it is best to set by, or forbear the needless Enquiry into them.

In one Person.

The Nature
of the Per-
sonal Union.

§44. That the most strict Conjunction therefore of God and Man in one Person may be express'd, the Things which are concrete of each Nature are predicated reciprocally one of the other. For since *the Lord Jesus Christ is one,* 1 Cor. 8:6. *One Mediator between God and Man, the Man Christ Jesus,* 1 Tim. 2:5. Add *Rom.* 5:17. it is equally said, *The Word or Son of God was made Man,* Joh. 1:14. as that the Son of the Virgin, or *what is Born of thee is call'd, or is the Son of God,* Luk. 1:35. *The Son of God, for whom are all Things, and by whom are all Things, took part of Flesh and Blood, as the Children are Partakers of the same, that he might be capable of dying,* Heb. 2:10, 14. *All the Fulness of the Godhead dwells in Christ bodily,* Col. 2:9. That we might be Members of his Body, and he might be our Mystical Head, which is what a meer naked Man could not represent, *Eph.* 5:30. That is to say, No one could be Mediator between God and Man, but he who was so God and Man, as to be one and the same Person. It would not have been of Advantage to Men if he had been only God, nor could he have sufficed to sustain the Office of Mediator if he had been only Man. It would not have been sufficient to this end that there might have been concerning him some Change or Reciprocation of Words or Expressions: But those very Reciprocal Expressions are founded in the Nature of the Thing, and do express what does really exist in the Person of the Saviour: But it must be said too, that because that Union exceeds the utmost Reach of the Humane Understanding, we must not let loose the Reins to Curiosity, nor determine too boldly any thing concerning that Mystery; by which it would be very easie for us to fall into such Mistakes as would overthrow, or be inconsistent with, the whole Mystery. Whence it is that all Similitudes, as for instance, that of a red hot Iron, or of the Conjunction of the Soul and Body, must be taken with due Qualifications. So also the Word περιχώρησις, which was used by some of the Grecians on this Subject, must not be strictly taken, as if there were a mutual and equal Permeating or local Co-extension herein of the Divine and Humane Nature, such as comes to pass, for instance, when Wine and Water are mingled. Which so gross a Conception does not agree with the Divine Nature, whose Immensity is not to be conceiv'd of after the manner of Corporeal Extension: Which has one part set beside another, and does besides destroy the very Form of the Humane Nature; that is, if one should affirm that this is extended through all the Extent of the Universe. If therefore any one should imagine that there is here such a Conjunction, as whereby the Humane Nature were plainly turn'd into the Divine, he would manifestly imagine a Contradiction, and would therein destroy the true Notion of a Mediator, in making him to be only God. Neither does the natural Conjunction which is between the Soul and Body less destroy that, forasmuch as that Conjunction is a thing naturally necessary; but the Conjunction of Two Natures in Christ is made by a previous Covenant. So also such a Conjunction, as whereby God might remain meerly God, and Man meerly Man, would also destroy the Nature of a Mediator, because in this Way the Bond of our Reconciliation with God would be broken.

§45. Further, it is a Consequence of this Personal Union, that the Proprieties of both Natures may be predicated of the whole Person of the Saviour, which is denominated by the Concrete of each Nature. So the Jews are said to have *crucified the Lord of Glory,* 1 Cor. 2:8. *The Son of Man is the Son of the Living God,* Mat. 16:13, 16. The *Word of Life, which was from the beginning this we have seen,* this we have handled, 1 *Joh.* 1:1, 2. *Jesus is before* Abraham, Joh. 8:58. *Jesus is the Son of David,* Matth. 22:42. *God sent his Son, made of a Woman,* Gal. 4:4. *God purchas'd his Church with his own Blood,* Acts 20:20. Neither does less proceed from the personal Union, and the Nature of the Mediator, that whatever either Nature has contributed to the Office of Mediator may be attributed to the whole Person, consisting of Two Natures. *There is one God and one Mediator between God and Man, the Man Christ Jesus,* 1 Tim. 2:5. *Christ gave himself for the Church,* Eph. 5:25.

§46. Finally, As the Humane Nature in Christ concurrs to all the Parts of the Mediatorial Office, for otherwise there had been no need that the Word should be made Flesh; so also the same must participate, and has participated, of those Divine Attributes of that Divine Eminency and Perfection which was requisite to the fulfilling the Office of Mediator; for otherwise the Efficacy of meer Man could not have risen to

The Consequence of that.

What is become belonging to the Humane Nature by vertue of this Union.

the producing so noble Effects. And because there is some Controversie among the Protestants in the Article of the Person of Christ, chiefly concerning the Communication of Idioms or Proprieties, I suppose the greatest Part of these Contentions might be avoided, if Men would confine themselves within the Bounds of this Simplicity, and not let their Curiosity proceed to those Matters which do not concern that Office, or either boldly deny or define how far the Humane Nature may participate of those Attributes: As also if they would set aside and leave out of the Dispute those Phrases and Propositions which are not contain'd in Holy Scriptures, since these alone are the Measure by which we are to understand and speak of those Mysteries. Where I would propose this to be examin'd and consider'd by honest and good Minds, and those who are well learn'd in Divinity, but without any Prejudice to my self, or the Doctrine receiv'd in our Churches; whether or no that Rule, anciently receiv'd, that *whatsoever is said to be added or conferr'd to the Son of God Incarnate, must be understood to be done with Respect to his Humane Nature;* forasmuch as his Divine one being most perfect is not capable of having any Accession, or any Addition to be made to it, may not admit of an Interpretation, saving the Orthodox Faith, which may prepare the Way to the removing of these Controversies. To insinuate such a Thing, we lay down this Foundation: As the whole Mystery of Redemption has proceeded from the Agreement or Covenant of God the Father, with God the Son, taking upon him to mediate for us: So also that eminent Dignity, and those Attributes, which accompany the Mediatorial Office are assign'd him, as we may speak by that Divine Covenant. Whence it seems not repugnant to say, that to Christ, even as God, by a certain, peculiar, Appropriation and Oeconomy, even the same Perfection of the Divine Essence which he had from all Eternity, may be attributed or given, with Respect to his Mediatorial Office which he has taken upon him to discharge; but yet so, as that the Humane Nature may be reckon'd to come into some Participation and Communion of the same. And that so Christ, as the Saviour of the World, obtains even what he had, as God before in a peculiar manner by Covenant or Agreement, and as committed to him; which same Things are properly given and communicated to his Humane Nature, which before had them not. If we may be allow'd to compare Divine Things with Humane, this Master I think may be thus conceiv'd of. Let us suppose Three Princes jointly exercising a Dominion belonging to them all: Their Subjects rise in Rebellion against their Government: One of these, with the Consent of the rest, takes it upon him to reduce these Rebels into Subjection, with this Condition, that those who shall submit themselves, and embrace the Favour and Reconciliation which he shall publish, shall constitute a Kingdom peculiar to himself, and become his particular Subjects. And when the Term of this particular Kingdom is finish'd, he also shall put off that Function or Office which hitherto he had from that Time borne. So if among Three such Princes One would undertake to make War, he would do this in his own Right, it being a Prerogative belonging to Government, which he is Partaker in, together with his Collegues; and yet if this were assign'd to him by Agreement to be manag'd by him alone, it would not be absurd to say, that the Power of making War were in a peculiar manner conferr'd upon him. So although God the Son did from Eternity enjoy all the Perfections of the Deity, insomuch that nothing can be added to him, yet when the same Person, by Covenant, has obtain'd the Office of a Mediator, that he might procure to himself a peculiar Dominion over Mankind, who were to be redeem'd by him, it would not be absurd to say, that those Things were conferr'd upon him, even as God, which belong to that Dominion to be exercised by him in a certain peculiar manner of Propriety by the Father, and the Holy Spirit; but yet so, as that the Humane Nature is by no Means to be excluded from the Participation of all those Things. Whence that Kingdom, which 'tis said God would give to him that should be Born of the Virgin *Mary, Luke* 1:32, 33. is not properly that Empire or Government which belongs to the Son of God, as God over the Universe, and so over Men, who are a Part of it, by his Divine Essence and Right of Creation; but it is that Empire or Government which is peculiarly join'd with the Office of Mediator. Therefore that may be said to have been bestow'd upon the Saviour, not only as Man, but also as God, in the Manner aforesaid. Which Kingdom however is nevertheless call'd the *Kingdom of God, and of*

Christ, Eph. 5:5. And in the Lord's Prayer we say, *Our Father, Thy Kingdom come.* To which Sence and Meaning that of *Mat.* 11:27. may be explain'd, *All Things are deliver'd to me of my Father.* Whence it immediately follows, *Therefore come unto me all ye that labour, and are heavy laden, and I will give you Rest.* Add *Mat.* 9:6, 16, 19. To the same Sence, as it seems, the Power of judging, which he has given to him, may be interpreted; which he enjoy'd as Son of God by Right of Creation, even before his Incarnation, *Gen.* 18:25. and yet *Joh.* 5:22, 27. it is said, *The Father judgeth no Man, but hath committed all Judgment to the Son, and hath given him the Power of Judgment, because he is the Son of Man.* Which last Words do not only infer that the Authority to judge is committed to Christ, as he is the Son of Man, but it is also intimated in them that the Authority of judging is committed to the Son of God by the Father, as he having assum'd the Humane Nature, has taken upon him the Office of a Mediator and Saviour, by which he constitutes to himself a Kingdom or Empire over Mankind; the last Act and Complement of which Kingdom is the final Judgment. And the Rule of that Judgment will not be the Law, but the Gospel publish'd by the Saviour, *Joh.* 3:18. 16:9. *Acts* 17:31. And the good Works which in the Day of Judgment shall be taken notice of in Favour to those that have done them, are not the Legal Works, bear the Fruits of Faith in Christ. *Mat.* 25:35, *Ye have given me to eat in giving to the Poor.* That is, with Regard to me ye did Good to the Poor; add 2 *Cor.* 5:10 so also it may seem to be with this Meaning said, *The Father is greater than the Son,* Joh. 14:28. Not only with Respect to the Humane Nature which the Son assum'd, but also by the Quality and State of the Covenant between them: Because he who by Covenant commits any thing to be executed to him who is in other Respects his equal, he is accounted to have something of Prerogative, by vertue of this Covenant before him to whom that is committed. Add *Joh.* 5:19, 20, 21, &c. 30, 43. 6:27, 38, 39, 57. 7:16, 17, 18, 28, 29. 1 *Cor.* 15:27, 28. So also Christ, after the end of the World, will again divest himself of his Mediatorial Office and Kingdom, and the covenanted Power which is adjoin'd to it. And to this meaning, as it seems, must that difficult Place be interpreted, 1 *Cor.* 15:24, &*c.* against the Socinians,[37] That in the end of the World Christ shall resign his Fiduciary and Covenanted Kingdom to the Father; so that the Faithful being now perfect, they shall from henceforth be subject immediately to God, having no further Need of a Mediator. Whence 'tis said, *The Son shall then be subject to him who hath put all Things under him.* Not for that the Son shall then become unequal to the Father, but because he shall then immediately subject his Kingdom to his Father, by laying down his Mediatorial Office, and the Government annexed to it. Just as when out of a Company of Collegues, who are equal to each other, the Command of an Army is committed to one, and the War being finish'd, and the Army disbanded, he who had the Command of it laying aside his Military Condition, and divesting himself of his Fiduciary Command, returns again to his simple, civil, Obedience. Add *Acts* 3:21. 1 *Cor.* 3:23. So from the same Foundation we may, I think, not unfitly explain that Place, *Mar.* 13:32. where the Son is said not to know the Time and Hour of the Day of Judgment: As meaning, that it did not belong to the Mediatorial Office, a Part of which is prophecying to reveal to Men the Day and Hour of his last coming to judge the World, which would put an end to his Mediatorial Kingdom, forasmuch as it would be of no Advantage to Men for Salvation to know this, as the following Things show. But rather it would be useful to them to be ignorant of it, that they might always watch. Add *Acts* 1:7. Further, that Majesty which belong'd to the Saviour by his Office, and which his Humane Nature was to partake of, was for some time to be conceal'd, and the Splendor of it in some measure to be laid aside, that some certain Works of his Mediatorial Office might be done; the which being finish'd, that Majesty fully shone forth. Whence that most eminent Name, and which is venerable to all Men, that he is *the Lord our Righteousness,* Isa. 45:24. was given to Jesus Christ for the Sake of his Mediatorial Office. Who nevertheless was to bear for a while the Form

---

37. Socinianism, which received its name from Faustus Socinus (1539–1604), is a "heresy" which denies the orthodox doctrine of the Trinity.

of a Servant, and a meer Man, because some Actions of his Mediatorial Office could not be discharg'd, if he had carried about in Triumph as a Spoil his Divine Majesty, *Phil.* 2:6. add *Eph.* 1:10. 4:9, 10. So also since it is requisite to the Office of a Mediator and King, that he do not depart or separate himself from his Kingdom; therefore does he, while his visible Presence and Conversation with Man is laid aside, yet confirm and assure to them that he will be present with his People to the end of the World, *Mat.* 28:20. 18:20. *Mar.* 16:2. Which Expressions are to be understood concerning the whole Christ, not of his Divine Nature alone, in which all Men Live, Move, and have their Being, *Acts* 17:28. For indeed it is a stricter, more gracious, and more efficacious, manner of Presence, by which Christ, God and Man, is with his Church, and the Faithful, than that common Presence of the Deity, by which this Universe is sustain'd. Further, *Joh.* 6:52. the Flesh of Christ is said *to give Life,* because it belong'd to the Office of Mediator, who must, as such, be himself an expiatory Sacrifice, that he should give his Flesh to the Faithful, that they might live by him. *Lastly,* Since Christ is our Mediator and Saviour, not only as God, but also as Man, the Worship of Adoration is due to him, even according to his Humane Nature, consider'd in Union with his Divine one. For without the Consideration of that Conjunction there does not appear to us any Case, wherein it may become a Question, whether or no the Humane Nature, consider'd separately and abstractedly, may be worshipp'd. For these Bodies of Christ which the Mass-men pretend to make of Bits of Bread we do not acknowledge, *Joh.* 5:23. *Phil.* 2:10. If Men would confine themselves to these Bounds, I think there might many vain Disputes be spar'd. Which because they do not concern the Mediatorial Office, nor is there any thing expressly said concerning them in Holy Scripture, it would become Men better to let alone, and to determine nothing concerning either side of them. Thus it is in vain to enquire whether or no the Power of creating the Heavens and the Earth be communicated to the Humane Nature of Christ, since the Business of Mediation was not appointed for any such End. And to what Purpose is to enquire whether or no Christ, according to his Humane Nature, be present to all the Stars, or to every Plant, Stone, and every other

Creature? For the Holy Scripture says nothing of these Matters, nor does such a Presence influence any thing towards the Redemption of Mankind. Neither is it necessary to assert these Things, that we may make good the Presence of the Body and Blood of Christ in the Eucharist. For when the Humane Nature was assum'd into One Person with the Word, it was advanced to a far more sublime Condition, than that it may be measur'd by the vulgar Qualities of Humane Bodies; or than that it may be said of it, that he can afford or yield his Presence no otherwise than as ordinary Humane Bodies can do it. For our Faith in this Article does not depend upon any such monstrous Extension, as is injuriously imputed to us. But because Christ can easily find a Way, wherein to fulfil what he has promised, and because the Humane Nature of Christ is assum'd into an Unity of Person with God the Son, to whom the Holy Scriptures ascribe an Omnipresence, we believe he can also afford a Presence of his Flesh in a particular manner, and such as exceeds the Reach of our Sences.

§47. But before we come to explain the Condition of this Covenant, it must be briefly observ'd, that altho' it is commonly in the Old and New Testament, express'd by the Word *Berith* and *Diathekes,* which has the Signification of a Covenant as a solemn Agreement in One only Place, as I remember, which is *Heb.* 9:16, 17, 18. that Word *Diathekes* has the Signification of a Testament or last Will. For it is not necessary that this Word be translated by *Testament* in *Gal.* 3:15. since it may be said of a solemn Covenant, that, being rightly made, it is not liable to change. And nevertheless, the vulgar Translation does almost everywhere give the Name of *Testament* to that which, in the Books we call the Old Testament, is call'd a *Covenant;* which Translation *Luther* also follow'd in that which he made in the German Language. When yet the Sence seems to be much more clear and manifest, by retaining the Word *Covenant.* Certainly there is a great Difference between a *Covenant* and a *Testament,* as by the Elements of the Civil Law is manifest to any one. Forasmuch as a *Testament* is the Act of One Party, that of Two Parties; or for the making a *Testament,* the Will of One Person suffices, but to the making of a *Covenant* there must

This Covenant is less properly call'd a Testament.

be a Concurrence of Two Wills. A Covenant is in Being between Two Parties that are existing, and when one is dead, it is at an end; but a Testament is not of Force unless he be dead who made it. In a Testament the Benefit which is dispos'd of thereby then passes to another, when the Dominion of the Testator ceases by his Death: But in a Covenant the Benefits agreed on are communicated on both Sides between Two living Parties. If any one does not embrace a Testament, but refuses it, he seems not to do any Injury to the Testator, nor to incurr any Punishment: But one Party cannot depart from a Covenant without Injury therein done to the other. These Things, with many more, perhaps, have no Place in that Engagement which God hath made with Man, nor can they be applied to it. So also in the Old Testament, as it is call'd, the Testator did not die; for the Death which was then interpos'd, as is acknowledg'd in the very Epistle to the *Hebrews,* was not that of the Testator, but of Bulls and Goats, which were used as Victims to confirm the Covenant. In the foremention'd Place then of the Epistle to the *Hebrews* we must understand St. *Paul* does not speak exactly according to the Law Sence of the Word he uses, but takes it in a larger Signification, and compares that Covenant of God with Man, as agreeing in this third Particular with a Testament; that as in this the Death of the Testator intervenes, and his Goods are devolv'd upon the Heir by the free Will of the Testator, without any equivalent perform'd by the Heir, whereby to purchase or deserve them, so Christ the Mediator of the Covenant has by his Death procur'd for us the Goods promised by the Covenant, without any equivalent Performance on our part. And as the Death of the Testator gives a particular Ratification and Solemnity to a Testament, so by the Death of the Saviour is that Covenant rendred much more August and Solemn. And the Case is the same with the Words *Heir* and *Inheritance,* which are frequently used in this Matter, but less properly, and in this Respect alone; that as a Patrimony descends from the Father to the Children by the Title of an Inheritance, so our Salvation proceeds from the Father, not by our Merit, but by the Son, whose *Co-heirs* we are said to be; and therefore also we are call'd the Sons of God, *Exod.* 4:22. That is, we are made Partakers of that Glory into which he by his

Death is entred. Otherwise an Heir does not enjoy the Goods of a Testator, but when the Testator loses his Dominion over them by his Death. Tho' κληρονομία does not precisely signifie an Inheritance, but also whatever comes to any one by Lot, or any the like gracious Assignation, as the Land of *Canaan* was divided by Lot among the Tribes of *Israel, Psal.* 16:6.

§48. Further, The Conditions or Things perform'd on the Part of the Mediator or Saviour, which by Agreement with God the Father he undertook to perform for the Advantage of Mankind, shall be now more particularly and distinctly consider'd. Of which he says, *John* 4:34. *My Meat is to do the Will of him that sent me, and to finish his Work.* The Sum of them lyes in this, that he took upon him the Sins of Mankind, and made Atonement for them, and did therein satisfie the Divine Justice with this Effect, that whosoever do believe on him, or repose all their Trust in his Merit and Satisfaction, and with Regard to that seek the Favour of God, they shall obtain Remission of their Sins, and a solid Righteousness, such as can subsist before the Divine Tribunal, with other Benefits which accompany those who are reconcil'd to God, and at length Eternal Life. And to this there are very manifest Testimonies in the Holy Scripture, *Isa.* 53:4, 5, 11. *Surely he hath borne our Griefs; we did esteem him stricken, smitten of God, and afflicted, who was yet to God a beloved Servant. The Chastisement of our Peace was upon him, and by his Stripes we are healed. All we like Sheep have gone astray every one hath turned to his own Way, and God hath laid on him the Iniquities of us all; by his Knowledge shall my righteous Servant justifie many. Mat.* 1:21. Jesus *shall save his People from their Sins.* Mat. 20:20. The Son gives his Life as *Ransom for many.* Acts 4:12. *Neither is there Salvation in any other, nor is there any other Name given among Men by which we must be sav'd.* Where we are not to enquire whether or no God might have found out some other Way for the Salvation of fallen Men. But it must suffice us, that he would not save us in any other Way or Manner than this, which we cannot doubt seem'd most agreeable to his perfect Justice, Mercy and Wisdom, tho' we are not able, by our Reason, to find out the Necessity of it. Add

The Conditions of the Covenant on the Part of the Saviour.

Joh. 1:12, 13, 29. 3:16. 6:33, 35, 51, 53, 54, 55, 56. 12:32. *Luk.* 1:77. 2:30, 31, 32. 9:56. *Rom.* 3:24, 25. 4:25. 8:32, 34. 2 *Cor.* 5:14, 21. *Col.* 1:12, 13, 14. *Tit.* 2:14. *Heb.* 2:9. 9:14. 10:5, 10. 1 *Joh.* 1:7. These Performances are commonly spoke of under the Name of his *Priestly Office.* Tho' otherwise there is a vast Difference between Christ and the common Priests; for he offer'd up himself for others, but they offer'd Sacrifices consisting of Beasts, both for themselves and others, *Heb.* 2:17. 7:27. Besides, that the Office of a Priest is confin'd within far narrower Bounds than the Duty of a Mediator and Surety which Christ took upon himself. To that Office it is join'd that the same Person should teach Men the Will of God, and the Benefits which he is willing to bestow, which is call'd the *Prophetick Office.* Compare *Exod.* 7:1, 2, 7. and *Joh.* 10:38. and that he should constitute a particular Kingdom of those who should undertake that Covenant, whom he should govern and protect, and at length translate them, being approv'd in the last Judgment, into his Eternal Kingdom of Glory, and this is what is call'd his *Kingly Office.*

The Promulgation of this Covenant.

§49. But that Men might come into that Covenant, and enjoy the Goodness of God which is offer'd them therein, which the natural Reason of Men could be no otherwise acquainted with, it was necessary that it should be publish'd to them as from God, and that they should be insisted to engage in it, and to enjoy the Benefits of it. For Man being fallen from the first Covenant, he cannot conceive that he may have any Trust in God, or Hope of Good from him; nor can he make any beginning of Return to him, unless he be prevented by the Divine Grace. *How shall they call on him in whom they have not believ'd? How shall they believe in him of whom they have not heard? How shall they hear without a Preacher?* Rom. 10:14. The Publication therefore of this Covenant was begun by God himself in Paradice immediately after the Fall, and was repeated afterwards by the Pious Patriarchs, who are said to have preach'd the Name of God; and *Noah* in particular is call'd a *Preacher of Righteousness,* 2 *Pet.* 2:5. that the Notice of the same might by them come to all that were then in Being, and might be propagated also to their Posterity. And when notwithstanding this came to be forgotten by many, *God did at Sundry Times, and in divers Manners, speak to the Fathers by the Prophets, but in these last Days he hath spoken to us by his Son,* Heb. 1:1, 2. *No Man hath seen God at any time, the only begotten Son, who is in the Bosom of the Father, he hath declar'd him,* Joh. 1:18. *He whom God hath sent speaketh the Words of God,* Joh. 3:34. *The Times of this Ignorance God winked at, but now commandeth all Men everywhere to repent,* Acts 17:30. And that this might be publish'd to all Men, Christ sent his Apostles into all the World to preach it, *Mat.* 28:19. *Mar.* 16:15, 20. Who faithfully fulfilling that Command, publish'd *all the Counsel of God* to Men, *Acts* 20:27. *We are Ambassadors for Christ, as tho' God did beseech you by us, we pray you in Christ's Stead be ye reconcil'd to God,* 2 Cor. 5:20.

§50. Furthermore, the Sum of those Things which Christ and his Apostles deliver'd, and with which they begun their preaching, lyes herein; *Repent ye, and believe the Gospel,* Mat. 3:2, 10. 4:17, 23. *Mark* 1:14, 15. *Luke* 3:3, 4, 16. 4:18, 24, 46, 47. Add *Acts* 2:22, 32, 36, 37, &c. 3:13, &c. 19, 26. 13:17, 39. 16:30, &c. And because that preaching was directed to adult Persons, whose Minds were dark with Ignorance of Divine Things, or possess'd with corrupt Opinions concerning them, and their Lives were corrupted with Wickedness, therefore it was begun with the urging of Repentance. Which strictly taken, consists in the Abdication of former Errors, *Acts* 19:19. and a Grief for former Sins, and a Purpose of forsaking them for the future. For by this the Way was to be prepar'd for the saving Reception of the Doctrine of the Gospel, and for Faith; and the Chamber must needs be first swept and cleansed into which so noble a guest was to enter. For the Profession of the Covenant in Christ requires another sort of Life and Manners than those of Heavens, and of them who follow the Inclination of the Flesh, or of the Corruption which proceeds from the Original Sin. 1 *Cor.* 6:9, 10, 11. *We must purge out the old Leaven, that we may become a new Lump.* 1 Cor. 5:7. *They who sit in Darkness, and the Shadow of Death,* must not shut their Eyes against the rising Light. Add *Eph.* 2:1, 12. 4:17, 18, &c. *Col.* 1:13, 2:13, 3:7, 8.

The Sum of those Things which are to be perform'd by Men.

By Faith we
are engag'd in
this Covenant. §51. But because only a Grief for the Sins we have committed cannot
suffice to an Atonement for them, or obtain their Remission, and therefore does not suffice to our Admission into the gracious Covenant of
God, nor can of it self produce a Conversion and Amendment of Life;
therefore the primary and essential Condition of this Covenant on the
Part of Men, and that, which being entertain'd Men become actual
Partakers of this Covenant, is Faith in Jesus Christ; or that we place
our Trust for Eternal Life only in him, and by his Merit seek Remission
of Sins, and a Righteousness, such as may be approv'd by God, and
eternal Salvacion. That Faith is call'd the Condition of the Covenant,
not for that we thereby deserve the Benefits of the Divine Covenant,
as by a Performance of equal Value, or as if we therein perform'd what
was equal to that which is done on the Part of God and the Saviour:
But because the Covenant and the Divine Benefits are thereby embraced; inasmuch as it is not the Pleasure of God to impose these upon
those who are reluctant and unwilling to receive them: Neither can
this be done without another Destruction of Morality. Whence it is
that in this Matter, the Words *Freely* and *Of Grace* are so industriously
inculcated in Holy Scripture. To which purpose the Scripture abounds
in very manifest Expressions, *Mar.* 16. *Preach the Gospel to every Creature; he that believes, and is baptized, shall be sav'd; he that believeth not
shall be damned.* Joh. 1:12. *To as many as receiv'd him, to them gave he
Power to become the Sons of God, even to as many as believ'd on his Name.*
Joh. 3:15, 16, 17, 18, 19, 36. *He that believeth the Son hath everlasting
Life, he that believeth not the Son shall not see Life, but the Wrath of God
abideth on him.* 20:31. Acts 4:12. *To this Jesus all the Prophets give Testimony, that whosoever believes on him shall receive Remission of Sins by
his Name.* 13:38, 39. 15:11. *Rom.* 3:23, 24, 25, 26, 28. 4:5, 6, 7, 8. 10:4, 9,
10. *Gal.* 2:16. 3:26, 27. 5:6. *Eph.* 2:8, 9. *Phil.* 3:9. *Heb.* 4:16. 1 *Joh.* 1:7.
2:1, 2. 3:23. 5:10, 11, 12, 13. And *Justification* is the Effect of this Faith
alone, by which Man is declar'd free from the Guilt of Sin upon the
Account of the Satisfaction perform'd by the Saviour, which by Faith
comes to be so imputed by God to him that believes, as if he himself
had perform'd it, whereby also he is adopted to be a Son of God, and
an Heir of Eternal Life, *Tit.* 3:7. *Rom.* 5:1, 9. *Phil.* 3:8, 9.

§52. It has pleas'd God to adorn our Entrance into this Covenant with the solemn Rite or Sacrament of Baptism; which Rite our Saviour did, as it were, borrow from the Jews; who also plung'd into Water, and wash'd those whom they made Proselites from among the Gentiles, or those whom they admitted to the Fellowship and Advantages of the Israelitish People, and receiv'd as Members of their Church and Commonwealth. By which Performance these were thought to be regenerated, and to become morally new Men, or new Persons. See *Selden de Jure Nat. & Gent. Sec. Discip. Hebr. L. 2. C. 4.*[38] Which Rite *John* the Baptist first, and after him our Saviour, advanced to a much more noble Nature and Use. Here we may observe concerning the Baptism of *John* what is said, *Acts* 19:4, 5. understanding the 4th and 5th Verses to be connected, and that the 5th Verse does not contain the Words of the Evangelist *Luke,* as continuing the Historical Relation of the Matter he speaks of, but the Words of the Apostle *Paul,* expounding what was the Nature of the Baptism of *John,* and with what Effect and Fruit he preach'd. But in the 6th Verse *Luke* goes on to relate what was done about those Disciples whom he speaks of. The solemn and immutable Form of this Sacrament is that it be done in the Name of the Father, and of the Son, and of the Holy Ghost. Because in this Article of Three Persons in One Divine Essence lyes the Foundation of Genuine Christian Religion; which being taken away, this falls to the Ground, and nothing will remain, but somewhat of an exact, moral, Philosophy. For if there is not more than One Person in the Divine Essence, there is no Saviour, there is no Redemption, there is no Faith nor Justification. Nor does it contradict this, that in *Acts* 2:38. 10:48. some Believers are said to have been baptized in the Name of Jesus: For it is not there said that this solemn Form was not used, but either the Authority and Command of Christ is express'd, or the Scope of Baptism, namely, the engrafting them into the Mystical Body of Christ, and their Entrance into the Divine Covenant, which is constituted by the Saviour. The

Baptism is the Sacrament of Initiation.

38. John Selden, *De Jure Naturali et Gentium Juxta Disciplinam Ebraeorum Libri Septem* (On the Law of Nature and of Nations according to the Doctrine of the Hebrews), 1665, book 2, chap. 4.

following Expressions speak of the Fruit and Efficacy of Baptism. *Christ sanctifies his Church, it being cleansed with the washing of Water by the Word,* Eph. 5:26. *Baptism saves us; not the putting away the Filth of the Flesh, but the Answer of a good Conscience towards God by the Resurrection of Christ,* 1. Pet. 3:4. *Ye are all the Sons of God by Faith in Jesus Christ. For as many of you as are baptized into Christ have put on Christ,* Gal. 3:26, 27. *He that believes, and is baptized, shall be sav'd,* Mark 16:16. *Unless a Man be born again of Water, and of the Spirit, he cannot enter into the Kingdom of God,* Joh. 1:3, 5. *According to his Mercy he hath sav'd us by the washing of Regeneration, and renewing of the Holy Ghost,* Tit. 3:5. *Be baptized, and wash away thy sins, calling upon the Name of the Lord.* Acts 22:16. *By one Spirit we are all baptized into one Body,* 1 Cor. 12:13. *As many of us as are baptized into Christ Jesus, as are baptized into his Death, we are buried therefore together with him by Baptism into Death, that live as Christ rose again from the Dead by the Glory of the Father, even so we also should walk in Newness of Life.* Rom. 6:3, 4. *By whom also ye are circumcised with the Circumcision made without Hands, in putting off the Body of the Sins of the Flesh by the Circumcision of Christ: Being buried with him by Baptism, in which also ye have risen with him by the Faith of the Operation of God, who raised him from the Dead,* Col. 2:11, 12. Which is as much as to say, As Christ being buried, did bid adieu to this mortal Life, or put off altogether his Mortality, and rose from his Sepulchre, to live a new Life, and such as was not obnoxious to any Infirmity or Corruption: So he who is baptized renounces all Carnal Lusts and Inclination to Wickedness, and coming from his Baptism, he rises again from the Death under which he was dead in Sin, to a new Life, which he now lives to God by the Benefit and Guidance of the Holy Spirit, and free from Sin. All which Things it seems to me may be comprehended in these few Words. As on the Part of God there is Conferr'd by Baptism the Right of Christian Citizenship, or that a Man may partake of the Benefits procur'd by Christ: So he who receives this Sacrament, does therein profess that he expects his Salvation from the Merit of Christ, the Complement of which was his Resurrection; and also promises that he will lead his Life conformably to the Doctrine of the Saviour, renouncing the former

Filthiness of Life, and cutting off those evil Fruits which are wont to be produced by the Corruption of his Nature. But altho' it is requir'd of those who receive Baptism, when they are come to the Use of their Reason, that they make Profession of their Faith; and so that they be actually prosses'd of Faith; *Teach ye* first *all Nations,* and after that, *Baptizing them,* Mat. 28:19. *He that believes, and is baptized, shall be saved,* Mat. 16:16. *They that gladly receiv'd the Word of* Peter *were baptized,* Acts 2:41. *When they believed* Philip *preaching the Things concerning the Kingdom of God, and the Name of Jesus Christ, they were baptized, both Men and Women,* Acts 8:37. 9:11, 19. Yet as in these their Faith is confirm'd by Baptism, so by the same it is generated in Infants who also *put on Christ,* which we cannot understand can be done without Faith. But that Baptism is to be bestow'd on Infants is to be concluded from *Gen.* 17:7, 10. compar'd with *Col.* 2:11, 12. *John* 3:5, 6, 7. 1 *Cor.* 1:16.

§53. Further, They who actually come under that Covenant are said to be therein regenerated, and to become, as it were, new Men. Which Word *Regeneration* is also borrow'd from the Jews: Among whom he also, who from among the Heathens became a Proselite of Righteousness, was accounted regenerate, and as an Infant new born, as if he were born of a new Mother: Inasmuch as being now, as it were, newly created, or come down from Heaven, he was reckon'd to become a new Man, having put off his former Consanguinity or Kindred no less than his Gentilism. Concerning which Matter, see *Selden de Jure Nat. & Gent. &c.* L. 11. C. 4.[39] Tho' the Jews wandred far, even into several Trifles, concerning this Matter. Unless it may be said that the ancient Jews understood many Things otherwise than as the Words found, and that their Sense of Things in this Case was very little different from ours. But the Things which the Holy Scriptures deliver concerning Regeneration may be reduced to what follows. Christ shews the Ne-

[margin note:] Regeneration attends the Entrance into the Covenant.

39. John Selden, *De Jure Naturali et Gentium Juxta Disciplinam Ebraeorum Libri Septem* (On the Law of Nature and of Nations according to the Doctrine of the Hebrews), 1665, book 11, chap. 4.

cessity of Regeneration, *Joh.* 3:3, 6. *Unless a Man be born from above, he cannot see the Kingdom of God: For what is born of the flesh,* that is, of that Stock or Race which is infected by Sin, *is Flesh,* and is it self defil'd with Sin. But *Flesh and Blood cannot inherit the Kingdom of God, neither can Corruption inherit Incorruption,* 1 Cor. 15:50. That Flesh, or that vicious and deprav'd Nature, which since the Fall of our first Parents is propagated to all their Off-spring, and is fruitful of evil Thoughts and Lusts, and such as are contrary to the Law of God, is so blinded, that it knows not Christ, nor can with its own Strength find him out, *Mat.* 16:17. According to which Nature and Quality Men are said to *be Carnal, and sold under Sin,* Rom. 7:5. and to *mind only the Things of the Flesh,* Rom. 8:5. and *to walk as Men,* that is, as such corrupted, being *full of Envyings, Strifes and Divisions,* 1 *Cor.* 3:3. Add also 2 *Pet.* 2:10. The Works of which Flesh are reckon'd up, *Gal.* 5:19, 20, 21. and 'tis said there, *They who do such things shall not inherit the Kingdom of God.* That Corruption also is signified under the Name of the *Animal Man,* and the *Earthly Man,* who *receiveth not the Things of the Spirit of God, because they are Foolishness to him,* 1 Cor. 2:14, 15, 48. *Eph.* 4:17, 18. But more frequently is it call'd *the old Man,* who *by Baptism is to be buried into Death;* that *like as Christ rose again from the Dead by the Glory of the Father, so also we should walk in Newness of Life.* And which old Man *is crucified with Christ that the Body of Sin may be destroy'd, that we may not henceforth serve Sin,* Rom. 6:4, 6. And this is *the old Leaven which must be purg'd out,* 1 Cor. 5:7, 8. and *which is to be put off concerning the former Conversation as corrupt, according to the deceitful Lusts of it,* Eph. 4:22. Add *Col.* 3:9. Therefore when we come into Covenant with Christ, that Flesh is not indeed altogether abolish'd, but yet the Dominion of it is destroy'd, that we should no more serve Sin, nor walk according to it, and that we should endeavour to crucifie and mortifie it. And on the other Hand we are said to be begotten of God, *of Immortal Seed, by the Word of God, who liveth and abideth for ever,* 1 Pet. 1:23. And we are said to become a *new Creature, Gal.* 5:15. and *new Men,* in whom God creates a *new Heart,* Psal. 51:12. and to whom he gives a *new Spirit,* and *takes away the Heart of Stone,* and *gives a Heart of Flesh;* that is, one that is soft and teachable, ready to obey God, *Ezek.* 36:26, 27. and in which the *Law of God is written,* Jer. 31:33, 34. Not that any new Physical Substance is created in us, but a new Disposition, a new Inclination, and new Powers, are put into our Minds from above, and are excited by the Spirit of God; such as are diverse from those which we have from our carnal Nativity. And this new Disposition is not built upon the old one as on a Foundation, as if there were hereby supplied what is wanting to Perfection in the Flesh: But altogether a new Creature is said to be produc'd, 1 *Cor.* 5:17. Repugnant to that old Disposition, and such as is bent and set to the utter Extinction of the other, *Gal.* 5:17. Which new Creature is also call'd the *new Man,* because these take in the chief Part of Man, that is, the Understanding and Will, the other Parts of Men being commonly but as Instruments to these, For by Regeneration new Light comes into the Understanding; so that they who *before mere Darkness are now become Light in the Lord,* Eph. 5:8. And a new Life takes Possession of the Will, and a new Inclination tending towards God, whom before it shunn'd, *Rom.* 6:13. When as before we were *dead in Trespasses and Sins God hath quickned us together with Christ.* Eph. 2:1, 5. And whereas the *Carnal Mind is Enmity to God,* Rom. 8:7. being now born again, we *delight in the Law of God in the inner Man,* and *with the Mind we serve the Law of God,* Rom. 7:22, 25. And this new Man is call'd the *inner Man,* as having its Seat in the very Soul; for the External Actions of it may be counterfeited by Hypocrites, and because other Things are common to the Regenerate with other Men, and do outwardly appear in both; but Regeneration is properly belonging to these alone, and is, as it were, hidden in the inward Recesses of the Heart, *Eph.* 3:16. 2 *Cor.* 4:16. Whence 'tis said by Christ, *The Kingdom of God is within you,* Luk. 17:24. *Rom.* 2:28, 29. 1 *Pet.* 2:4. To this Purpose serves what is said, *Mat.* 15:17, &c. *Mar.* 7:1, &c. *Mat.* 23:25, 26, 27, 28. To this the *outward Man* is opposed; and 'tis said, *As that decays, this is renewed Day by Day,* 2 Cor. 4:16. and it is *strengthened by the Spirit of God,* Eph. 3:16. So then by Regeneration is a new State or new Condition conferr'd on a Man; and we who before were *by Nature Children of Wrath,* and those upon whom as Children of Unbelief *the Wrath of God did abide,* now we are the *Sons of God, Joh.* 1:12, 13. and we *receive by Adoption the Privilege of Sons,* Gal. 4:5. are *beloved in the Beloved. We are made Partakers of the Divine Nature,* 2 Pet. 1:4. *We are engrafted as Branches into Christ the Vine,* and by his Vertue *bring forth much Fruit,* John 15:1, &c. So that *not we live, but Christ liveth in us,* Gal. 2:20. *And we live not to our selves, but to the Lord we live or die,* Rom. 14:7, 8. *Are freed from the Law of Sin and Death,* Rom. 8:2. *Being freed from Sin we are made the Servants of God,* Rom. 6:17, 22, with which is conjoin'd that, *because we are Sons we are also Heirs, Co-heirs, with Christ,* or are to be Partakers of the same Glory, *Gal.* 4:7. *Rom.* 8:17. *That we should be no longer Strangers and Foreigners, but Fellow-Citizens with the Saints, and of the Houshold of God,* Eph. 2:19. *Whose Conversation or Citizenship is in Heaven,* who are free of the Heavenly *Jerusalem,* Phil. 3:20. and who have Admission into the House of God, where there are *Mansions prepared for us,* Joh. 14:2, 3. *Here indeed we have no enduring City, but we seek one to come,* Heb. 13:14. Lastly, By Regeneration there are put into the Regenerate new Faculties, new Inclinations, and Powers, so that their Understanding is illuminated, and their Wills come to *take Delight in the Law of God,* and they are *renew'd in the Spirit of their Minds,* Eph. 4:23. *To the Acknowledgment and Image of him that created him,* Col. 3:10. That they should *walk in Newness of Life, and from thenceforth no longer serve Sin, but should live to God,* Rom. 6:4, 6, 11. That as *Spiritual they should mind the Things of the Spirit, and should by the Spirit mortifie the Deeds of the Body, or the Flesh,* Rom. 8:5. 13. That they might be *turn'd from Darkness to Light, and from the Power of Satan unto God,* Acts 26:18. *Created unto good Works,* Eph. 2:10. *And bring forth the Fruits of the Spirit in all Goodness, and Righteousness, and Truth,* Eph. 5:9. *That they may be strengthened with Might by the Spirit of God in the inner Man,* Eph. 2:16, &c. *That taking the whole Armour of God they may be able to stand in the evil Day, and having done all, to stand,* Eph. 6:13. *That the Spirit may help our Infirmities, and intercede for us with Sighs that cannot be utter'd,* Rom. 8:26. *That they may bring forth Fruit unto God, and serve him in Newness of Spirit,* Rom. 7:4, 6. *That they may cry* Abba, *Father,* Rom. 8:5. Gal. 4:6. *That they may mind this one thing, forgetting those Things which are behind may press forwards towards those Things which are before,* Phil. 2:13. *That the Law of God may be put into their Hearts, and written by God in their Minds,* Heb. 8:10. 10:16. Jer. 31:33. That *Sin may not reign in them,* Rom. 6:14. *Lastly,* That *their Body may be the Temple of the Holy Ghost dwelling in them which they have of God, and are not their own,* 1 Cor. 6:19. But this must be observed concerning Regeneration strictly taken: That this, as also Justification, is done, as it were, in an Instant, and is not done Day after Day, or can be said to be capable of Degrees, or to be more or less done. But it is otherwise with Sanctification, and the Renewal of a Man, which may receive successive Degrees, and ought to do so. But from all these Things there is this Consequence to be gather'd: If any Man calls himself a Christian, and yet is not govern'd by another Impulse and Guidance than that of his Carnal Concupiscence, or his natural Reason, such as is found even in Heathens, and has for the Scope and Aim of his Actions nothing but what is pleasant, or profitable, or becoming in the Sight of the World, such an one either never was regenerated, or is fallen from his Regeneration again. For in Truth the Regenerate are carried by a diviner Instinct, and have a nobler Scope and Aim set before them.

§54. But altho' the Covenant establish'd in Christ comes in the Place of the Primitive Covenant which was broken by the first Parents of Mankind; yet there remains from that Covenant an Obligation to Holiness of Life and Manners, as a thing inseparably annexed by God to the Humane Nature. Which Obligation, after the Fall, would draw Men into Damnation, because the Power to fulfil it is lost, and yet the Justice of God does not cease to exact it; and we have lost also by our Imperfection, and inherent Corruption, all endeavour to resist what is corrupt and wicked in us. Now therefore by the Covenant of Christ there is such Provision made against the Misery of Men, that the Satisfaction of the Saviour supplies what the Rigour of the Divine Justice demands, and by Faith and Regeneration new Powers are produced for the doing of those Things which that Obligation requires; and through the Satisfaction of the Saviour the Imperfections are not imputed to Damnation, but are as it were overlook'd, as are also the Faults committed without our Choice, and the evil Motions proceeding from

Of Sanctification as the necessary Fruit of Justification and Regeneration.

the original Pollution: The malignant Operation of which the Faithful have Power in this Life utterly to extinguish, tho' this is what they ought continually with all Diligence to endeavour. From whence there is no small difference between the Primitive Holiness which Man had preserv'd, if he had persisted in his State of Innocence, and that which is perform'd by the Regenerate. The Rule indeed of both is the same Law, as to the chief Heads of it, which include the Love of God, and of our Neighbour: Only the Law of loving our Neighbour must be extended, by reason of the Corruption which is fallen upon Mankind to many Cases, which there was no Place for in the Primitive State. As for instance, there would have been no Place in that State of Mankind for the Vertues of Patience, Mercy, Beneficence to the Poor, or the like, because it would have been perfectly free from all Misery. Whereas now the doing Good to Religious Poor, or the Brethren of Christ, makes an eminent Part of the Love to our Neighbour, which is requir'd of us. But the Primitive Holiness differs much in point of Perfection from that which the Faithful are now able to perform. For the Primitive Righteousness, as being in all Respects perfect, could approve it self to God by it self. But the Sanctity of the Regenerate being in it self imperfect, and blotted with the Contagion of Original Corruption, *Rom.* 7:14, &c. is acceptable with God for the full Satisfaction of the Saviour: So that *there is now no Condemnation to them that are in Christ Jesus who walk not after the Flesh, but after the Spirit,* Rom. 8:1. Therefore whereas otherwise, even *he that breaks the Law in one Point is guilty of all,* Deut. 27:26. *James* 2:10. Christ hath freed us from that Curse, *Gal.* 3:1, 11, 12, 13. As also the Obedience of the Regenerate does not proceed from the Compulsion of the Law, because Christ hath satisfied that both actively and passively; and they are no more the Servants of the Law, but they by a free Spirit yield a filial Obedience to God from the Powers bestow'd upon them by Regeneration. *We are freed from the Law, that being dead, wherein we were held, that we should serve in Newness of Spirit, and not in the Oldness of the Letter,* Rom. 7:6. *That we should yield our Bodies a living Sacrifice, holy, acceptable to God, which is our reasonable Service,* Rom. 12:1. *And being renewed in the Spirit of our Minds, we put on the new Man, who after God is created in Righ-*

teousness and true Holiness. Whence also our Saviour is not to be accounted a new Lawgiver, but a Fulfiller of the Law, *Mat.* 5:17, 18. and its last and most accurate Interpreter. Who also has thus taken away the Terror and Curse of it, and clearly explain'd the Sublime and Spiritual Nature of it, as tending chiefly to a Purity of the Mind; but which was wrested by the Jews almost wholly to External Works, *Mat.* 5:6. From thence also it is that Holiness of Life and Manners is not inserted into the Covenant of Christ, properly as a Primary Condition, but it is reckon'd only as a Fruit and necessary Consequent of Justification and Regeneration. But so notwithstanding, that the Necessity of it is not at all the less; forasmuch as this is the very End of the Redemption purchas'd for us by Christ, that we should serve God *in Righteousness and Holiness,* Luke 1:74, 75. *That we should be the Workmanship of God created in Christ Jesus unto good Works, which God hath before ordain'd or prepar'd, that we should walk in them,* Eph. 2:10. *Col.* 1:22. *Tit.* 2:14. Yea, tho' in the last Judgment the Saviour in his final Sentence will appeal to good Works, this he will do, not because we are not to be justified by Faith, but because good Works are Things that fall under the Notice of the Sences, and those will be present then, and bear Witness of them to whom they were done, *Mat.* 25:35. *Rom.* 2:6. *Luke* 16:9. *Gal.* 6:7, 8. Whence both the Practice of Repentance, and believing in Christ, and the Endeavour after Holiness of Life, or the Vertues, Actions and Works, which are worthy of the Christian Calling, are so twisted together, that no one of them can be, or take place, without the other. For Repentance, unless Faith be added, leads to Despair. And it is a Mockery to pretend to Faith if Repentance does not attend it; that is, if a Man persists to wallow in his former Sins. And Faith, if it be not attended with Holiness of Life, is a vain and presumptuous Perswasion, a dead Tree without Fruit, which shall be hewn down, and cast into the Fire, *Mat.* 7:19. &c. But good Works, unless they proceed from Faith, are not acceptable with God, yea, indeed are not good. So that those Divines are altogether void of Reason who are sollicitous only about the Theory of Christian Religion, or who inculcate only Faith in Christ, and make no Account of Holiness of Life. For as true Faith *is effectual by Love,* Gal. 5:6. so *Faith*

without Works is dead, James 2:17. And as in *Mar.* 16:16. and *John* 3:18.
he is said to be condemn'd already who does not believe; so no less is
it said of them who profess Faith in Christ in Word but deny him in
their Deeds, that *Christ knows them not,* Mat. 7:22, 23. *Luk.* 13:27. *Eph.*
5:5. *Gal.* 5:19, 20, 21. *Rev.* 22:14, 15. Where, among those *who love and
make a Lie,* I believe may be put the Mass-Priests and Monks, who
deceive the People with Fables and false Opinions, driving them from
reading the Scriptures themselves. They love a Lie who gain by it. But
what it is to make a Lie, or commit Sin, may be sufficiently gather'd
from *Rom.* 7:4, 5, 6, 15, 17, &c. 8:1, 10. and 1 *Joh.* 2:8, 9, 10. compar'd
with *Ch.* 2. *Ver.* 1. and *Ch.* 1. *Ver.* 8. that is, to sin with Endeavour, and
to profess, as it were, a Liberty of sinning, but not to labour as yet
under the Sins of Weakness. *Lastly,* As above we have said of Faith,
that altho' it is the Primary Condition of the Covenant, yet it has not
the Nature of Merit, so the same thing must be said concerning Holiness of Life. Neither has this Covenant the Nature of a Contract of
buying and selling, or of letting out and hiring, or of any unnam'd
Contract, as when I give that thou may'st do, or I do that thou may'st
do; in which Case there is requir'd an Equality between the Things
perform'd on both sides: But it has some Agreement with a Feudal
Contract, wherein one Party does out of Favour confer something upon
the other; but what is perform'd on the other Part has not the Nature
or Quality of Retribution, but only of Acknowledgment, and of a
Testimony and Proof of a grateful, faithful, and devoted, Mind, *Rom.*
11:35. And that the rather, because the one side here might require the
Performance of the other Party in this Covenant by meer Command.

The chief   §55. Holiness of Life consists of two Parts; which are the *Abstaining*
Heads of   *from Evil, and the Performance of what is good,* Psal. 34:15. For the
Holiness are
to abstain   Abstaining from Evil, is not only to be done in the beginning of Con-
from Evil.   version, as by which a dirty and thorny Way is cleansed and clear'd,
that there may be a free Access to the Saviour by Faith, *Mat.* 3:3. *Mark*
1:3. *Luke* 3:4, 5. from *Isa.* 40:2. He that sate at the Receipt of Custom
must rise and depart thence, *Mat.* 11:9. *Luke* 19:8. But it must also be
continued through the whole Life, *Rom.* 13:12, 13, 14. 1 *Cor.* 5:7, 8. 6:9,

10, 11. *Gal.* 5:19, 20, 21. *Eph.* 2:1, &c. 4:17, &c. 5:3, 4, 5, 11, &c. *Col.* 3:5, &c. 1 *Thess.* 1:9. 2 *Tim.* 2:19. *Tit.* 2:12. 1 *Pet.* 1:14, 15. 2:1, 2, 11, 12. 24:4, 2. *Heb.* 12:1. And this is to put off the old Man; that is to lay aside the former Vices, evil Habits, and evil Actions, proceeding from the Original Corruption, and afterwards confirm'd and made frequent by Custom. But as for those, who in their Infancy were dedicated to Christ by Baptism before they could commit actual Sins, and be sensible of their so doing, or could make any Reflections upon their Actions, and so cannot be possessed with any Grief for what they have done; with them Repentance takes place when they have wandred from the right way by gross and voluntary Sins, and have fallen from the Grace of the Covenant. And they must seek to return again to the Favour of the Covenant, by a Godly Sorrow for the Sins they have committed, by ceasing to commit them, and by a Reparation of the Loss and Damage which they have done to others by their Sin, and also by their trusting in the Merit of Christ, and renewal of their Desire and Endeavour after Holiness. But because even they who have once put off their former Filthiness, and are by Baptism and Faith ingrafted into Christ, are not so perfectly purg'd from their Original Pollution; but that by reason of this evil Desires, as Vapours from a filthy Lake, and Motions towards Sin will arise in them, and these may produce at least sudden slips, which yet may not throw a Man out of a State of Grace, 1 *John* 1:8, 9. *Rom.* 7:22, 23, 24. 8:1, 3, 4. Therefore the whole Life of Christians ought to be pass'd in perpetual Pennance and Strife against the evil Desires of the Flesh. Which Strife the Holy Scriptures every where express in most emphatical words, which imply partly the difficulty of suppressing these; partly the earnest Endeavour, and fervent Desire which should be imploy'd and concern'd herein. So *Rom.* 6:6. Our old Man is said to be *crucified with Christ, that the body of sin might be destroy'd, and that we might not henceforth serve sin:* So we are commanded *to crucifie the flesh with the affections and lusts.* So we are said to be *dead unto sin, that it should not reign in our mortal body, to make us obey it in the lusts thereof,* nor *yield our members instruments of unrighteousness unto sin,* Rom. 6:11, 12, 13, 14. But *by the spirit we must mortifie the deeds of the body,* Rom. 8:13. or our *earthly members,*

Col. 3:5. and *beat down the Body, and bring it into subjection,* 1 Cor. 9:27.

And to do good, and practice the Christian virtues.

§56. But as for positive Holiness, which consists in the Christian Virtues, and good Works, or Actions, that is every where in general requir'd and enjoyn'd, *Mat.* 3:8. 5:3, &c. 16:20. Chapters 6 and 7 throughout. 12:35. 18:6. 24:42, 44, 46. 25:21. *Luke* 1:74, 75. 3:8, 9. 8:15. 11:28. *John* 15:2, 4, 14, 15, 16, 17. *Acts* 24:16. *Rom.* 6:4, 19. 12: throughout, 1 *Cor.* 3:16, 17. 6:19, 20. 2 *Cor.* 7:1. *Gal.* 5:16, &c. 6:10. *Eph.* 1:4. 2:10. 3:16, 17, 19. 4:1, &c. 25, &c. 5:15, 16. 6:10, &c. *Phil.* 1:11. 4:8. *Col.* 1:10, 22. 1 *Thess.* 5:23. *Tit.* 2:12. 14:3, 8. *Heb.* 10:22, 23, 24. 12:1, 14. 2 *Pet.* 3:3, 4. 1 *John* 2:4, &c. 15, 16. 3:3, &c.

But among the several Virtues, Charity is the most eminent, as the main Test or Mark of the Christian Profession, *Luke* 6:35. 12:33. *John* 13:34, 35. 15:12. 1 *Cor.* 13. throughout, *Gal.* 5:6, 13, 14, 15. *Eph.* 4:15, 16. 5:1, 2. *Col.* 3:14. 1 *John* 4:11, 20, 21.

Hope *Romans* 5:5. 12:12. 15:4, 13. 2 *Thess.* 2:16, 17. *Rom.* 8:24. 1 *Tim.* 4:10. 5:5. *Eph.* 1:10. *Heb.* 1:6.

Patience, *Job* 5:17, &c. *Mat.* 5:39. *Rom.* 5:3, 4. 12:12. 15:4. 2 *Cor.* 6:4. *Eph.* 4:2. *Col.* 1:11. 1 *Thess.* 5:14. 1 *Thess.* 1:4, 7. 1 *Tim.* 6:11. 2 *Tim.* 2:3, 12. 2 *Pet.* 1:6. *Heb.* 10:36. 11:25. 12:7. *James* 5:7. *Rev.* 1:9. 13:10. 14:12.

Humility, *Mat.* 11:29. 18:1, &c. 20:26. 21:5. 23:7, 10, 11, 12. 14:11. 16:15. *Gal.* 5:26. *Mark* 9:34, &c. *Luke* 1:51, 52. 9:47, 48. 18:13, 22, 26. *John* 13:14. *Acts* 10:26. *Rom.* 11:20. 12:16. 1 *Cor.* 4:6, 15. 8:9. *Phil.* 2:3. *Col.* 3:12. 1 *Pet.* 5:5. *Rev.* 4:10. 19:10.

Meekness, *Mat.* 5:5, 11, 29. *Gal.* 5:22, 23. 6:1. *Eph.* 4:2. *Col.* 3:12. 2 *Tim.* 2:24. *Tit.* 3:2.

A Readiness to forgive Offences, and abstinence from Revenge. *Mat.* 5:24. 18:15, &c. *Luke* 6:12, 14, 15, 27, 28, 29. 17:3, 4. *Mark* 11:25, 26. *Eph.* 4:26, 32. *Col.* 3:13. 1 *Pet.* 3:8, 9. *Rom.* 12:19. 1 *Thess.* 5:15. *Heb.* 10:30. *James* 5:9. *Rev.* 6:10.

The Love and Endeavour for Peace. *Mat.* 5:9. *Mark* 9:50. *Rom.* 12:18. 1 *Cor.* 1:10. 3:3, 14, 33. 2 *Cor.* 13:11. *Eph.* 4:3. *Phil.* 2:1, 2, &c. *Col.* 3:15. 1 *Tim.* 2:2. 1 *Pet.* 3:11. 1 *Thess.* 4:11.

Contentment, and Acquiescence in the Condition assign'd us by

God, and the avoiding Covetousness. *Psal.* 62:10. *Mat.* 6:25, &c. *Luke* 12:15, &c. *Mark* 8:17. *John* 12:5, 6. *Acts* 8:20, 24, 26. 1 *Cor.* 6:10. *Eph.* 3:5. *Phil.* 4:11. *Col.* 3:5. 1 *Tim.* 6:6, &c. 17. *Heb.* 13:5.

Acquiescence in the Will of God, *Job* 1:21. 2:10. *Mat.* 26:39, 42. 19:21. *Mark* 10:21. *John* 12:26. *Phil.* 1:29. 3:7. *Acts* 21:13, 14.

The Denial of ones self. *Mat.* 10:37, 38, 39. 11:29. 16:24. *Mark* 8:34. *Luke* 9:23. 14:26, 27, 33. *John* 8:54. 1 *Cor.* 7:29, 30, 31.

Chastity. *Job* 31:1, 9. *Acts* 15:20. *Rom.* 1:26, 27. 1 *Cor.* 5:1, 11. 6:9, 13, 15, 18, 19. 10:8. *Eph.* 5:5. *Col.* 3:5. 1 *Thess.* 4:3, 4, 5. 1 *Tim.* 1:10. *Heb.* 13:4.

Temperance. *Luke* 2:37. *Rom.* 13:13. 1 *Cor.* 5:11. 6:10. 7:5. *Gal.* 5:21. *Eph.* 5:18. 1 *Pet.* 1:13. 5:8, 1 *Thess.* 5:9.

The Love of Prayers. *Mat.* 6:5, &c. 7. 7:18, 19. *Mark* 11:24. *Luke* 11:1, &c. 18:1, &c. 22:40. 1 *Cor.* 14:15. *Eph.* 6:18. *Col.* 4:2. 1 *Thess.* 5:17. 1 *Tim.* 2:1. 1 *John* 5:14.

To these are added the most Holy Precepts which relate to Duties of the Principal States and Orders of Men, and the Relations which they stand in to one another, which are very frequent and obvious in St. *Paul's* Epistles.

Concerning this Sanctity of Manners, enjoyn'd by Christian Religion, we may by the way observe, Not only that all those things which are deliver'd by the Philosophers for the Regulation of Manners, if compar'd with them are plainly insipid, and unsavory: But also that if all Men would universally endeavour to entertain and practice it as they ought, this would increase the Felicity of this Life to all Men, as far as is consistent with the present Frailty of our mortal Nature. For since the greatest part of the Evils with which this mortal Life is infested, proceed from the Vices of Men which are opposite to the Virtues enjoyn'd, and taught by Christian Religion: Such as Avarice, and Ambition, Pride, Hatred, Envy, the Thirst of Revenge, Fierceness, *James* 4:1, 2. And on the other hand, a great part of the Inconveniencies to which our present frail Condition is obnoxious, might be either remov'd, or much alleviated by Patience, Charity, and the other Christian Virtues: Certainly, if Men would live according to the Rules of Christian Love, there would be no Wars waged among Christians, which bring with them always a vast Inundation of Woes and Miseries; and on the other hand Peace would always flourish among them, and with Peace, Plenty, and the Abundance of all things. So also how many Troubles and Cares might we set aside, and be free from, if Men knew how to measure the things of this World by the Rule of the Christian Law! How many Weaknesses and Diseases might be prevented, if Men would govern their Appetites, and the Motions of their Minds, by the Virtues which are recommended to Christians. These things, and many more of like sort, any one must be sensible of who can conceive what the present Life and Condition of Men would be, if all did duly endeavour to conform themselves to the Precepts of Christianity, and what Evils proceed from hence; That the greatest part of Men suffer themselves to be govern'd by their wicked Lusts, and the Manners of the Age, or the Craft of prophane Politicks. So that if ever there is to be a better Condition of Mankind, and a happier State of the World, it is not to be expected but from a serious and universal Practice of Christian Piety and Virtue.

Of the Holy Eucharist.

§57. Further, That the Memory of this Covenant, confirm'd by the Death of the Saviour, may be frequently renewed, and impress'd the more strongly upon the Minds of Men by the help of some external Action which can fall under the notice of the Senses: And that it may be assur'd, and seal'd by a certain singular Monument: And the Grace of it at the same time be confer'd to the Faithful; it pleas'd the Saviour just at the instant of his Passion to Institute the Rite or Sacrament of his Supper. For the better understanding the Nature of which, it would conduce not a little, if it were observ'd, That this Rite was borrow'd by Christ from among those which were used by the *Jews* at the eating of the Pascal Lamb, and was advanced by him to be of a Nature far more sublime. For with this Rite the Master of the Family distributed the unleavened Bread, which he had blessed, and broke to those who stood about the Table, saying these words: This is the Bread of Affliction which our Fathers did eat when they went from the *Egyptian* Bondage. Our Saviour improv'd this Sentence, as if he should say; hitherto in the Celebration of the Passover ye did eat Bread, which

exprest the Misery of your Fathers when they went in hast out of *Egypt*.
But I now reach to you a far more noble Bread, which is my Body
which is given for you for a Sacrifice, to bring you, being freed from
the Service of Sin and the Devil, into the Liberty of the Covenant and
my Kingdom. So also in the Celebrating of the Pascal Solemnity, a
Cup full of Wine was distributed, joyn'd with the praising of God for
that he had made so noble a Creature for the chearing and refreshing
of Mankind. But instead of this another federal Cup was substituted
by the Saviour, as if he should say; Hitherto ye have drank meer Wine,
but I now mingle for you a more noble Cup, For this is my Blood, or
the Cup of the new Covenant in my Blood which is shed for you for
the Remission of Sins. Thus it appears that the solemn words of the
mystical Supper are taken from two Rites of the *Jewish* Covenant: One
from the Pascal Solemnity Instituted when the *Israelites* became a free
People, and subject to the supream Dominion of God himself; and the
other from that by which *Moses* Establish'd the Obedience of the People to the Laws, as the noblest part of the Divine Common-wealth.
Exod. 24:8. *Behold this is the blood of the covenant which the Lord hath
made with you, concerning all these words.* But 'tis not now the Blood
of Bulls and Goats that is shed or poured out, but that of the Saviour
himself. *Heb.* 9:10. And whereas, otherwise, Blood is a thing which
makes unclean, and the eating of which is accounted among things
forbidden; yet the Blood of the Victims had a Virtue of Cleaning and
Purifying, as it did prefigure the Blood of the Federal Victim. And this
Blood much rather must have this Virtue, *Heb.* 9:13, 14. *To cleanse us
from all sin,* 1 *John* 1:7. *Rev.* 1:5. So that in this Sacrament, Christ reaches
out to us, not only his Body, but also his Blood, as the Vehicle of his
Soul, or Life, *Lev.* 17:11. from which things the Genuine End, and Fruit
of the Sacrament does appear; which is, on the part of him that uses
it, that he should repeat his Promise by which he entred into the
Covenant in Christ, and should therein apply to himself the Benefits
procur'd by the Passion and Merit of Christ; and testifie himself very
thankful for them, and so publickly declare himself a Subject of the
Kingdom of Christ. And on the part of Christ these are conferr'd and
seal'd, and by a certain Divine Power bestow'd on those who rightly

use this Sacrament. Which is agreeable to the ancient Custom of making Covenants with a Sacrifice, and a Feast annexed to it. See *Gen.* 26:28, 29. 31:44, 46, 54. Whence we judge the Genuine sense of what is said, *John* 6:53, &c. to be this, That his Discourse must not be understood strictly to concern the Lord's Supper; for otherwise there could be no Salvation for Infants and Children, who before they partake of it depart from this Life; neither could the Thief on the Cross, nor many of the Catechumens of the Primitive Times of Christianity be sav'd. Neither is the whole force and meaning of his Discourse exhausted, if it be said, that to eat the Flesh of Christ, and to drink his Blood, is the same thing as to believe in Christ, or to place our Hope, and trust for Salvation in the Satisfaction of Christ. And I suppose there cannot be found in all the Holy Scripture, or any prophane Writers a Translation of this sort. Therefore it seems to me that the Sacrament of the Supper is also comprehended and included, and thereby after the manner of a Synechdocical Expression the whole Confederation, or as it were Incorporation of the Faithful Man with Christ, which is seal'd by the Sacramental eating the Body and drinking the Blood of Christ. In the same manner as the whole Instrument of a Contract is spoken of under the Name of the Hand and Seal: To strike a Covenant, signifies the whole Composition of the Covenant as it is taken from the Rite of striking a Victim for the Confirmation of a Covenant.

Concerning the Invisible Matter of this Sacrament.

§58. But there is very sharp Debate among Christians concerning the Invisible Matter of this Sacrament, because the words are very plain, *This is my Body; This is my Blood;* and yet there is nothing that appears to the Senses but Bread and Wine. To us it seems most natural and easie to proceed thus in this Matter: Since the Sacrifice by which the Covenant of God in Christ was confirm'd, being once slain on the Cross, is not to be repeated, *Heb.* 7:27. 9:12, 25, 28. it is not necessary nor agreeable, that the Body and Blood of Christ be present in this Sacrament, with the same Qualities which they were endow'd with when he offer'd himself to God on the Cross, nor that it should here have the same Effect as it had there. Yet, because St. *Paul* teaches us,

1 *Cor.* 10:6. That the *Bread which we break is the Communion of the Body of Christ, and the Wine which we drink is the Communion of the Blood of Christ,* we must say, that Communion or Communication does not signifie a naked Sign or Symbol, and therefore that not only Bread and Wine are present, but also, and conjointly, the Body and Blood of Christ: Where it is not to be overlook'd as inconsiderable, that upon the account of this Conjunction, the Attributes of the Body of Christ and the Bread, and of the Blood of Christ and the Wine, are reciprocally predicated of Both. So 1 *Cor.* 11:24. it is said, the Body which was *broken* for you, when properly the breaking belongs to the Bread. *Luke* 22:20. It is said, the *Cup which was shed* for you, when properly the shedding, or being pour'd out, belongs to the Blood of Christ. For if the word *shed,* there, should be referr'd to the Blood, it should have been said, *In my Blood shed for you.* And that Cup, or the Wine alone, is not the Covenant; but as it is in *Matthew, This is my Blood of the New Covenant, which is shed for many for the Remission of Sins:* And in *Mark, This is my Blood of the New Covenant which is shed for many.* When therefore the clearness and emphaticalness of the words will not permit us to deny, but that the Body and Blood of Christ are receiv'd in the Sacred Supper, the only Question that remains is about the Manner of the Presence: And this seems what may be left undecided, provided only it be simply believ'd, that in this Sacrament the Body and Blood of Christ are truly given to us, and are verily and indeed taken and receiv'd, eaten and drank by us. For altho' Christ was in a visible manner advanced into Heaven, yet since his Humane Nature by virtue of the Personal Union, is inseparable from the Divine, and is now not only possess'd of the Condition and State of a glorified Body, 1 *Cor.* 15:44. but also advanced to the right Hand of God, not to a certain Place, but to the right Hand of Power: He who considers the Truth and Omnipotence of God, may reasonably be ready to put off that Curiosity concerning the manner of the Presence, and may simply acquiesce in the Divine Word.

§59. The whole Body of them who come into this Covenant, make up the Kingdom of Christ, which is assign'd to him by the Father as his Peculiar. Into which he invites and calls all Men; and those who do not despise his Invitation, and call, he takes to be his Beloved Subjects, and them he governs and protects, *John* 10:27, 28, 29. 17:24. *Rom.* 8:34. *Eph.* 2:6. 4:11, 12. *Luke* 1:33. *Acts* 10:42. *Rom.* 14:7, 8, 9. He who is a genuine Subject of this Kingdom, which is also known under the Name of the Church, is a Partaker of all the Benefits purchased by Christ, and so is a Member of the Mystical Body of which Christ is the Head, from whom a vital Spirit flows into all the Members: So that all the Actions of these derive their Value from Christ, and are pleasing to God in him: And also, what is done to any one of these, does as it were touch himself, in like manner as a Prince reckons himself concern'd in the Injuries which are done to his Subjects, *Acts* 9:5. 2 *Cor.* 1:5. 4:10. *Rom.* 8:17. *Col.* 1:24. To this Matter belong all those Expressions which speak of the Union of the Faithful with Christ, which is not to be understood of a naked Conjunction of Substances on both sides, since in God all things are, and live and move; but after the manner of a Moral Conjunction, whereby many Persons come together into one Moral Body; and from that Coalition or Conjunction they partake in certain Rites and Benefits, *Eph.* 5:25, 26, 30, 32. 1 *John* 2:24, 27, 28. 3:2. *John* 6:56. 14:23. 15:4, &c. 17:21, &c. 1 *Cor.* 15:15, 17. *Gal.* 2:19, 20. 3:27. *Eph.* 4:15, 16. *Rom.* 10:10, 11. They who shall persist to the end of their Lives in this Covenant, to them Death will be a Passage to a better Life, *Phil.* 1:21, 23. And their Soul shall be receiv'd by Christ, *Acts* 7:56, 59. 2 *Tim.* 4:8, 18. who at the end of the World shall enjoy a glorious Resurrection; and after they have in the last Judgment, heard a most mild Absolving Sentence pass upon them, shall enter into a most happy Life which shall endure for ever, *Mat.* 22:30. 25:34, &c. *Luke* 10:35, 36. *John* 5:28, 29. 6:39. 11:25, 26. *Acts* 24:15. 1 *Cor.* 15. throughout. 2 *Cor.* 5:1, &c. *Col.* 3:4. *Phil.* 3:21. 1 *Thess.* 4:14, &c. 2 *Tim.* 2:11. *Rev.* 20:12.

§60. In this System which we have composed, tho' but in a rude Draught, and capable of much polishing, we suppose all the Articles of Faith necessary to Salvation are contain'd. So that none of them can be deny'd or call'd in question, but the whole Chain or Connexion of the Faith would be broken, and the Body of Christian Doctrine be render'd maim'd and imperfect. We also think this System to be so perspicuous and clear, that the whole Contents may be easily comprehended by any one, and easily retain'd in memory: And also that the Reason of the Articles, and their Connexion with one another, may appear to any one. And there can be no doubt, but that if all the Protestants would consent to it, which why they should not I can see no good Reason, many Controversies would fall of themselves, and the way to Concord and Union would be not a little advanc'd thereby. But this System must not be accounted lame and imperfect, because we have slightly past over the Questions about Grace and Predestination. The reason of doing which was, because we had a desire to find out such a System, as wherein both the Parties of the Protestants might easily consent and agree. For if I had thought fit to express the Opinion of the Lutherans upon these Heads, it had been easie to have found a place where those Principles might have been inserted. But what the Reform'd do deliver concerning Predestination, and the Grace which is suited to it, could find no place in our System. For we judge it to imply a Contradiction that a Covenant should be made by God with Men, and yet that they should be sav'd or damn'd by virtue of a certain absolute Decree. For if God has without respect to any thing decreed to save certain Men, and to damn the rest, a Covenant seems superfluous and illusory. Whence it seem'd better to set aside those Opinions for the present, to see whether the Parties that differ about them, may not in process of time be brought into Union by an amicable Conference. Unless the Consequences of those Points did reach to other Fundamental Articles of Faith: it seem'd that they might be abstracted from them, and those Points being set aside, there might be an Agreement and Concord about the rest. Especially since we may observe that Christ and his Apostles in the beginning of their Preaching make no mention at all of any Predestination, and in the Process of it they are

What are Fundamental Articles.

very sparing in doing this; which yet, it had been very fit they should have mention'd, if any absolute Decree ought to have the place of a Fundamental Proposition in the System of Divinity. And it may very well suffice a Christian, that would be duly modest, to acquiesce in those things which God hath in time reveal'd, and to conform himself to the Order which he has prescrib'd, and not to doubt but the Effect of them which God hath promised shall certainly be fulfilled in him, and not to break in upon the secret Counsels of God, but to join them with his reveal'd Will. To which purpose is that, 1 *Tim.* 6:3, &c. compar'd with 2 *Tim.* 1:13. But neither is it requisite that every thing be exactly contain'd in a System of Christian Faith, which is deliver'd in the sacred Scriptures. For in these there are many other things to be found, the Knowledge of which, tho' it be an Ornament, and might conduce to the Perfection of a Christian, yet if a Man be altogether ignorant of them, or entertains any Errours concerning them, he does not therefore presently fall from a State of Salvation, nor may it be thought that he should be excluded from the Society of the Faithful. Tho' in a Teacher of the Church it is manifest a larger Knowledge is requir'd then in an ordinary Christian. But this is to be taken with due Qualification, as meaning that those Points which are for a while set aside, do not oppose the undoubted Fundamental Articles, either directly, or by Consequences deduced from them; nor are those Articles weakened or overthrown by these Consequences. As also this is universally requir'd, That no Point or Principle whatsoever, which is clearly propounded in the Canonical Books be denied: For when any Truth clearly expess'd there is oppos'd, the Authority of Sacred Scripture is therein denied, and so the whole Foundation of the Faith is overthrown. But they who dispute only concerning the Genuine and true Sense of some places of Holy Scriptures, they are not for this to be thought to call in question their Authority, especially if the Sense which they contend for is not contrary to the Analogy of Faith, nor such as that for the maintaining of it the whole Context of Scripture must be wrested. Lastly, That also is by some well observ'd; That an Erroneous Opinion may be deliver'd by an Orthodox Person, when tis such an one as the fault of it does chiefly appear in the Consequences which are deduced from it. If he who proposes that Erroneous Opinion does not see those Consequences, he cannot be condemn'd as holding the Errours which are deduced by Consequence from thence; and therefore he has right to desire that those Consequences may not be imputed to him. But when afterward those bad Consequences are demonstrated to follow truly, and without any Sophistication from that first Erroneous Opinion it is not lawful to others who take upon them that first Thesis to protest that they do not acknowledge those Consequences. And so the Errour which before any Controversie about it, or at the beginning of it is admitted through Imprudence may be pardon'd; it may afterwards, when the Controversie is search'd to the bottom become a Fundamental one.

§61. It remains that we suggest some things concerning the Controversies which are maintain'd between the two great Bodies of the Protestants, and that we give our Opinion, whether or no any Temperament may be found out whereby they may be compos'd. Which, yet, not only contains our private Speculation, but also is what we shall not obstinately adhere to; and we publish our Thoughts about this Matter for this End alone, that hereby an Occasion may be offer'd to others to inquire more carefully into this Matter. Whence I would not have the things which I shall propose to create any Prejudice against my self, or the Church in which I was born, and have been Educated, and in the Doctrine of which I have design'd to persevere to the end of my Life. Neither yet am I influenced by any Hatred against the Reform'd Church, to which three most Gracious Lords whom I have serv'd have been addicted. The most Serene Electors of the Roman Empire, *Charles Lewis Palatine,* and *Frederick William,* and *Frederick* the 3*d.* of *Brandenburg:* And no less have I made use of the Friendship, Favour, and good Offices of many of that Religion. But what I endeavour here, proceeds only from a Concern for Truth, and the Publick Good, when, therefore, in the foregoing Age from a very small Occasion, as it appear'd at first, the Corruptions of the Romish Religion were brought to light, a great part of *Europe* fell, as by an Instinct to reject these, and having cast off the Yoke of the Pope of *Rome* to Reform Religion

Of the Controversies among the Protestants.

to its Primitive Purity, according to the Holy Scriptures: But because that Affair was undertaken in divers places by several Men, and not by Compact or Agreement: It so happen'd, that the same Rites were not every where Retain'd, which yet add nothing to the Substance of Religion, nor was there a Consent to the same Confession of Faith Compos'd by a Common Agreement. And there having been an early Dissention about some Points, between *Luther,* who made the beginning of Reforming in *Saxony,* and *Zwinglius,* who a little while after fell upon doing it among the *Helvetians,* and the Doctrine of the former being propagated through *Germany* and the Northern Tracts, and that of the Latter among the *Helvetians,* the *Belgick* Provinces, *England* and *France,* those Dissentions were spread among the Followers of both, and hindred them from ever joining in one Communion: Which thing was no small Obstacle to the Progress of the Reformation, the common Enemies taking occasion thence to exclaim against the Hereticks, as they falsly call them, and to say they were acted by the Spirit of Confusion, and they knew not what to believe, or not to believe. But especially did that Division cause great Mischiefs through all *Germany.* For when all that, so far as it shook off the Pope's Yoke, professed the Principles of *Luther,* express'd in the *Augustan* Confession,[40] and at length obtain'd the publick Peace and Liberty for them: After this, they began to creep in amongst them who would needs spread about the Principles of *Zwinglius* and *Calvin,* and did here and there prevail, that the ancient Rites which were tolerated by *Luther,* should be abrogated, and introduc'd a Reform'd Doctrine according to their mind amongst them: At this the Papists began to quarrel, and to say, the Peace of Religion did belong only to them who profess'd the Doctrine exhibited in the *Augustan* Confession, and therefore these new Men were not to be tolerated in *Germany.* From thence there began to be sharp Disputes among the Divines, the *Lutherans* condemning the *Reform'd* as erroneous, and the Reform'd arguing that they also were comprehended under the *Augustan* Confession, and ought to be partakers of the Priv-

40. See note 14.

iledges then obtain'd. The *Lutheran* Princes urg'd, that altho' it was
not to be denied but these Men dissented from them in some things,
yet they should not be excluded from the Publick Peace, especially
since there might be some hope that they might forsake their Errours,
and return to their former Communion. But when the Papists cherish'd this Discord, and flatter'd the *Lutherans* that they might forsake
the Reform'd, and then when these were oppress'd, they also might
the more easily be reduced into their Order: The *Reform'd* began to
provide for their Security by Leagues, and fell into several Counsels,
which gave Matter for a horrid Civil War; after that, the chief of the
Reform'd Party, the Elector Palatine accepted of the Crown of *Bohemia*.
Which Endeavours succeeded so ill, that the whole Protestant Cause
was in imminent Danger, had not the Providence of God immediately
interposed to restore it. For altho' by the Peace of *Osnabrug*,[41] the
Reform'd had an equal liberty of Religion confirm'd to them with the
others, yet without doubt it had conduc'd very much to the establishment of the Affairs of both if the Dissention between them could,
saving the Divine Truth, have been utterly taken away. In that Dispute
the *Reform'd* condemn the *Lutheran* Divines as guilty of too much
Sharpness, and of Rashness and Rigour in condemning them. The
Lutherans on the other side aggravate the Errours of the *Reform'd*, and
load them with odious Consequences: And charge them with acting
insidiously, and unsincerely, and that they soften hard Expressions, and
cover their Principles with specious Colours, and make show of an
Opinion agreeing in words with them, and all the while, that they have
secret Reserves to themselves, and cherish still in their minds their old
Opinions. And altho' the *Reform'd* frequently use the Name of Brethren, yet they omit not to impute to the *Lutheran's* monstrous Opinions,
how much soever they contradict them, and where ever they prevail,
they oppress them either openly or by oblique Arts and Methods, and
extend as much as is possible their own Bounds by the diminution of

---

41. The treaty of Osnabrück, between the German empire and the Protestant
states, along with the treaty in Münster between the empire and France, made up
the Peace of Westphalia (1648), the general settlement ending the Thirty Years' War.

those of the others: When they should rather endeavour to deserve that Applause, which would be given by all Men to those who can gain any Advantages against the Common Enemy. Nor is it worth while, say they, to receive the Rites of the *Reform'd* into the place of those of the *Lutherans:* Because, whatever of good there is among the *Reform'd,* that they have in common with the *Lutherans;* and what they have that is peculiar to them, conduces nothing towards a solid Piety; and it is so candied over, and adorn'd with specious Interpretations, that they themselves do even seem to be asham'd of it. I am not willing to excuse or reprove any of these things on either side, since the first Rule to be observ'd by those who would promote Peace and Concord, is to commit to oblivion the things that are past. These things therefore being dismiss'd, we shall come to the Controversies themselves.

§62. Those Controversies may be referr'd to two Heads or Ranks; For some of them are particular Ones, and touch only one Article of Christian Religion: But some are dissused through the whole System of Divinity, and do greatly alter, if not utterly overthrow it. To the former Rank we refer the Controversies concerning the Person of Christ, and the Sacrament of the Supper: To the other, the Questions about Predestination and Grace. Upon these, the other things controverted do commonly depend: So that these being compos'd, the other will fall of themselves. The Controversies concerning the Person of Christ, do seem to have their rise from Human Curiosity, while it would needs bring that Mystery, more than it ought to be, to the Test of Human Reason: When yet it may be said of that, no less than of the other Mysteries of Divine Wisdom, and Goodness, and Justice, discover'd in the Method of Salvation, that the Angels *desire to look into it:* or, that such is the Splendour and August Sublimity of it, that even these Holy Spirits, who enjoy a far greater Light and Clearness of Understanding than we do, dare not observe it but as it were at a narrow Passage, lest they should be dazled with the direct Beams of so great a Glory. When yet the confidence of some Men in defining concerning this, is no less than that of the Physicians, in describing the Parts of the Human Body when they lye dissected before them. But I believe

And indeed about the Person of Christ.

those Contentions would die of themselves, if, as I have given my Advice above, we would proceed no further in this Mystery than the plain Assertions of Holy Scripture call, or than the Office of a Mediator leads us. Whatsoever exceeds these Bounds, should be left undetermin'd, nor should any take the presumptuous Pains to define concerning them. But besides, The Crime of Heresie must not be imputed by one side or other, for any difference in the Method of handling this Article, and in Scholastical Distinctions. The chief Debate seems to concern the Omnipresence of the Body of Christ. The *Lutherans* seem to maintain it chiefly for this Reason, that they may not divide and take away the Union of the Natures, which, according to the Expression of the Ancient Church concerning it, is inseparable. The *Reform'd* on the other hand seem to fear, least if this should be granted, the Humane Nature of Christ would be utterly destroy'd, since 'tis of the Essence of a Body to be extended and bounded by certain Limits. But before they had contended on both sides with so much Heat, they ought first to have defin'd what may be the Nature and Quality of the Omnipresence of God. Which indeed is in no wise to be thought to consist in the coextension of the Divine Essence with all the Bodies of the World. As neither is the mutual περιχώρησις of the Natures as the *Greek* Fathers speak, to be measur'd by a certain coextension of the Human Body with the Divine Essence: But it implies another most close manner of Conjunction which transcends our feeble Thoughts. Therefore we may believe, that Christ even as Man or his Human Nature, and his Body and Flesh, which we suppose ought never to be consider'd out of a Personal Union with the Divine One, is at least present there where he has promis'd he would be present, because of the indivisible Union of the Natures in one Person: But yet so, as that 'tis in no wise necessary to imagine such an Extension of this Body as would interfere with the Dimensions of the Bodies to which it is said to be present. But when on both sides the greatest of all Mysteries, the Personal Union is acknowledg'd, or that the Human Nature is assum'd into the Person of the Word, never to be put off again by this, nor to be separated or divided from it, why should the Consequence of that Union be call'd in question? And why may there not, by reason of it, be a more sublime manner of Presence granted to Christ as Man, than that which may be ascrib'd to common Bodies present to one another, altho' the manner of that Presence cannot by us be exactly defin'd? So because Christ hath promised, *Where two or three are gathered together in my Name, I will be in the midst of them,* Matth. 18:20. And, *I am with you to the end of the World,* Matth. 28:20. Why should the Nature and Quality of Human Bodies hinder, but that we may believe whole Christ, and even as Man to be present to all the Assemblies of the Faithful, and even to every particular Person of them? Especially, since while he was conversant on Earth both before and after his Resurrection, he perform'd such Actions as other Bodies are not capable of. And it is not to be doubted, but that hereafter the Bodies of the Blessed shall be advanced far above the present Condition of our mortal Bodies. On the other hand, we judge it superfluous and rash to enquire nicely concerning the Presence of the Man Christ Jesus, beyond or out of the Kingdom of Grace; As whether or no Christ be present with his Human Nature, or how he is so present, there where he has not promised his Presence: As for instance, with this or that Star, or with all the Stars together, or with this or that Stone, or the like. For what does it signifie to the Covenant of God with Men in Christ, and to their eternal Salvation, to define concerning such Questions? Nor is it repugnant, that Christ should afford his Body and Blood to those that receive the Sacred Supper in a singular Manner, and by a kind of Presence imperceptible to us, and so as he is not present to any other Creatures. For those things are to be referr'd to the Will of God, which being discover'd in the Case, it does not become weak Men to question either his Power of performing his Promise, or to be solicitous about the Manner of his performing it, *Luke* 1:37. For otherwise, since the Lord Christ is no where without his Humanity, there would follow of it self an Omnipresence of the Body properly so call'd.

About the §63. The other particular Controversie concerns the Sacred Supper;
Lord's Supper. about which tho' there was little Dispute that we read of in the next Ages after Christ, yet the Christians in the *Western* Parts have for an Age or two last past very sharply differ'd about it. Concerning which Controversie, it may be observ'd, That so far as it is about the manner

of the Presence it is more curious then useful, provided there be a Consent only concerning the Substance of the Sacrament, and the end and use of it. For the *Manner* both in Naturals and Morals lies often times hid, and is unknown; and for all that there may be no less Profit and Advantage from the right use of them. And further, this is to be taken for granted, That the Substance of the Sacrament, and what is therein exhibited and receiv'd, does not depend upon the Perswasion and Credulity, or Belief of the Men that use it, but upon the Disposition and Appointment of him that Institutes it. And therefore neither a true nor a false Interpretation of the words of Institution can make that the Body and Blood of Christ is present, or not present in the Supper, but the Will and the Veracity or Truth of him that hath Instituted it. To which these words may be applied, *Rom. 3. Shall their unbelief make the faith of God of none effect?* So, for instance, If any unknown sort of Meat or Drink be given to any Man, tho' he should entertain a belief that it is otherwise than it truly is; yet is not that Meat or Drink therein alter'd or chang'd; and the Man does not receive that which he perswades himself he receives, but that which was offer'd to him by his Entertainer. So tho' it signifies much towards the Fruit of this Sacrament with what Perswasion a Man comes to partake of it, yet that Perswasion, whether too large, or too narrow, does not change the Substance of the Sacrament. From whence it follows, That they who receive this Sacrament whole, and according to the Institution of Christ, do receive the same thing as to the Substance, and neither more nor less, altho' they think diversly concerning that which is invisible. And so in this Supper there is not more receiv'd among the *Lutherans,* than among the *Reform'd;* nor is there less receiv'd among these then among the former. So that there is no need to dispute so fiercely concerning this Article under which is included in the Opinion of all Antiquity an awful Mistery, which cannot be perceiv'd by our Senses, and which ought to be consider'd and handled with a sort of Sacred Horrour. As for the differing Opinions about this, 'tis certain, that the *Lutherans,* no less then the *Reform'd* abhor the monstrous Transubstantiation of the Papists, and the Consequences which are deduced thence: For as much as hardly any thing more absur'd and horrid, then that Opinion can be invented either in Divinity or Philosophy. For

what can be more monstrous, then that the Body of the Saviour which
is partaker of Divine Adoration, should be produced from a bit of
Bread at the pronouncing a certain Form of Words by the Priest?
Which Body too must not be reckon'd born of the Virgin *Mary,* besides
which Body the Saviour has no other, but is anew produced upon the
Altar: Or that this can be infinite times in a day produc'd by the words
of Priests, which heretofore was with such solemn Preparation by Almighty God, and with such Expectation of the faithful People, born
of the Virgin, and hang'd on a Cross, to make Attonement for Mankind. And since according to their Opinion the Body of Christ made
of Bread, remains even after the Celebration of the Sacrament, and is
to be ador'd. It does not appear how it can be that that Body should
be obnoxious to Corruption, when in the Sacred Supper it is receiv'd
by the Communicants. Therefore, whether they say the Body of Christ
is digested by them, and turn'd into their Substance, or that it continues void of Alteration or Corruption, both of these is attended with
very great Absurdity. For from thence it would come to pass, that either
the Flesh of all those who receive the Supper must become adorable,
and fit to be worshipped, or they must be as the Repositories wherein
this Body is laid. But the *Lutherans* stay at the naked words of the
Institution, without any Interpretation, lest they should seem willing
to limit and confine the Truth, and the Omnipotence of God. Therefore they determine that the Bread and Wine remain what they are, as
well in the use of them, as afterwards, and yet so that in the use of the
Sacrament the Body and Blood of Christ are verily present together
with the Elements, and are indeed taken and receiv'd with the Mouth
of the Body, but in a manner that cannot be perceiv'd by our Senses:
And so indeed as that there is not any new and peculiar Body produced
for every Communicant, and given to him, but so as that all the Communicants do truly partake of that one Body of Christ which hung
upon the Cross, and of that Blood which he there shed. Yet neither
the one nor the other does loose any thing, nor is it therefore torn,
lessened, or consum'd, 1 *Cor.* 10:17. For the establishing which Opinion, it is not necessary to fly to the Omnipresence of the Flesh of Christ.
Which if any should so rudely assert, it would follow that the Body of

Christ would be eaten, and his Blood drank with all our Meat and Drink; that I do not mention any more of the Absurdities that would attend this. But to those Reasonings which are objected from the Judgment of the Senses, and the Nature of Natural Bodies, the Truth and Omnipotence of God is justly oppos'd, by which this may easily be perform'd, that this Body may be present after a manner which is Imperceptible to us, which through the Assumption of the Son of God, and the eminent Degree of Glorification which it has attain'd, does far exceed the Nature and Quality of other Bodies. Therefore if there were any Errour in this Opinion (which is in no wise granted) it would yet be therefore very innocent, because we bear such Reverence to the words of our Saviour, that we suffer our Reason to be Captivated to the Obedience of Faith, and chuse rather simply to receive those things, then curiously to interpret them. On the other hand the *Reform'd,* that they may cast away that simple Sense of the Words, and seek a Figurative Interpretation of them, have used Reasonings taken from the Testimony of the Senses, and from the Nature of Bodies, both because Christ is ascended into Heaven, and sits at the right Hand of God, and upon that account is no longer present upon Earth; and also because 'tis contrary to a due Reverence to say, that the most Holy Body and Blood are receiv'd by the unworthy and the Wicked. For as for that Cavil, that if the Body of Christ were present in the Supper, it must have been long since eaten up; it is so silly as is not worthy to have any regard in a Discourse of Divinity. From whence they believe that in this Sacrament there is nothing else receiv'd by the Mouth of our Body, but the Bread and Wine: But the worthy Receivers, and the Faithful, lifting up their Thoughts by Faith into the Heavens where Christ is, do in a spiritual manner eat of him in this sacred Ceremony, and so are made partakers of the Benefits purchased by him. But since the Sense of this Interpretation reaches no further then this, That in the use of the Sacred Supper the Saviour is call'd to mind by an Act of Faith; it does not appear what occasion, or need there was for that Sacrament, since the Faithful might in every place, and at all times call to mind the Saviour, or how such a calling him to mind could possibly be express'd in these words; *eat ye, this is my body.* Some seem to them-

selves to argue with more subtilty, and say, The first Supper Celebrated
by Christ himself, must be reckon'd the Rule of all other Celebrations
of it. But in that, Christ did not offer to the Disciples to be eaten by
them that Body which then sate at the Table; nor did he give them his
Blood separated from his Body to drink. For it cannot agreeably be
said that in the same Act there was a double Presence of the Body of
Christ, which was yet in its low and humble State, the one visible, the
other invisible, and so that the same Body sate in a local and visible
manner at the Table, and was eaten by the Disciples in an invisible
manner, and as without place. But since they were to eat of a Federal
Victim, we must know that the Saviour in this Sacred Rite substituted
Bread in the stead of his Body, and Wine in the stead of his Blood.
Especially since for preserving the Memory of any Person, it is not
necessary to have the Person himself, but some other thing is put for
this purpose in the stead of the Person himself. Yet we must not believe
the Bread and Wine to be a naked Symbol, but a Communication, or
Mean by which we come into Participation of the Body and Blood of
Christ, as St. *Paul* speaks, 1 *Cor.* 10:16. But of what sort that Communion, or Communication is whether Physical or Moral, may be very
well gather'd from that very place of St. *Paul.* By a Physical Communion, or Participation, must be understood the Conjunction of two
Bodies, as of Water and Wine, of Meal and Sugar: But by a Moral one
is meant, such as when any thing partakes of the Virtue and Efficacy
of the other, and in that respect is accounted the same with another,
or connected with it. As among the *Jews,* they who did eat of the Flesh
of the Victim, were made partakers of the Altar, that is of the *Jewish*
Worship, and of all the Benefits which did accompany that Worship,
so also they who did eat of things Sacrificed to Idols, were partakers
of Devils; not for that they did eat the Substance of the Devils, but
because they did derive upon themselves the Guilt of Idolatry. From
all which things, we may learn to understand the words of the Institution in this Sense; *This is my body, this is the cup of the new covenant
in my blood:* That is, This Bread eaten by the Faithful in the Ceremony
of this Supper, this Wine also therein drank by such, shall have the
same Virtue and Efficacy, as if ye should eat the Substance it self of

my Body, and drink the very Substance of my Blood: Or this Bread is put in the stead of the Sacrificed Flesh, this Wine is in the stead of the Sacrificed Blood, whereby the Covenant between God and Men, having Me for the Mediator of it, is establish'd. But neither are such sort of Expressions signifying an Equivalence, or Substitution, unusual either in Sacred Scriptures, or Prophane Authors. For Instance, *Job* 31:24. *If I have made gold my hope,* 2 Kings 11:12. *Elijah* was the Chariots of *Israel,* and the Horsemen thereof, *John* 19:26, 27. *Woman behold thy son, son behold thy mother,* Mat. 12:49. *He that does the Will of my Father, he is my Mother, my Sister, and Brother,* Phil. 3:18, 19. *Their Belly is their God,* said of those who are Enemies of the Cross of Christ. So in *Virgil* we have a like Expression, *Thou shalt be to me the great* Apollo.[42] For in Articles of Faith, it is better to follow that which is simple and easie, than to indulge to the Exercises of Wit, in seeking Subtilties. And it has been observ'd, that while the Reins have been let loose too much to Human Reason in discoursing upon this Article, the other Mysteries of Christian Religion have been struck at, so that by degrees *Socinianism* is at length sprung up. But if on both sides it is sincerely profess'd, That in the Lord's Supper the Body and Blood of Christ are truly and properly eaten and drank, and there is a participation of the Benefits which he has purchased, the Controversie that remains is about the manner of Eating and Drinking, and of the Presence, of the Body and Blood of Christ, which both do acknowledge transcends the reach of Human Reason; and so they make use of Reasonings in a Case where Reason cannot determin any thing.

§64. But the Controversies which are maintain'd concerning Predestination and Grace, are diffused almost through the whole System of Divinity, and alter the Whole, and therefore seem to be of the greater Importance. And this will be obvious at first sight, if it be observ'd in what Order in their *Hypothesis* both Parties place the Principles which they build upon it, and in what order indeed they must place them

The Controversies concerning Grace and Predestination.

42. Virgil, *The Eclogues,* III, verse 104.

according to natural Consequence. With the *Lutherans* this is the *Hypothesis* which is assum'd. That we must suppose the same Order of the Decrees of God, in the Divine Mind, as there does appear to be in the Execution of them: Or, that God has decreed from all Eternity to save or damn Men in the same Order and Manner as in time their Salvation or Damnation is produced and brought to Effect. For we can no otherwise have the Knowledge of what is the Will of God, but by Revelation, and by his Works. But in preaching to Men and calling them to Salvation, there was never a beginning made at the Doctrine of Predestination, but with Exhortations to Repentance, and to embrace the Means of Salvation which God has appointed. No where do we find, that Christ, or any of his Apostles, began their Preaching in that way; by telling Men, that God has by an absolute Will elected some to Eternal Life, and others by a like Decree he has reprobated, therefore Repent and believe the Gospel. And it is very obvious, that such a way of urging Men to embrace the Gospel, is most unreasonable. But it ought to suffice us to embrace what God offers in time, whom we must believe to deal sincerely with us, and to use no Dissimulation in his Applications to us. So that we should not be solicitous what God has before-hand decreed in his secret Counsel, which it is not in our Power ever to determin, at least with respect to this or that Person in particular. And certainly, a Man may be in the Favour of God, and in Covenant with him, and may be saved, tho' it never came into his Thoughts that God form'd a Decree before-hand concerning the Salvation of Men. This Foundation being laid, the first thing built upon it is the Creation of Man just and holy. Then follows his voluntary Fall, which came to pass without any Fault on the part of God. Then must be set the New Covenant, or the New Way of Salvation in Christ, as the Saviour of the whole Human Race; after which, came his Death and Merit on the behalf of all Men; after this, his Invitation of all Men to embrace the Saviour, and the affording efficacious Means for this End: But this Invitation, only a part of Mankind do embrace, by Powers implanted in them, the Means being afforded by God; others by their own Wickedness and Resistance reject it. And when God from all Eternity, foresaw both these things, he chose the former, and predestinated them to Eternal Life, and the latter, being excluded from Salvation by their own Fault, he appointed them to Damnation. Whence, as the former are *chosen in Christ,* Eph. 1:4, 5. so by the Grace of God, and the Merit of Christ, they actually obtain and reach eternal Salvation, the rest by their own Fault pull upon themselves their Damnation. So that the Covenant of God in Christ is Universal among them, and his Merit, and Calling, and Grace, is for all: But the particularity in the Case, proceeds from the Wickedness of Men, who resist the Counsel of God for their Salvation. These things some express thus: There is in this Matter to be consider'd, a Purpose, and then a Prescience, and then a Predestination. The Purpose is the Decree, by which God hath determin'd to procure the Salvation of Fallen Men by the Saviour, apprehended by Faith. Then God foreseeing from all Eternity, who would admit of that Faith, and who would reject it, he elected the former, and reprobated the latter. On the other side, the *Reform'd,* the first of them especially, dispose all these things in a quite different Order. And they set in the first place, the Decree of God, of manifesting his Mercy and his Justice. And that he might have Opportunity or Occasion so to do, it pleased him to create Men, on whom he might exercise his Mercy and his Justice. These must be for this purpose thrown into the Condition of the Fall; out of which miserable State they must be drawn, whom God by an absolute Decree had appointed to eternal Life, the rest being left to perish for ever. And the Means of Salvation were design'd only for the former, and are not to be to the benefit of the latter. But that Doctrine of an absolute Decree, seeming too horrid to some, even of those that are join'd to that Church, as intimating, that God of his own accord brought it to pass that Men should be wicked, that he might have occasion to exercise his Justice against them; They have bethought themselves for the mitigation of this Method, to begin theirs only after the Fall, and to rise no higher. And therefore, they suppose Mankind already fallen into Sin and obnoxious to eternal Damnation. And that he has selected some certain Persons by his absolute Pleasure, out of that common guilty Mass who are all in a like condition, and decreed to bring them to eternal Salvation, and has determin'd, that the Means of Salvation should only be profitable and effectual to them; The rest he suffers to perish in their Misery, and will not give them any Way or Mean of being sav'd. But tho' these latter Persons seem to think more mildly than the more ancient Ones did, which ancient Ones go by the Name of *Supralapsarians*, and the latter by that of *Sublapsarians*, yet 'tis evident they both maintain one and the same *Hypothesis*, with this only Difference; That the Ancients expound their *Hypothesis* whole: The other cut off the first part of it, as too horrid to be maintain'd. When yet the Matter comes to the same thing; And when these latter Ones are urg'd about the Causes of the Fall, they find it necessary to return back to the Opinions of those that went before them.

The Original of these Controversies.

§65. But that we may the more truly and intimately understand the nature and quality of these Controversies, it must be known, that they derive their Original from the Disputations of *Augustine* against the *Pelagians*.[43] For when the *Pelagians* would needs attribute more than was just to the Powers of Human Nature, and of the Free-will in Men: He, as is wont to happen in the Heat of Dispute, and from the Desire of Victory, inclin'd to another Extream; and that he might the more depress the Powers of Human Nature, and extenuate them, did exalt the Grace of God so far, that he referr'd all things to the absolute Will and Pleasure of God. After his time, during the barbarous Ages, and while the Superstition of the Kingdom of Darkness was prevailing, it was for the interest of those Times to incline to the Opinion of the *Pelagians*, so that there might be the more abundant meritorial Power and Force attributed to good Works. Tho' for all this, there were some found even in that Synagogue, but with an eminent Proof of their

43. Pelagianism received its name from Pelagius (late fourth to early fifth century) and designates a "heresy" according to which man can initiate his own salvation apart from divine grace; eventually this led to outright denial of original sin. Augustine wrote extensively against Pelagianism, e.g., *On the Merits and Remission of Sins and on the Baptism of Infants, On the Spirit and the Letter, On Nature and Grace, On the Perfection of Man's Righteousness, On the Grace of Christ and On Original Sin, On Marriage and Concupiscence, On the Soul and its Origin, Against Two Letters of the Pelagians, Against Julian of Eclanum.*

Stupidity, who maintain'd the Opinion of the absolute Decree, since nothing does more contradict the Merit of Men than the absolute Decree of God. On the other hand, they who in the last Age labour'd in purging Religion from the Errours and Abuses of the Papists, that they might the more effectually destroy the Opinion of Human Merit, as conducing to eternal Salvation, they return'd to the Opinion of *Augustine;* and among these was *Luther* himself, as being in his Education a Disciple of *Augustine.* To which Opinion, some hard Expressions were annexed by some, not with an ill Mind; as it is reasonable to believe, but that they might take away all Force and Power from Human Strength and Merit in the Matter of Salvation, and ascribe it only to the Grace of God. And I am willing to believe, they did not at first foresee what a multitude of absurd and hard Consequences, might be drawn, or would easily follow from those things so inconsiderately laid down. Therefore, when afterward that Opinion began to be oppos'd, and, as it is the fault of Human Nature, they were unwilling to depart from the Principles they had once espoused; the next thing to be done, was, that they would argue those Consequences were reproachfully imputed to them, and deny, that they asserted or approv'd them: And from thence they would proceed to soften some Matters, and interpret them with some Variations, but yet so as to think it would be a Disparagement, should they openly reject their first Principles from whence those hard things do proceed. And here this thing seems to be certain, That if I sincerely lay down any Principle, and do not in the Beginning foresee, that this or that ill Consequence can be deduced from it, I am not to be accused as if I did approve those ill Consequences, and held them too for my Opinion. But that Doctrine from whence such things follow, cannot with at all the more Reason be accounted found. And when those Consequences are plainly demonstrated, and their Connexion cannot be denied, it is in vain to interpose a Protestation, that the Consequences are not acknowledg'd when the Premises are admitted from which they follow. For that which may be accounted true, must not be that which has a falshood Consequent upon it. And if any Opinion was approv'd at the beginning, but afterward being more throughly search'd into, it is found to produce evil Consequences, it ought either to be intirely rejected, or to be so limited and explain'd that the Spring or Source of those ill Consequences may be stop'd up.

In these Controversies there are some things unsearchable by Men.

§66. Further, There is this also which no sober Man can deny. That in this Matter there are some questions the Reason of which can never be found out by Men, and to which we have nothing to say but *O the depth!* As for Instance, why it pleased God so long to wink at the Times of Ignorance, *Acts* 17:30. *Rom.* 16:25. *Eph.* 3:5. *Col.* 1:26. Why he hath caused the Doctrine of Salvation to be Preached to one Nation sooner, and to another later, *Acts* 16:6, 7. Since very many of the *American* People, many in the more undiscover'd Parts of *Asia,* and *Africa,* continue under an invincible Ignorance of the Gospel, what is the Reason why these are damn'd. Tho' otherwise we do not suppose it to be requisite to the Universality of the Vocation that it be made to all in every City, or Village, or in every particular House, *Col.* 1:6. And other Questions there are of the like nature, But it does not follow, because we are not able to give an evident Reason from the common Rules of Justice and Equity, why such Men who lie under such Ignorance should be damn'd, that therefore God has in the damning them follow'd nothing but a naked Will, and such as has no Reasons attending it. If any Man be not pleased with this, I would say to him, *What have I to do to judge them that are without?* 1 Cor. 5:22. And to be willingly ignorant of those things which our good Master is not pleas'd to teach us, is a learned Ignorance. Add *Tit.* 3:9. But that no other Reason may, or ought to be given, why among those who are born and educated in the Church, and to whom the Word of God is continually Preach'd, some are saved, and some are damn'd, but only the absolute Decree, and Will of God; is what can in no wise be reconcil'd with a Genuine System of Theology, certainly it had been in vain that God should go about to accomplish the Salvation of Men by certain Means, in vain altogether had he made a Covenant with Men, if it had pleased him to save some by an absolute Will, and so to damn the rest.

§67. This therefore is what I cannot see, How it can be hoped there should be an Agreement and Union between the *Lutherans* and the *Reform'd*, so long as these latter do so obstinately adhere to their Principle of an absolute Decree, and the Consequences of it; and do set this among the things which must be expresly believ'd, and give it the first place among the Articles which represent the Method of our Salvation. Indeed the chief Cause why the Salvation of Men is not to be determin'd to proceed from an absolute Decree, and a Will abstracted from all manner of Respects, and by which the second Causes, and their Operations and Effects are determin'd by an unalterable Necessity, is this; That God is pleas'd to bring Men to Salvation in the way of a Covenant, with which Way or Method such a Necessity cannot consist. For that which I produce, and effect by my own indispensible Will and Disposal, it is Contradictory, and Superfluous, and Illusory; that I should pretend to make a Covenant about it. In truth, it is not my Purpose to allow nothing at all to our own Powers, in the Business of Salvation, nor to withhold from the Grace of God the Glory of our Salvation. But this at least must be left to our Will, that it can resist and refuse the offer'd Grace of God; since without this all Morality would be utterly extinguish'd, and Men must be drawn to their End after the manner of working of Engines. To which may be applied, that in *Ps.* 32:9. No longer then would Theology be a Moral Discipline, but a Physical one, and the Operations according to it, must be accounted for by the Laws of Motion. It is true, that in Creation God only said *Let it be,* and it was so, and the same thing is daily done in the Government of Nature: See *Ps.* 148:5, 6, 8. But in the Conversion of Men God does not act in such a manner but Morally, and by Inducements or Perswasions. Whence it is that we every where read in Holy Scripture of Men's Resistance to the Divine Will, *Gen.* 6:3. So the *Pharisees* are said to have *despised the counsel of God against themselves,* Luke 7:30. Nor do we ask any thing more, then that it may be taken for Truth which is expressed by God. *O Israel, thy destruction is of thy self, but in me alone is thy help.* Hos. 13:9. Add *Jer.* 10:23. Also, *The wages of sin is death, but the gift of God is eternal life.* Also, *I would,*

The Absolute Decree cannot be admitted.

but ye would not. Mat. 23:27. Add *Acts* 7:51. *Rom.* 10:21. *Phil.* 1:6. And
those things which *Georgius Calixtus* has Commented[44] on this Place,
Eccl. 7:10. *Wisd.* 2:23, 24, 25. *Isa.* 5:2, 3, 4. *Jer.* 2:21. 7:13, 24, 25, 26, 27.
Ezech. 3:7, 27. But neither is it to be thought that the Will and Power
of God are confin'd by this Power of Resistance, or that in asserting
this, we assert any thing to be stronger then He. That indeed might
perhaps take place, if God were concern'd about acquiring any Advantage to himself, and this could be intercepted, or hindred by any one.
But we are now Treating about Benefits only, which God, who is in
himself most blessed, and sufficient to himself, is willing to bestow
freely on others: But which he will not force upon those who are
unwilling, and refuse to receive them. And in this God does not act
with all his Power, or to the utmost of what he is able to do, as Machines, and Brutal Powers are wont to do. But he acts as a free Power,
and such as can exert its Strength within a certain Measure, and either
intend, or remit it at Pleasure. And so since it hath pleased him to deal
with Man in a Moral manner (for Christ heal'd the Sick, commanded
Storms into a Calm, call'd the Dead to Life with a word, but is never
read to have Converted Men in like manner.) It was necessary that he
should so attemper and adjust his Operation about our Salvation, as
that there might at least remain to Men the Faculty of casting away,
or of refusing it. For which Reason it is not necessary that God must
Will all things absolutely, but he may Will some things under a Condition, and so suspend the Effect of his Will upon that Condition.
Also tho' the Prescience of God is never deceiv'd, and that which God
does foresee will certainly come to pass; yet it is not to be imagin'd
therefore that any Necessity is laid upon things by his Prescience, for
as much as that includes with the Events the Causes of them, and he
also foreknows those things which are to come to pass under a certain
Condition. Some times also God determines a certain end, but yet so
that he does not determine the Means immediately which lead to that
end, but only foreknows and permits them. As God determin'd the

44. See note 4.

Death of the Saviour, but he only foreknew and permitted the Wickedness of the *Jews,* and of him that betraid him; because that Death
might also have come to pass by other, and those innocent Means, *Acts*
2:23. But neither may we imagine that there is any such Predetermination of things in God, or such a Disposition beforehand of Causes
and Effects as laies an absolute Necessity upon all Events. For in a
Disposition of this sort we are speaking of, we must understand him
to have disposed the Causes that act Morally, so as that there may be
a Morality consistent with their Operations and Effects. And the
Words, Providence, Prescience, and Predetermination, and the like
must be purg'd from that Imperfection which is imply'd in them when
they are apply'd to Men; in which Case there is a space of Time interpos'd between the previous disposition, and ordering, and the producing of the Effect. Which space is not to be conceiv'd as interpos'd
in the Providence of God, for as much as in him there is no succession
of time after the manner of former and latter, but a pure Eternity or
Everlasting now: And so all things past, present and future are to God
as this day, *Psal.* 90:4. And therefore we must understand the Direction
and Disposition of God, who is as it were settled in a Center, always
accompanying the Operations of things, as moving about in a Circum-
ference, and going with an equal pace along with them. Which Opinion may be very well illustrated by what is said in several places of the
Psalms, Lead me that I may *walk? Show me thy way O Lord, that I may
walk in thy truth. Thy word O Lord is a light unto my feet.* Which cannot
be said by him, or of him who is mov'd irresistibly, and like an Engine.
Further, The *Reform'd,* that the Morality of Humane Actions may not
be said to be taken away by the Physical Predetermination which many
of them assert, have fled to this: To fain that the Liberty of the Will
of Man consists only in a Spontaneity, or Absence of Violent Constraint, not in an Indifferency, tho' not always set in an Equilibrium.
But if the Physical, or Natural Act of every Humane Action is so
predetermin'd, as that it must needs exist, and if the Physical Act existing Man cannot chuse but he must morally influence to it, I must
confess I cannot conceive that there is more Liberty in Men then there
is in Water, flowing down within its Channel, or in a round Stone

placed just at the descent of a Hill, in the motion of which things there is nothing of Force or Constraint appears.

§68. But in this too, does the Opinion of the *Lutherans* differ as widely as can be from that of the *Reform'd:* That when the Effect of Salvation is not produc'd upon all Men, The *Reform'd* refer the Cause of this Particularity ultimately to the Pleasure of God, who they say did therefore appoint only the particular Operation of the Means of Salvation. The *Lutherans* on the contrary acknowledge that the things which are conferr'd towards that end on the part of God are universal, but the Particularity in the Event proceeds from the Fault of Men who despise the offer'd Means. And this Opinion is favour'd both by the things already said, and also by the very Nature or Quality of the Covenant of God in Christ. For as God from the beginning made a Covenant with *Adam* that was universal without any Exception: So also by reason of the Violation of that was Destruction propagated to all without Exception. The Covenant with the Mediator the Son of God was made in the room of that Covenant; which we are expresly taught does reach as far as the Effect of *Adam's* Fall, *Rom.* 5:12, 15, &c. And indeed, so that the Universality in the Grace purchas'd by Christ, should be much more favourable than the Universality of the Corruption proceeding from the Fall of *Adam.* But neither does there appear in that Covenant the least footstep of Particularity. For if God had design'd that it should belong only to a certain and determin'd Part of Mankind, this Part ought to have been distinguish'd from the Reprobate by certain Nations, Places, or other Marks. But nothing of this sort is found here: *Go ye into all the World; Teach all Nations.* When on the other side, the Saviour was pleas'd for Experiment-sake, to send his Disciples to some certain Places only, he told them to whom they ought not to go, *Matth.* 10:5. And so when *God hath chosen us in Christ,* Eph. 1:4. the cause of Damnation can be no other than not to believe in Christ, and in no wise can it be any absolute Decree. And also the Expressions in Scripture of the Universal Mercy of God, of the Extent of the Merit of Christ to all, of the Vocation and Preaching of the Gospel, from which no Man is excluded by any Divine Order or Command, *Col.*

Of the Cause of Particularity.

1:23. *Mark* 16:8. are so clear and manifest, that they must be wrested
and forced, if they are restrain'd to certain particular Men only. It is
indeed argued, that it was not fitting or just to give a Ransom of so
great Price in vain. At least it cannot be said, that Christ shed his Blood
for them who were already damn'd before his Passion, and thrown into
Hell, from whence there is no Redemption. But such Reasonings might
take place, if the Redemption of Mankind were made by any thing
which might be rated at a certain Price, or by a Price which might be
divided into certain Parts. As for instance, If there were an Agreement
at a certain Rate for the Redemption of Captives, it were prodigality
and profuseness to pay a Price for more than are actually restor'd to
liberty. But the Merit of Christ is Indivisible, and is an Universal Price
of Ransom for all Mankind, which exerts it self both backwards and
forwards, and from which nothing is lost altho' upon some particular
Persons, by reason of their Fault it does not take effect. And when 'tis
a thing above the Strength and Riches of all Mankind, to redeem but
the Soul of one, *Psal.* 49:7. there was need of a Price of Infinite Value
for the Redeeming of all Mankind. But that which is Infinite is not
capable of Division; and so it is nothing to the Merit of Christ, whether
Mankind consist of an hundred or of a thousand thousand Persons.
So the Virtue which was put into the Brazen Serpent by God, to which
Christ resembles himself, *John* 3. was not vain, tho' some should have
despised to use that Remedy, and therefore should have perish'd, or if
that Virtue was not to be utterly spent by being diffused to more than
were actually cured by it. Therefore the Grace and Mercy of God, and
the Merit of Christ, is by no means to be measur'd by the Rules of
good Husbandry, which weak Mankind may govern themselves by;
which will not suffer that any thing should be bought or procur'd to
perish in vain, or be of no use: But it is rather to be conceiv'd of,
according to the Magnificence and Abundance of the Works and Benefits of Nature. As for instance, the Light and Heat of the Sun, the
Water, and the Air we breath, do so abound, that much the least Part
of them is taken or consum'd by Men, or other Animals, or is apply'd
to any use by them. Nor did they more sparingly dispence themselves
when Mankind consisted of only two Persons, than now that they are

multiplyed into many Myriads. Nor for this can it be said, that God, who is the Author of so many Benefits, is profuse therein or prodigal, *Mat.* 5:45. And if the Benefits procur'd for Mankind by the Covenant in Christ, are to be measur'd by such Parsimony, it were fitting and requisite that some Mark and Note should be establish'd, by which it might be known to what Individuals among Men they do belong, and to whom not, that Holy Things might not be thrown to Dogs, nor Pearls cast before Swine. Lastly, It has been necessary also to the *Reform'd,* that they may elude the Universal Expressions, and save their own Position, to devise the Distinctions of a *secret* and a *reveal'd Will;* of a *Will of Good-pleasure,* and a *Will signified,* a *Legislatorial,* and a *Decretory Will.* Which, however they may be speciously set off, and adorn'd, are such things as hardly any good Man can suffer should be apply'd to his Promises and Covenants. It is true indeed, they are not wanting in something to say for the mitigating their Principle of the Particularity, which is as follows: That every Man comes into the Covenant in Christ for himself, and singly, not in a whole Society or Communion with other Men. Whence the Faith by which particular Persons are saved, is this; *Christ hath lov'd me, and given himself for me. I live by the Faith of the Son of God,* Gal. 2:20. Altho' he should abstract from, or not consider this Proposition, Christ hath lov'd all, and given himself for all. As also no Man builds his Faith upon that Condition. I will believe in Christ, if also all others will believe in Him, and if also all others are to be sav'd. Whence, since every Man lives and is sav'd by his Faith, it is sufficient if particular Persons are persuaded firmly that they are in the Number of the Elect, provided they have firm and unshaken Foundations of that Persuasion. But tho' we should grant, that the Error of Particularity is not damnable in it self, if any Man sincerely holds it; that is, if he be persuaded indeed that it is the Sentence of Holy Scripture, because he may by Himself be in Covenant, and may enjoy all the Means of Salvation which are sufficient to him; Yet is the Principle of the Universality much more safe, and more useful to promote the Christian Practice, and for the affording of Comfort to the Mind of Men, than the opposite one of Particularity. Certainly, he will be less liable to Scruples and Doubts, who knows God is willing all Men should be sav'd, and the Means of Salvation are offer'd to all, and that they exert their Efficacy upon all but those who reject them by their own Fault: Then he who is persuaded that God has elected some, and those in truth the lesser part, by an absolute Will from a Company equally damnable, and has left all the others in that Misery. For those Signs by which the particular Persons are willing to presume that they are elected, that sense of Faith, and internal Testimony of the Spirit may fail, and many have fallen who seem'd to themselves to stand very sure, *Col.* 1:23. Also so long as the manifest Sense of Faith is felt in him, who is possess'd with the Principle of Particularity, he may comfort himself with it: But if that be interrupted by the force of Temptations, from whence then shall he derive any Consolations? And a secret Will that is contradistinct to the reveal'd One, will never suffer any Man to be secure, that the Faith which he now thinks himself to feel, does proceed from the secret Decree of God. As if a Pardon were in this manner publish'd to a Community of Rebellious Subjects: The Favour of the Prince shall be yielded to all of you, who do not obstinately reject it; There must needs arise a greater Confidence of obtaining it among the Subjects, than if the Offer were thus form'd: The Expressions of an Amnesty seem indeed to offer an Universal Pardon, but in truth the Prince has determin'd to receive but some of you into Favour, the rest shall remain under his Displeasure, nor shall there any infallible Token be given by which every one may judge whether they are in the Number of those that are to be pardon'd, or those that shall be punish'd. Lastly, How can it be, that Incredulity can be alledg'd as a Cause of Damnation, *John* 3:18. if by an Absolute Pleasure or Will of God, the Saviour and his Merit must not belong to the Reprobate? Certainly, no Man can deny but it is contrary to the Goodness and Clemency of the Creator, who is as a Common Father to Men, to destine the Rational Creature to inevitable Destruction by an Absolute Will; or to take some from among a Company of Fallen Men, and leave the rest in their miserable Condition, without any particular Cause, Respect or Merit of this: And notwithstanding, to invite all without Exception, to practice Repentance, and believe the Gospel, when nevertheless, where certain Persons are destin'd to a certain End, without any respect it signifies nothing to this Matter, whether they be brought to that End either by Means or without them. But to invite others, whom you absolutely reject, is a Mockery join'd with the sharpest Cruelty. It seems to me worth observing, what *Jurieu* confesses in his Book about *Peace amongst Protestants,* p. 221.[45] The Ancient Reform'd Doctors, (says he,) *Oecolampadius, Bullinger, Gualter, &c.*[46] preach'd, That the Death of Christ was a Price sufficient to the Salvation of all, and procur'd a Possibility of Salvation to all that believe; Yea, it was given for all Men, and God wills that all Men should be sav'd, and come to the Knowledge of the Truth. *For this is the very Doctrine of Holy Scripture. But at present we interpret the Scriptures according to those things which the same Scriptures reveal to us concerning the Absolute Predestination.* But I ask, Does not the Scripture speak much more clearly concerning the Universal Mercy of God, and the things which belong to it, than of an Absolute Decree of which there is no where an express Mention made? And do not they tread more securely, who measure the Predestination from those clear and manifest Expressions, than they who from the Predestination, by Vertue of a preconceiv'd Opinon, or from obscure and ambiguous Expressions, do in a violent manner wrest those most clear Expressions as they have deform'd them?

The Controversies of lesser Importance.

§69. And these indeed are the chief Controversies which are maintain'd between the Protestants; For the composing of which, if a proper Method could be entred upon, it would be easie to correct or dissemble the rest. For as the *Lutherans* urge the *Reform'd* with the Consequences about the Article of Predestination; so these again, the Vulgar especially, object against the *Lutherans,* some Relicks of the Popish Rites not sufficiently purg'd away. Into the Number of which, they put the *Exorcism* retain'd in Baptism, the Private *Confession,* and, what is wont to accompany it, the Sacred *Peny,* the *Round Wafers* used in the Lord's

45. See §70.
46. Heinrich Bullinger (1507–75), Johannes Oecolampadius (1482–1531), Rudolf Gualther (Walther, Gwalter) (1519–86).

Supper, which hardly retain the Nature of Bread, *Altars* also and *Candles,* and many *Images* retain'd in their Churches, and among others that of *our Saviour hanging on the Cross,* the particular *Garments* of Ministers, the *Bending the Knee and Uncovering the Head at the mention of the Name of Jesus,* the superfluous *Festival Days,* the Exorbitant use of *Musick,* and other things of like nature. For about the difference of Ministers and the external Government of the Church, they do not so much differ with the *Lutherans* as among themselves, chiefly in *England.* About which things, it is to be observ'd, they are all of them such as do not touch the Foundation of the Faith, and so are wont to come under the Name of Things indifferent. And as there might easily be a yielding in these Matters, if by that Means a way might be made to a solid and sincere Concord; so if a change or abolition of them is to be taken as a Sign of the Approbation of the Religion in the whole of it, it would be unprofitable as well as also hardly becoming to shew by such a yielding any thing of Uncertainty or Wavering. For in such a Case, those things become the Symbols of the Sect, and if the Principles of the Sect are not approv'd, the outward Signs of it cannot be taken up with a safe Conscience. But if all these things are consider'd in themselves, they will certainly appear by no means worthy, that for them there should be so mischievous a Dissention cherish'd. Especially, since in many of the *Lutheran* Churches very many of these things are not observ'd, which Churches, the other where those things are still retain'd, do not upon that score condemn. As neither do the other of the Reform'd Churches exclude from their Communion the Church of *England,* which uses yet more Ceremonies than the *Lutherans.* And as for the *Exorcism,* however that came to creep into the Form of administring Baptism, no *Lutheran* is so mad as to believe, that Infants are spiritually or corporally before Baptism, possess'd with an Evil Spirit, in a proper Acceptation of that Phrase, and that this is expell'd by that Adjuration. But since by Baptism we have admission into the Church and Kingdom of Christ, out of which the Power of Satan exerts it self, and no less does Original Sin out of the Church rule with full Right and Power: By that Ceremony it is not unfitly intimated, that Satan has now no Right remaining in the Baptized Person, who is now become a Subject of the Kingdom of Christ: And also, that the Impure Spirit which rises like a Vapour from the Lake of the Original Corruption, must now give place, since this new Subject of Christ must hereafter be govern'd by the Holy Spirit. And when it is very Expedient that we should be admonish'd of that Fruit of Baptism in the Administration of it, the Question only is, Whether or no it is not best to express this thing by a convenient, and no way frightful Ceremony? But here if by any Temperament any thing may be done that can promote Concord, I do not see why we ought to make any difficulty about it, provided the Sense and Meaning of the Thing which I have express'd be retain'd. The *Private Confession* may have very great use to admonish and correct those whose Life and Fame does not conform to the Precepts of Christ, and whom there could otherwise be no Opportunity gain'd to admonish particularly. As also, that they may be furnish'd with proper Information and Consolation, who have their Consciences troubled with any Scruples. The small Gift or Offering which is given to the Ministers upon this Occasion, is a part of their Salary. If this offends any one, either let their Salary be establish'd by the Publick, from whence they may sustain themselves and their Families honestly, or let their Auditors be accustomed to exercise their Liberality towards them under some other Name, who being call'd to such an Office, it would be a great shame to the whole Congregation to suffer them to want. The *Round Wafers* used in the Lord's Supper, are made of the same Matter with the other Bread; and the small Form of them ought not to offend any one, since 'tis not the End or Design of them in that Sacrament to fill the Belly. Tho' to the wisest Persons it may be all one what kind of Bread is used, yet it hardly appears how a Change in this Matter can be introduced without great Offence of the common People; the Weakness of whom is not to be altogether despised. Nor is it necessary that the breaking of the Bread in the very Celebration of the Supper should be ridgedly requir'd. For to break Bread, is properly to divide greater Masses of Bread into little Parts, that it may be more fitted to be eaten. Which Division it matters not whether it be done before the Supper, or at the Celebration of it. So we are bid to break our Bread to the Hungry, *Isa.* 58:25. But no Man can be so absur'd, as to believe that, for the fulfilling that Precept we must needs give broken pieces of Bread to the Poor. To urge for the Necessity of that Rite, that it may appear that the Body of Christ does not lie hid in the Bread, is what I want a Name for, as thinking it not Decent to use a Ridiculous one in a serious Matter. For neither are the *Lutherans* so stupid, as to believe that the Body of Christ lies hid in the Bread, as what might be seen if the Superficies of that were taken away. In the Hymn of *John Husse,* in these Words, *Verborgen im Brodt so klein:*[47] The Word *Verborgen* is not a Participle, but an Adverb, and so it signifies not the Body of Christ hidden in a little Bread, but secretly, in a hidden manner. It is of no Concern, or Importance, whether the *Table* upon which the Holy Supper is Celebrated, be of Wood, or of Stone, or of what Figure it is: And all Men know that these Tables of Stone are not used by the *Lutherans* for a Sacrifice, who where they cannot so conveniently have Tables of Stone, are not afraid to use common Tables of Wood. Among many of them there is no use of Wax-candles. But where these are still retain'd to signifie the Nocturnal Time of the Institution of this Supper, he would be too nice who should cavil against such an innocent Rite. To loath and abhor the setting up the *Image* of a Crucifix for meer Remembrance, without any Veneration in the Churches does not become those, who ought to glory in the Cross of Christ. No one had taken it ill, if other Images had long since been remov'd, and if Rottenness does destroy them no Man will be griev'd. He would be too Morose, who could not endure what serves for innocent Ornament: For neither is the Form of Churches prescrib'd to Christians, as was that of the Tabernacle to the

---

47. John Huss (Jan Hus, c. 1372–1415), professor of theology in Prague, priest, proponent of John Wycliffe, and radical critic of the church. Huss denounced various church abuses in his sermons, especially concerning Holy Communion, and taught that the office of the pope did not exist by Divine command. In his conflict with the Church, Huss got caught in the schism that arose when Alexander V and Gregory XII both claimed the papacy, and in 1414 he was summoned to the Council of Constance with an assurance of safe conduct from Emperor Sigismund. The Council arrested Huss, found him guilty of heresy, and had him burned at the stake in 1415. It also settled the schism in 1417.

Israelites. If any are displeased at peculiar Habits of Ministers in the Church which are suted to Modesty, and have no Superstition; let them, if they think fit permit their Ministers to mount the Pulpit in a Lawyers Bar-gown, or a Military Habit, and to set themselves thus dress'd at the Holy Table, and then ask of prudent Persons whether or no this be decent. It should be hard certainly to perswade a Christian that too much Honour can be given to Jesus Christ our Lord and Redeemer: When Persons of good Manners are wont to uncover their Heads, even at the mention of the Name of our Princes. And when we are by him deliver'd from a Pernicious Slavery, and call'd to the Cap, as we may speak of the Liberty he gives us, why should we be so sparing of giving to him the Respect and Honour of the Hat at the mention of his most acceptable Name. It was of Use and Importance too to take away the Multitude of Festival Days where they still remain'd, as which serve for and Occasion only the cherishing of Vice and Wickedness among the common People. It is worthy, and fitting to be forbid that the Church should sound with the meer noise of Musick; but no Man can condemn the seasoning our Sacred Hymns with the Sweetness of Harmonious Musick. And with relation to the External things of the Church, there is nothing else commanded, but that all things be done decently, and in order, 1 *Cor.* 14:40. And that Modesty be observ'd. No Man can approve that the new conceiv'd Hymns of any one should be receiv'd into the Publick Use of the Church: But to insist stifly, that only the *Psalms* of *David* should be used, is a Pertinacy that has no Reason for its Foundation, since the greatest part of these does not sute the present Times of the Church, or the Necessities of particular Christians. As I should hardly refuse that the ordinary Texts which are wont to be explain'd on the Lord's Days, according to ancient Appointment might be digested into a better and more concise Order, and with greater choice: So to leave it to the free Choice of every Minister, what Text at every turn he shall be pleas'd to explain, is a thing, I think has no less Inconveniencies attending it. Lastly, Since the Questions concerning the External Government of the Church do not touch the Foundation of the Faith, nor does it concern the Doctrine of the Covenant, whether a Man believes the Ministers of the Church to be equal among themselves, or Subordinate some to others: Certainly it were not fitting to contend with so much Fervour about Episcopal, or Presbyterian Government, unless the contending Parties were willing to expose themselves to the Reproach on one side of Ambition and Covetousness, or on the other side of Obstinacy, and another kind of Ambition, which cannot endure a Superior. At least from that Strife it does appear that the Obstinacy and Stifness of Mind, which is objected to the *Lutherans,* is not altogether a stranger to the Ministers of the *Reform'd Party.* But it is enough for us, that we have, according as we were able, describ'd the Foundation of the Faith, and the Nature of the Controversies which are agitated among the Protestants. I now leave it to the Judgment of the Pious and Prudent Minds, and those well acquainted with Holy Scripture, whether or no both the Parties might not consent in the System propos'd, and Transact with Sincerity about the Controversies mention'd, if Ambition, Stubbornness, the Contempt of others, and a Hatred unworthy of the Christian Name, and Prepossession of Opinions, were taken away, or allay'd.

§70. But while we are meditating these things, there is fallen into our hands, *A Consultation about making Peace among Protestants, by* Peter Jurieu *a Divine of* Rotterdam.[48] I think fit to bestow a little Pains in the Examination of what he therein delivers, to try whether or no a further light may thence be fetch'd to this Controversie. Who tho' indeed he seems to have omitted none of these things which can be said to recommend the Opinion of the *Reform'd* upon the Article of Grace and Predestination; yet it is to be hoped that those who are free from Prejudice will acknowledge, that those things which our Party

Remarks upon the Consultation about making Peace among Protestants, by Peter Jurieu.

48. Pierre Jurieu, *De Pace inter Protestantes ineunda consultatio* . . . (Utrecht, 1688).

profess upon this Article do much better sute with the Sense and Meaning of Holy Scripture, and the Notions which this requires us to entertain of Almighty God. Certainly as no *man hath seen God but the only begotten Son, who is in the bosom of the Father he hath reveal'd him,* John 1:18. So we know nothing concerning God and his Will, and the Order Establish'd concerning our Salvation, but what is reveal'd to us by him in the Holy Scriptures. In this way we shall walk with most safety, and it is certainly rash, and slippery to forsake them and follow humane Reasonings, with however subtle Distinctions they are supported. Therefore, that *Jurieu* pronounces, That *Inefficacious Wills do contract the Idea of a Being infinitely Perfect, because they argue either Mutability, or Ignorance, or Impotence.* We on the contrary think that Inefficacious Wills, that is, such as do not reach the extream Effect of a thing, do not contradict the Notion of a Being Infinitely Perfect. For God is not to be conceiv'd of after the manner of a Brutal Power, such as a weight is, which always exerts its utmost Force in an uniform manner; but after the manner of an Agent that is Intelligent and Free, and which can intend, and restrain, and moderate as he sees fit his Power and Force of Acting. But when it pleased Him to Create not only Irrational Creatures which Act after the manner of meer Machines, but also such as have in their Nature some Degrees of Liberty, so as that they may and ought to give an account of their Actions: Therefore the Will of God did not exert all his Power about these, but proceeded within a certain Order design'd by it self. Otherwise it would have involv'd a Contradiction to create a free Creature which must give an Account of his Actions, and yet to determine his Actions beforehand by his own absolute Will. Therefore it is not any unconsider'd Change, or unforeseen Event, or any external Cause which comes across as it were, that renders the Will of God Inefficacious; but he himself suspends his Will upon the Event of the Action, or Omission of another, which is indeed foreseen by him, but which he does not Will to bend or induce by all Means the Will of the other to undertake, or omit, but leaves it intirely to its liberty. Certainly no Man can deny but God can do more than he actually does; therefore his Will does not reach so far as to the utmost of what he is able to do.

§71. From thence *Jurieu* has taken upon him to show that *there is in* Of the
God a twofold Will, one as he is consider'd as a Legislator, the other as he Legislatory,
is consider'd as Determining an Event. This Distinction seems to be what and Decreetory
we admit in a certain Sense. As for Instance, that God Wills and Com- Will of God.
mands some things to be done by others, so as that those Actions may
be imputed to them to whom they are enjoyn'd, or may be accounted
for their Actions: But some things God Decrees that they shall come
to pass, or be; so as that these Events are to be accounted for the Effect
of the Divine Will, and of which God may be said to be the Author.
But *Jurieu* has in his Eye another Sense of that Distinction, and he
says that these two Wills do *sometimes seem to oppose one the other.* For
(1.) *According to the Will of a Legislator God cannot permit Sin:* For that
would be, as if he should declare Sin to be Lawful, which implies a
Contradiction. But God as Decreeing Events *does at least permit Sin;*
that is, he does not do all he can to hinder it from being. But we think
there is no Repugnancy at all between these two Expressions: I do not
give Liberty, or grant an Impunity of doing a thing, and I do not with
all my Power hinder that such a thing should be done. (2.) (*p.* 10.)[49]
We can never resist the Will of God as a Lawgiver, without a Crime, true,
But the Decreeing Will of God may be resisted, not only without a Crime,
but also sometimes out of Piety. This I deny: For Proof of it he adds; *A*
Son sees his Father Sick, all Symptoms signifie that his Death will shortly
be, that is the Will of God Decreeing the Event; yet he resists this Will:
The Son humbly Prayes, he uses Remedies, he leaves nothing untried that
he may delay the Event which God Wills. But we deny, that if the Death
of the Father appears inevitable, the Endeavour and Prayers of the Son
can be recommended as Pious, unless they are done upon Condition,
if the Will of God be for the Recovery, *Matth.* 26:38. *Acts* 21:14. And
it seems very evident from 2 *Sam.* 12:20, 21, 22. That *David* supposed
this Condition in his Prayers for the Son begotten of *Bathsheba.* (3.)
The Legislative Will does not settle the Event of things, or determine be-
forehand whether the thing shall come to pass or no: But the Decreeing

49. This and the following page numbers in the text refer to Jurieu's work
mentioned in the previous note.

Will of God makes that the thing shall certainly come to pass. I add, but yet not so as that all Conditions are excluded, and that the thing shall absolutely come to pass. (4.) *For the fulfilling his Will, as Legislator, God does not dispose of Means, for these things are permitted to the free Will of Man.* These things are spoken ambiguously, and cannot be admitted, but with this Meaning; God does not so dispose the Means, as that the Action cannot be imputed to the Man as his. Otherwise, in truth the Legislator supposes Means, that is a Possibility of Performance, which either is present, or will be. For all Laws are about possible things. *But God that he may execute his Decreeing Will, prepares and sets in order the Means.* (5.) *The Will of a Legislator, signifies what is the Duty of Men which God must be perform'd by him: But it no way signifies what God himself will do.* These words are insnaringly laid; 'tis true the Legislative Will abstracts from the Decree of Futurition: But this even the Legislative Will signifies, that God has not Decreed to effect that the thing must of necessity not be which he has commanded, or that the thing should be which he has forbidden. For in this manner the Legislative Will of God would be Contradictory, and most Unjust. (6.) (*p.* 11.) *The Will of the Legislator is not settled, fixed, or immutable, but with respect to the Laws which have their Foundation in the Divine Nature: That Will is changed for the time, and several Dispensations.* Here *Jurieu* seems desirous to insinuate, that there is a difference between the Laws of God which are Eternal, and Temporary, and so which are Immutable, and Mutable. But this Distinction is nothing to the present Purpose. (7.) *The Legislative Will is something Extrinsick to God, as Creation, Revelation by the Word.* Here *Jurieu* confounds the Declaration of the Legislative Will, with the Legislative Will it self. That is indeed a Transient Act, but why this may not as well be call'd an Immanent one, as the Decreeing Will, I cannot see; When even this also presupposes something out of God in the Exercise of the Divine Mind, as we shall hereafter more largely show. From all these things *Jurieu* infers; *The Legislative Will of God is not, properly speaking, the Will of God, but a Law given to the Will of Men, and in God Figurative and Metaphorical only: But the Decreeing Will is truly and properly so call'd the Will of God.* We on the contrary do assert, That altho' we may conceive a difference between that which God as a Legislator will have another do, and that which he Decrees as his own Act; yet we must not devise such a difference, as by which these things which are commanded by God to be done, are almost wholly excluded by his serious Will; and so that a great part of what God has said in Holy Scripture should be eluded. Which is a vile Abuse of this little Distinction. For as much as on the contrary, God does in earnest, and seriously, and properly Will, not Figuratively and Metaphorically, that his Legislatorial Will should be fulfill'd: But he does not Will it in such a manner, as that the Aptitude to be imputed should be taken from the Action, or so as that a Man cannot any longer be Responsible for the Action, or the Omission of it. Whence it was that God Created the first Man with Powers which were sufficient to his fulfilling the Law which he laid upon him. Which Powers having been lost by the Fall, God afterwards with the renew'd Covenant offer'd so much of Power, as by which he might be able to fulfil also this Covenant. Therefore when God is said to Will, for Instance, that a Sinner should turn and live, it is not to be believ'd that he does deceive Men, and determine the contrary, by a Tacite Exception, or secret Decree: But with the Precept he offers fit Strength and Power for Conversion, but in such a manner, as that the Moral Nature of it may be consistent. Whence it can by no means be admitted. (*p.* 12.) That the Legislatorial Will of God does coincidate with *the Will of the Sign,* or the signified Will which differs from the Intrinsick Pleasure, which is in truth illusory, and by which all the Force of the Divine Promises might be taken away; just as all Force of Truth is banish'd from among Men by the Jesuitical Reservations. And which indeed is not necessary to the Genuine Sense of those things which are spoken Figuratively, and after the manner of Men, which things even the most stupid Person can discern from what is properly spoken. Whence 'tis very falsly said, *God indeed does seriously Will that such his Legislative Will should be a Rule to Men of what they are to do, and the Rule according to which they shall sometime be judg'd: But it is not his serious, true, and real desire that all Men do obey his Legislative Will.* But such things may be said of Tyrants, who make Laws on purpose to squeeze Money from their Subjects.

But such ungenerous Deceit must be infinitely unworthy the Majesty of God. And what is the Reason given for that Assertion? *Otherwise all would obey; for who can resist his will?* Indeed no Man can resist the Absolute Will of God, but that is what has no place here; for otherwise there could no Action be perform'd by any Man, which could justly be follow'd with any Approbation, or Reward, or Punishment. Of the same sort are these things which follow; *The Legislative Will does not declare the Propension of God to these, or the like Events, but it signifies in general that God loves Holiness, and Purity of Manners, as it is defin'd by his Laws. And when the Holy Scripture says, God would that all Men should be obedient to his Law, this does not signifie that God vehemently desires that all should obey, but only that he has laid this Law upon all Men, that they Subject themselves to the Divine Laws, or else render themselves deserving of Eternal Death.* That is it suffices to God in giving Laws to have declar'd what he approves, and for the rest it is all one to him, whether Men obey them or not; for in the latter Case he has those who may suffer Punishment. But certainly a good Prince among Men would take it as the highest Injury to impute such things to him. Whence 'tis false, *that the Legislative Will is only Extrinsick and Metaphorical; for that a true Will in God, and such as is really Existing, cannot but be Efficacious, nor can want Success.* But the Legislative Will of God is a true and serious Will, and it is also Efficacious, and which always attains the End and Term which is intended, and towards which it is carried: Which is to lay an Obligation upon him to whom it is Publish'd, to do that which the Law prescribes, and if he will neglect it to render him obnoxious to Punishment. But that those things which are commanded by Laws, should be, or not be done, cannot be absolutely Decreed by the Legislatour, nor but with this Temperament, that at least a Physical or Natural Faculty be left him upon whom any thing is enjoyn'd, of neglecting the things commanded at his Peril, in as much as without this the Action cannot be understood to be Moral. And so the Decreeing Will is not to be so oppos'd to the Legislatorial one, as that the Faculty of Acting contrary to this is taken away, which is a thing presuppos'd by the Legislatorial Will. For otherwise it would be Illusory to propose to the Subjects one or the other, either Obedi-

ence, or Punishments, which is that we see every where done in Holy
Scripture. See *Gen.* 2:17. Where the Threatning had been altogether in
vain, if there had not been a Physical, or Natural Faculty of Neglecting
the Command, *Levit.* 26. throughout, *Deut.* 11:26, 27, 28. *Jos.* 24:15.
2 *Chron.* 7:17, &c.

§72. It will further afford no small Light towards the discussing this
Controversie, to consider well the Nature of the Divine Prescience, and
how that differs from the Predetermination, and the Decrees of God,
which of them precedes the other in the Exercise of the Divine Mind,
and whether or no this, or that do lay any Necessity, both upon other
Events, or upon the Will of Man, and so whether both of them may
consist, or not with the Liberty of the Humane Will. Concerning the
Divine Prescience, then it must be observ'd, that altho' this is very
clear, and cannot be deceiv'd, yet it lays no Necessity upon things, nor
causes them to be. But that this signifies no more then the Intuition
of things that are to be, or that are possible, as Inspection is of things
present, and the remembrance of things past. And it also happens to
those who can contribute nothing to the Production of the things
foreseen. For the Production of Things is the Work of Power and Will,
Prescience is the Work of the Understanding alone. Production Determines and Constitutes according as the thing must exist: This abstracts from the Necessity of Existence, and beholds the thing simply.
As for what concerns the Order of Prescience, and the Divine Decrees
concerning the future Existence of things, which of them precedes the
other: It is certainly manifest it cannot be said without Contradiction,
and Absurdity that the Decrees of God are before his Prescience. For
that were all one, as to say, I have determin'd to produce a certain
thing, but I know not what, or of what Sort it is to be. Whence it
must be said that the Act of the Intellect precedes in the Exercise of
the Divine Mind, which represents the Possibility, or what may be
done saving the Wisdom, Justice, and Holiness of God. From that
Contemplation, as it were of the Possibility and Congruity God Decrees and Determines what is to be, and shall come to exist. But in the
Forming of Decrees, it must be observ'd that the Power of God is

*The Nature
of the Divine
Prescience.*

join'd together with Liberty, Wisdom, and Righteousness; or that God does not always exert himself to the utmost of his Power, but that he of his own accord does as it were restrain, or moderate his Power, that he may leave something of liberty to other Powers created by him, and also that his Power in no wise tends to any thing contrary to his Wisdom and Justice. Whence it is that God could Create a Creature endow'd with a certain Degree of Liberty, all the Actions of which he could foreknow, and which nevertheless he might not predetermine by an Irrefragable Decree, and what would overthrow the Liberty of it. For it would be plainly Contradictory to give Liberty to any Being, and yet to impose upon it before hand such a Necessity, as it can in no wise decline. And because God is Holy and Just, he cannot Decree that any thing shall come to pass, he being the Authour of it, and making it necessary to be, which yet is repugnant to his Holiness and Justice. Whence God can foresee, and he can permit the Evils which are to be committed by free Creatures; that is, he is able not to hinder with all his Power but that they may be. He can also Decree that some good Effect shall follow from that which is Evil. But saving his Holiness and Justice, he cannot command Evil, or before-hand lay a Necessity upon it to be. For that of which 'tis said, *Acts* 4:28, that God had Decreed that it should be was the Death of the Saviour, not the Unjust Judgment of Pilate, whom he admonish'd by the Suggestion of his own Conscience, and by a Dream sent to his Wife: But because he thought fit rather to indulge the Fury of the common People which he might have restrain'd with his Souldiers, or by deferring the Sentence he might easily have eluded, God used that evil Action to a good End, which End however might have been obtain'd even without that. But that a good Action should be commanded by God, and he should afford Strength to perform it, and indeed so as that such Action may after a certain manner be attributed to Man, and he upon the account of it may acquire a Reward, has nothing in it disagreeing with the Goodness, Holiness, and Justice of God, *Mat.* 25:14, &c. When therefore the calling of God to embrace the Gospel, and the way of Salvation is propos'd in the manner of a Law, as *Acts* 17:30. God is said *to command all Men every where to repent,* it is absur'd to say that God decrees that some Men shall not obey his Call. But about this Matter, that he may not extinguish the Morality of it, God does not use an irresistible Force, but leaves at least a Liberty of rejecting the offer'd Grace. Whence, consistently with the Power and Wisdom of God, it may be rightly said. That God wills a thing seriously, and affords fit means to bring it to pass, and yet that which he wills does not come to pass, but the contrary to it is done: And this because it pleases God to moderate his Power whereby the Rational Creature can exert its native Liberty. As also God can will a thing under a certain Condition, which it is in the Power of a rational Creature, either to fulfil, or not to fulfil. From these things I think it may with sufficient clearness be gather'd, How the Prescience and Power of God can consist with the Liberty of Man, namely, because it does not lay any Necessity upon Things, but his Liberty does as it were moderate his Power about the moral Actions of Men, least their Liberty being extinguish'd, the Morality of their Actions should be destroy'd too. These things well observ'd would prepare the way for dissolving many Sophistries about this Matter.

§73. Further, concerning the calling of the Reprobate, *Jurieu* delivers himself thus: *God has had indeed a Will to call them, because he has call'd them, but he has not had a Will to draw them to Himself, because he will not draw any one but his own. For among these whom God externally calls, there are some whom God calls so, as that with the Force of his Grace inclining their Minds, he sweetly allures them to himself. Others there are to whom the Invitation and Offer of Salvation is made for this end, that they may be rendred inexcusable, and may perish by their own Fault.*[50] But they seem to us to think much more Reverently of the Goodness and Sincerity of God, who say that God seriously Wills that all should obey his Call, and that there is nothing wanting or omitted on his part but that they may do so. But yet he does not so far intend the Power of his Grace, but that they who are call'd can reject the Call, and by their own Fault fall short of the offer'd Benefit. Tho' *Jurieu*

Concerning the Calling of the Reprobate.

50. Jurieu, *De Pace*, p. 15.

presently afterwards endeavours to moderate the harshness of his Assertion by subjoining, *Never has God properly speaking propos'd to himself*
this end of the external Vocation, to wit, that he might render Men unex-
cusable. God does not call the Reprobate but by accident, because they are
mingled with the Good and the Elect: All things are done in the World
for the sake of the Elect: The Vocation is of the Elect, as also the other Gifts
of God. But the Elect cannot be call'd alone, they lie hid in a Multitude.
The Call is made by Men who know not the secret Purposes of God.
Therefore the Word and Preaching are directed indifferently towards all,
and the Ambassadour of God ought to suppose that all are Elected, or at
least may be.[51] This Reasoning perhaps shows why he who speaks to a
great Congregation, may frame his Discourse so as supposing them all
to be Elected. But it is not for this Reason necessary that the Holy
Scripture must speak thus, That God would have all Men sav'd, that
he calls them all, that he requires Repentance of all. But on the other
side it must be said God does directly and seriously call even the
Wicked, that he may demonstrate his Goodness, and may take from
them all Pretence for Complaint, as if it came to pass by him that they
Eternally miscarry: And it is not either the manifest, or secret Decree
of God, but their own Wickedness which is in fault, that they do not
enjoy his Goodwill. So *Ezeck.* 2:3. The People to whom the Prophet
is sent by God, is universally said to be Stiff-necked, Obstinate and
Rebellious: To whom nevertheless he is commanded to declare the
Word of God, whether they would hear or not hear. And nevertheless
in that very Prophet, *Chap.* 33. *Ver.* 11. and *Chap.* 18. *Ver.* 13. God
solemnly testifies that he desires not the Death of a Sinner, but rather
that he would turn and live. But if it pleas'd God to afford his serious
Call only to certain Men, it would not be at all difficult to difference
them by some certain Note or Mark, that what is Holy might not be
thrown to Swine. As when the Saviour sent out his Disciples to make
their first Essay at Preaching, he appointed the particular Places where
they should Preach the Gospel, and where they should not do it, *Mat.*

51. Ibid.

10:5, 6. And when God at a certain time would not that *Paul* should Preach the Word in *Asia* and *Bithynia,* he forbade him the doing it.

§74. From the same Foundation that God does not always act as it were to the utmost of his Power, but can temper and moderate it, and is wont to do so, it also is that God does not Will all things absolutely, but some things under a certain Condition; which that it may exist, or not exist, is in the Power of him to whom he has granted some Degrees of Liberty. Which Condition not existing that Effect which was to have follow'd upon the Existence of the Condition does not follow; but so that there is not for all that any Mutation in God, since he did not determine his Will, but in case of the Existence of that Condition. Whence 'tis with too much Boldness, that a *Velleity* in God, or *Antecedent-wills* are rejected by *Jurieu,* upon the account that they are Inefficacious. For those Wills have always this Efficacy that they testifie concerning the Good-will, or Benignity of God. But they are not to have that Efficacy, whereby the Benefit offer'd by God is actually to be given and confer'd by the Intention of God, any other wise then upon the taking place of that Condition which depends upon the Will of him to whom the Offer is made, *Psal.* 81:11, &c. *Jer.* 38:17, 18. Whence 'tis falsly said, *That a Being Infinitely Perfect, can never say I would. For this must belong to a Being, either ignorant of the future, or that is weak, and bound under Laws,*[52] none of which things can be in God. But there is a fourth part which may be added to this Division, and that is, or it must be said of him who does not always exert the utmost Force of his Power. In which Respect it is not at all repugnant to God, to say *I would.* Therefore 'tis needless to deny that there are in God *Conditional Decrees,* as if they did not *well agree with the Idea of a Being infinitely perfect,* Jurieu indeed says, *whoever frames a Decree under a certain Condition, he therein declares himself ignorant of the Future, or else Impotent.* But there may be added a third part to this Division, and it may be said, Or he is not willing to constrain the Liberty of

Of the Conditional Will of God.

---

52. Ibid., p. 19.

another by an inevitable Necessity. But neither is that Condition, tho'
it be foreseen that it will not come to pass, *a meer Mockery,* since it
declares the Benignity and Good will of him that makes the Offer,
who omits nothing necessary on his part, and who puts off from himself all the Blame, why such a Man perishes. Neither may such a Condition be said to be *impossible,* which it was foreseen would not come
to pass, since the foresight of things lays no Necessity upon them, and
the Condition would indeed come to pass if Man would not abuse his
Liberty. It cannot be deny'd indeed, but that God has a Power of
effecting that the Condition also should exist: But he was not bound
to apply that Measure of Power, nor was it necessary that he should
do so, by which the Morality of that Action, and the Aptitude of it to
be imputed to the Actour had been extinguish'd. And God truly Wills
the Salvation of such Men provided they are not against it. Yet he does
not hold it agreeable to his Wisdom to continue them within the
immutable Laws of Motion, after the manner of Self-moving Engines,
so as that they cannot but produce that Condition. And so he *permits*
that the contrary may be, that is, he does not in that manner hinder
it, that it cannot be. For that permission has not the Nature of a positive
Decree, but it is a pure Negation of an Impediment which he was not
bound to interpose. But a Conditional Decree is not a simple Legislative Declaration, or Rule by which any one is to be judg'd; nor is it
a naked Sign to which the Internal Intention does not correspond. But
it is a true Genuine, and sincere Declaration of the Internal Benignity,
which yet he has not Decreed to exert, but under a certain Condition:
But so as that, he has in no wise form'd a Decree by Vertue of which
that Condition cannot exist. *Jurieu* proceeds, *A Man that makes Laws,*
ought to desire and wish that Men would live according to the Laws made
by him, that it may be well with them, because Man is by the Divine Law
bound to wish and afford all good things to all Men: But God, as he does
in a most holy manner give Laws, so he freely determines concerning things
future, nor is he bound by any Laws, nor constrain'd by a fatal Necessity,
nor is he bound to wish, or do good to any Creature, or Man; for he does
what he will with his own. So that he bestows his Benefits with the most

perfect Liberty.[53] Which things must be qualified from *Mat.* 7:11. But what then? May God therefore with a perfect Liberty inflict Eternal Torments, only because it pleases him so to do? Truly *Abraham* Judges quite otherwise, *Gen.* 18:25. *That be far from thee to destroy the righteous with the wicked, that be far from thee who art the judge of all the world.*

§75. From thence *Jurieu* endeavours to prove that God does not foresee future Contingencies, and so all things proceed from a Previous Decree of God, and every Prescience in God presupposes a Previous Decree. To this Purpose he thus Reasons: *Future Contingencies cannot be certainly and infallibly foreknown from all Eternity, unless they are seen by God in themselves, or in their Causes: But God cannot, before all Decree of his, know the future Contingencies, neither in themselves, nor in their Cause. For there can be found in God but three ways of knowing things future.* (1.) *He knows things in his own Will, because he Wills they should be done; or he knows the things in themselves, and without their Causes after that they exist; or lastly, he knows them in their Causes, as he sees their Determination to such an Effect.*[54] That God does not foresee things in the first and second manner is easily admitted, because to assert this would be Contradictory. But why he cannot foresee them in the third Way and Manner, this Reason is added: Because *the Causes are as yet undetermin'd.* But this seems to us not sufficient. For as *David* rightly reasons, *He that made the Eye, shall not he see? He that planted the ear, shall not he hear?* So it is also rightly Collected, He who hath given to the Creature the Liberty of determining its own Actions, why cannot he foresee these Determinations? For God who is from Everlasting, always immutably beholds all things as present, and from all Eternity he beholds the free Action of his Creature, not as Decreed by himself, but as to be determin'd by the Creature. See *Psal.* 139:2, 4, 5, 23, 24. 81:13, 14. *Acts* 14:16. *Rom.* 1:24. And that there may be the less fear of a Contradiction here, it must not be said that God foresees future

Of Future Contingencies.

---

53. Ibid., p. 23.
54. Ibid., p. 27.

Contingencies as determin'd, but as to be determin'd by a free Cause which has its liberty from him, and liable to his Direction. Whence the future Contingencies which God hath not determin'd by his Decree, because such a Decree would contradict his Goodness and Justice, do pass from the Possibility to be, to what is to be by the Intervention of the Determination of a free Creature. But it is very absurd that double Decrees are invented. *Operative,* and *Permissive, and they Efficacious*[55] when it manifestly implies a Contradiction to say a permissive efficacious Decree. When the Permission of God signifies nothing else but the Denial of a Prohibition of a certain Kind and Degree. Whence when God Decrees to permit any Evil, he does not Decree that that Evil shall be; but only he decrees that he will not apply all the Means which might effect that it could not in any wise be; which things indeed he could not apply, nor was he bound to do it, saving the Morality of the Action and the Liberty which he had granted. But also no Man ever could have it in his Mind to assert that *Sins which are defects and privations of Being, rather then Beings have a virtue of determining themselves to Existence.*[56] But Man as a free Agent determines the Existence of his Sins. It cannot be denied but God as Creatour and Preserver of Nature and Motion does concur to that which is Natural in Evil Actions: But so that he does not predetermine that Physical, or Natural Motion, or beforehand define and decree that it must exist, to which Man is to add the Morality of it: But that it shall be left to the liberty of Man to direct that natural Motion, and apply it to something that is Evil.

Concerning
the Universal
Good Will
of God. §76. Those things which are urg'd by *Jurieu,* concerning the *universal good will of God* to Mankind, and *his will* that they should *be sav'd,* and so about that common distinction between an Antecedent, and a consequent Will, have a very easie Solution if the Sense of them be rightly explain'd. For we deservedly give Credit to the Holy Scriptures, when they assert that God has lov'd the World, that he wills not the

---

55. Ibid., p. 28.
56. Ibid., p. 29.

Death of a Sinner, that he is not willing any one should perish. Which Benevolence, or good Will does not stay within a meer Complacence and Approbation; but it proceeds even to such an Efficacy that God has afforded fit and sufficient Means for that End, and perform'd all things which can be desir'd on his part. So that the Reason why some Men perish, is not in God, but in the Men themselves. But it must be well observed, as also we have suggested before, that God as a free Agent does not every where exert the utmost Force of his Will and Power, but does so moderate it, as that a Liberty is left to his free Creatures, at least not to accept of the Good which is offer'd. So that a Man cannot be sav'd indeed but by the Benefit of God, but he perishes by his own Fault; and so he has as it were a Negative Vote about the Matter of his Salvation. Whence God has neither absolutely will'd to bestow Salvation upon Men, nor that their Perdition shall come upon them, nor has he decreed either but under a Condition, if they will not hinder or refuse the Means of Salvation. Whence if any Man refuses the Means of Salvation offer'd by God, and perishes, the Antecedent will of God is not frustrated, because this did not determine to proceed absolutely any further, then to the producing and offering Means of Salvation. And if any one whom God hath lov'd with his universal Good will, does afterwards perish, there happens no Change in God, because he did not absolutely will to save that Man, but under a Condition, which that it might exist, God on his part perform'd what was sufficient thereto. But the Conditional Will, whether the Condition exists or no, is not chang'd, but always remains uniform, and consistent with it self. Which things being laid down, it is not difficult to dissolve the Sophistries of *Jurieu.* (p. 53.) His first Evasion is, *That the general Will of saving Men in God is only Legislatory.* But God does not in the Expressions of that sort, intimate any Law according to which he intends Men should be judg'd, but declares what on his part he is about to perform. Therefore if at the most it should be granted that some of that sort of Expressions have the Force of a Law, yet 'tis certain the Legislatour cannot, saving his Justice, apply an Impediment whereby it may come to pass that the Law given by him cannot be fulfill'd; nor can he withdraw the Means, without which it is altogether impossible that the Law should be satisfied. But to this Question, *Whether or no the Legislative Will speaks, and has annexed to it a serious desire, and good will to bestow Salvation upon all,* it is to be said it is so; but that Good-will is Conditional, not Absolute. Certainly unless God invited all Men seriously to Salvation, the Opposition were ridiculous in the Expression, *Mat.* 23:37. and such like, *I would, but ye would not.* For without doubt it was very seriously that the *Jews* would not. But how impertinent an Expostulation, were it to say I have call'd thee to my Supper, not seriously, but for Forms sake, and thou wouldst not come. And if that Thread-bare Distinction of *the Will of the Sign,* or the signified Will must be of force to elude the Expressions, which in so clear words, speak of the universal Good-will of God, the Satisfaction of Christ, and his Call; why may it not be able to elude the other Particular Expressions, and allow us to say that God does nothing else through the whole Scripture but impose upon Men by pleasing Dreams. *Jurieu* proceeds to argue, (*p.* 45.) *Either God has that Will now, or he has it not, which without doubt he had from all Eternity.* If you say the former there will be in God at the same time two contradictory Wills, to wit, that general one of saving all Men, and the Will of damning many for their foreseen Impenitence. But now others teach that the Antecedent Will is not to be made to reach beyond the first Call by the Gospel, and the voluntary Choice of Men, and that it is not to be extended to the last end: That is, God has been willing thus far to bear a Good-will to all Men, that he has prepar'd Means of Salvation for them, and offer'd Salvation, but he suspends the actual Attainment of Salvation upon the not rejecting his Grace. From whence there is no change in God, if by the fault of Man that end does not follow which God suspended upon a Condition which was in the Power of Man. *Jurieu* further asks, (*p.* 55.) *Why if God would have all Men to be sav'd under the Condition of Faith and Obedience, did he not decree this to be according to his wish, when it was in his power to fulfil and give the annexed Condition? Why has he not bestow'd so much Grace as might easily overcome the Rebellion of the Will, which also he could easily have done?* To which things we answer, That we must know and judge of the Will and Disposal of God by what he has reveal'd in his Word. To which 'tis vain and foolish to oppose the Reasonings of Humane Wit, by which Man presumes to judge of Almighty God, according to his own sense of things. Nor can such things be any more approv'd by sober Minds, than that bold Expression of *Alfonsus* King of *Arragon;* That he would have given the World a much better Frame and State, if he had been Counsellour to God in the Creation of it. But in my Judgment it seems a sufficient Reason why God made the foreseen Non-resistance a Condition in this Case: Because it does not please him to draw Men to Heaven after the manner of the working of a Machine, and because by such an irresistible Grace all Morality in the Business of Salvation would be taken away. But that Question too may be much more justly retorted upon the Adverse Party: Why has God, when it was in his Power to have sav'd all Men by an Absolute Will, decreed to bring only some to Salvation by an irrevocable Necessity, who are in themselves no better than those who are Reprobate, and to condemn the rest to Eternal Torments. He enquires further, (*p. 57.*) *Why was not God before the Fall mov'd with that general Philanthrophy, or Good will to Men, as to decree to preserve all Men free from Pollution, that so he might bestow Happiness upon them all?* But did God suffer any thing to be wanting on his part, unless he would have exceeded the Measure of a Rational Creature, which might be capable of Morality? And if we will measure all things by that which we judge God to have been able to do, we must say God was able to have sav'd all Men after the Fall into Sin by an Absolute Decree, no less then a few of them. He enquires in the last place, *why God should begin to be mov'd with the desire that all Men should be sav'd after the foreseen Fall, and the decreed Permission of the Fall, when the thing was now become impossible, according to the Laws which God had given both to Himself, and to Men.* To which we return: It is falsly said God now at length begins to be mov'd with the desire of saving all Men, (which desire was certainly in him from the beginning, and is not risen up since the Fall,) when the thing is now impossible according to the Laws which God had given to Himself and Men. For who can say it is absolutely impossible that all Men should be saved? Or that it is impossible the means of Salvation appointed by God should not be rejected by some?

Or what these Laws are which God has laid upon himself and upon Men, which bring, or cause a Necessity that many cannot but refuse the Means of Salvation. In truth I can read nothing of any such Laws in Holy Scripture. But it seems a more expeditious way to *Jurieu* to solve all these Questions, if it be said, that God after he foresaw and permitted the Fall made this Law, *I will that all they who believe, on my Son whom I intend to send shall be sav'd.* But still we must needs greatly doubt of the Equity of the Law, if God by an absolute Decree will not give that Faith to all which cannot be exerted by the Natural Power of Man. So therefore there seems to be nothing to hinder, but that we may say, that the general Will of Saving all Men always was, and is in God, both yesterday, to day, and for ever.

Concerning the manner of Reconciling the Expressions which seem to contradict one another in this Matter.

§77. But there are very many Expressions occurring in the Holy Scriptures, which declares the universal Will of God, for the saving of all Men. As for Instance, 1 *Tim.* 2:4. 2 *Luke* 10. *John* 3:16. *Ezek.* 18:23, 32. 33:11. To which others are wont to be oppos'd, which seem to restrain the Good-Will of God to a few. Such as *Rom.* 9:15, 18, 21. *Isa.* 53:17. *Ps.* 141:4. *Job.* 12:20. *Mark* 4:11, 12. To each of these, the Place where they are being well consider'd, I believe there may be very fit Answers given, and this seems to us to have been every where done by our Divines. And here we shall add, by the way, that the Expression of the Potter in *Rom.* 9:4. may very well be explain'd from *Eccles.* 33:10, &c. So as that the Similitude of a like Power of a Potter is not to be extended beyond Temporal Things, about which we do not unwillingly acknowledge an absolute Disposition, *Eccles.* 9:11. But *Jurieu* with one blow cuts asunder all those Knots, in saying, That *there is in the Mind of God a double Will, and in his Mouth a double Speech. And as those Wills seem to be contrary to each other, so those Speeches adapted to those Wills seem to sound altogether contrarily too. God as a Legislatour now Wills and Commands all Men to yield Obedience to his Commands, and by these to live. But as to what he has from all Eternity foreseen, known, and decreed, the contrary is fixed and establish'd with him. Nor is God therefore contrary to himself: But he gives Laws by the Will of a Legislatour, according to which Men are bound to act, and according to which they shall be judged; by the Wills of his Decrees he orders Events which are to be directed by himself for his Glory through all Ages.*[57] And so he will have the Expressions of the former Rank to belong to his Legislative Will, and those of the latter to his Decreeing Will. To these things we return; There is indeed a difference between a Law and a Decree, between a Law-giver, and him that Decrees. The former Commands that somewhat be done by another; the latter determines to produce somewhat himself, or to effect, and cause that it be. But it ought to be settled with us, that these two Wills are never contrary the one to the other. For a humane Legislatour presupposes Powers of performing in him upon whom he lays his Law. Therefore if he should command things purely impossible, he will be thought to act against Reason and Justice, and only to seek a Pretence that he may inflict Evil upon an innocent Person; and much rather must this be, if he himself should effect, or Cause that the Law could not be fulfill'd, which would certainly be the extreamest Degree of Tyranny. Further it is confess'd that the Conversion of Man, and his Salvation are things which cannot be attain'd, unless God himself affords Powers for them. But if God by his secret Decree has determin'd not to afford such Powers to the greatest part of Mankind, and yet commands all Men to Convert and Believe, with the threatning of Eternal Punishment if they do not, he would commit a Mockery, and that joyn'd with the greatest Cruelty; and would do just as if I should command a Man to mount a Tower, and take away the Stairs. Therefore the Expressions in which there is a seeming Repugnancy, are not to be oppos'd to each other, but to be rightly explain'd: Since it can in no wise agree with the Goodness and Perfection of God to say and command one thing, and in his secret Will to Decree another. Lastly, If at the most one or two general Expressions may be explain'd after the manner of Laws, for Instance, *Acts* 17:30. Yet there are some of them that will plainly not admit of such an Interpretation, but do simply declare the thing as it is: Such, for Instance we have, *Luke* 2:10. *Ezek.* 18:23. *John* 3:16. And what reason is there why the former

57. Jurieu, *De Pace,* p. 62.

Expressions must rather be explain'd by the latter, then the latter by them; Of-what is there more of Figure in the Expressions of the former sort, then in those of the latter. And how can that be the Rule according to which the most Righteous God is willing to judge, which God by a secret Counsel has decreed shall not be. And it is a very dangerous saying, (*p.* 63.) That, *But one place in which God speaks as Decreeing, and in which he discovers his true Will is sufficient to declare and direct to the true sense of those places in which he speaks as a Legislatour.* In truth if it be fit to Establish such a Rule for the Interpreting of Scripture, why may not some prophane Person determine concerning *Eccl.* 3:19. That the true Will of God is there express'd, and all other things deliver'd in Scripture proceed from the Legislatorial Will. And why does not God as often and clearly discover his secret and serious Will about the Salvation of Men, as that Legislative Will according to which Men are to be judg'd. Since the latter would be not only Vain, but most Unjust, if the former appoints what is contrary to it. I command after the manner of a Law, that something be done by a Man, and yet in my secret Will I decree and determine that it be not done, which secret Will too Causes that the thing cannot be done. Is it indeed true that the most perfect Being does act thus? But that all Scruple may be remov'd, *Jurieu* delivers some Observations to show that the Expressions of Holy Scripture which speak of the Legislative and Decretive Will, do not oppose one another. The first of them is; That *the Divine Promises, and Declarations concerning the Salvation of Men, are made in general words, and conceiv'd in Terms of Universality; as if they did comprehend all Men, and all things within their Compass, but they are fulfil'd and made good, but only in the Elect.* This Rule may in a certain Sense be admitted: As that God offers Salvation to all in general under the Condition, if they do not reject it, which Condition is perform'd in the Elect, but not that God Wills absolutely not to bestow Salvation upon the Non-elect. The Expression, *John* 12. Seems not to speak *of all Men,* but of Disciples, as appears by 25:26, &*c.* Nor is it to be gather'd from thence that Christ drew his Disciples to Faith in him from an absolute Decree, or that he had determin'd in the same manner, not to draw others to this. Also from the Expression in *Luke* 2:10.

It cannot be gather'd that some Absolute Decree of God was the Cause why either all the *Jews*, or all Men did not partake of the Joy which God afforded Ground for to all People. And 'tis a very weak Reason which is brought for it, That *Denomination is from the better part*, and that *the Godly are the better part of Mankind, but the Reprobate are before God as nothing, and of no account*. But another thing is insinuated, *Mat.* 5:45, &c. The second Rule is this, (*p.* 64.) *It is an easie Passage from Universal to Indefinite Propositions, and the latter are put instead of the former*. But so violent a way of Interpreting, no Man will easily admit. The third Rule is, (*p.* 65.) *Men cannot be otherwise call'd to Salvation, then in general Terms and Expressions, by reason of the Condition of those that are called, and those that call them. Those that are call'd are Men who are bound to believe that which is most true, which is, that the offer'd Salvation belongs to them all, if they believe and obey God that calls them.* Which Condition, whether it be understood in the Sense of *Amyraldus*, or whether it supposes an absolute Decree not to give that Faith, is Illusory. But neither is it most true that Salvation belongs to all; which according to the Opinion of *Jurieu*, is by an absolute Decree withheld from the greatest part of Mankind; nor is any Man bound to believe such a Declaration. *Those that call are Men also who not knowing the Secrets of God, are bound to believe by a Judgment of Truth that all those whom they call, may for ought they know be Elected, and by a Judgment of Charity that they are truly Elected.*[58] But those that call are ignorant indeed of the secret Will of God, concerning the several Individuals of the Elect, or Reprobate; but yet they know that secret Will in general, that God according to the Opinion of *Jurieu*, by his absolute and secret Decree, is not willing to save all Men. Whence they cannot believe with a Judgment of Truth that all those whom they call, may, for ought they know be Elected, unless it be antecedently to the absolute Decree; which yet is set by these Men in the first place among the Decrees of God about the Salvation of Men. And further, it is false, that he who calls is bound by a Judgment of Charity to believe that all whom he

58. Ibid., p. 65.

calls are Elect: For Charity obliges to nothing else but that we damn no Man, unless from Tokens that cannot deceive, and that we always presume on the milder side, and leave the Judgment to God. But from these things it in no wise follows that the Invitation must be conceiv'd in Universal Terms according to the Mind, that is, of *Jurieu,* and his Followers. For according to the Opinion of our Divines, without doubt it must be made in this manner. But if according to the Opinion of *Jurieu,* any one should thus invite a great Multitude of Men; God indeed will have all Men to be sav'd, if they believe: And according to this Rule he will Judge them all. But in his secret Counsel he has Decreed not to give Faith to all. But it does not appear to me to whom among you God has by his Absolute Pleasure Decreed to give Faith and Salvation, and to whom not to give these. Nevertheless I Preach Salvation to you all, and I invite you all to Faith. What Success do we believe such a Preacher would have among his Auditors. But according to the Opinion of our Men it may with some Truth, and rightly be said; God has rejected none of you by his Absolute Pleasure, but offers you all sufficient Means of Salvation, which if you do not reject, he will truly bestow upon you all Salvation. With him is your Help, but your Perdition is of your selves. *Jurieu* proceeds; *If God should himself immediately call and invite Men to Salvation, it might be objected to him, why do you call to Salvation this or that Man, who you certainly know does not belong to you?*[59] But the Apostle, 2 *Cor.* 5:29. Says, *we are Ambassadours for Christ, as tho' God did entreat you by us.* Whence the things commanded to the Ambassadour ought to conform to the In-tention of him that sends him, otherwise that Ambassadour might be said to be sent to lie and deceive others. Nor may a secret Intention of him that sends, differ from the Commands given to the Ambassadour. Otherwise he that sends would deceive both the Ambassadour, and those to whom he sends him. Therefore if there be a secret Will which disagrees with the reveal'd one, *such an Invitation is both false and fallacious: Come all of you, the Remedy is prepar'd for all that are sick,*

59. Ibid.

and whoever will take it shall be restor'd to perfect health. For how can
they take it, if by an Absolute Will it be Decreed that it shall not be
given to all to be able to take that Medicine. It is also very doubtful,
whether or no the Observation deliver'd by *Jurieu* will serve his turn.
The Holy Scripture is dictated, not as proceeding immediately from the
Mouth of God, but as what is to proceed from the Mouth of Men through
all Ages, and is to be as it were dispensed by Men. For it must be added
that the Holy Scripture is nevertheless so formed, not only as that it
may be understood by Men, but as that Men may from thence perceive
what is the Will of God; and so as that the genuine Sense of Holy
Scripture which is perceiv'd by Man, does not disagree with the Intention and Sense of God. But if the secret Sense of God should differ
from the Revelation of Holy Scripture, the Scripture would be un-
useful, and would prove invented only to deceive Men. Whence 'tis
false that *the Spirit of God does not speak in that manner in the Holy*
Scripture, as God himself would speak, if he should immediately speak to
Men, but only as Men might speak to other Men. For how can an Expression so bold, and of such Importance be prov'd? Certainly God
spake with *Moses face to face,* that is immediately. After what manner
the Impression from God was made upon the Mind of *Moses* by God,
I leave undetermin'd. But yet this cannot be doubted, but that from
that Revelation, *Moses* perceiv'd what it was that God Will'd. But Men
ought so to speak to other Men, and so to form their words, as that
the same Sense may be express'd to the hearer, which is in him that
speaks. Otherwise a Lie and Deceit is committed. It is also a very weak
Reason why the Invitation must be made in universal words, altho' the
Intention of God was only particular, to say, (*p.* 66.) It must be so *that*
the Unbelievers may be rendred unexcusable, lest they should say it was
not possible to accept the Salvation which was offer'd. For he is at last
unexcusable to whom all Means to any End have been offer'd, and he
only is in fault why he has not accepted them, and by using them
obtain'd that End. But if the secret Decree of God does disagree with
the external Vocation, this Vocation in whatever words it is conceiv'd,
does not render a Man unexcusable. And if it be so, that it is not
known to the Unbeliever what is the secret Decree, and so he cannot

appeal to that in Judgment, and he must confess he has done those things which deserve Damnation, yet when God according to the Opinion of *Jurieu* has deliver'd some by an Absolute Will of those who lay in the same Mire, and offered them efficacious Means for that End, and has suffer'd others no worse in themselves, then they to perish in the Mire, and hath not when he could design'd Efficacious Means for the saving them, the Reprobate at least having knowledge of the Absolute Will will be unexcusable. Lastly, *Jurieu* endeavours in a violent manner to impose a particular meaning upon that Expression, *God would have all Men be sav'd:* For that Declaration, or Expression, he says must be put among the Prophesies; and of these, as they reach to what is future *the Events are the Interpreters, and before the Events Men can hardly gain the true Sense of them.* But we deny that that Expression may be referr'd to the Prophecies. For it is not said that all, or some Men shall be sav'd, or shall in effect obtain Salvation; but it is said what the Will of God is at present concerning the Salvation of Men: Not indeed his absolute Will, but that which is confin'd to a certain Condition, and a certain Order. That we should moreover assert and vindicate what is the Nature of Prophecies is not to our present Purpose. It is also false that it is every where in Scripture said, *I Will not that all should be sav'd.* (p. 67.) For that most abus'd Expression, *I have Mercy on whom I will, and whom I will I harden,* has not that meaning nor is it therein express'd, that God out of his meer Will and Pleasure, and without regard to any thing does show Mercy to some, and harden others. The Repetition of one and the same word, does not signifie the Absense of all Respects, but Constancy and Immutability. *What I have written I have written,* does not signifie that *Pilate* had written without any respect, but that he would not Retract what he had once written. Add, *Jer.* 15:2. So *Exod.* 33:19. *God hath mercy on whom he will have mercy:* That is to whomsoever he once hath promised Mercy, to him he will truly perform, and will not Retract it. And indeed *he has Mercy on whom he will;* but he does not Will to have Mercy on any but those that believe in Christ, *John* 6. *He hardens whom he will,* but he does not Will to harden any one from an absolute Pleasure, but only those who by some peculiar foregoing Wickedness have deserv'd this. So the

hardening of *Pharaoh* was preceded by an excessive Pride and Contempt of God, *Exod.* 5:2. Let there be one Example produced, if it can
be, of a Person hardned by the meer Pleasure and Will of God, and
who had not perversely despised the first Grace of God. Thus, therefore, the Expressions of the latter sort do not contradict the former,
nor is the Universality of these restrain'd by those, but both may very
well consist, and so both do declare *the true and genuine Will of God,*
but neither of them an Absolute Will, but such as is limited by certain
Conditions and Respects. Therefore *Jurieu* might have written more
calmly then thus: *The thing speaks of it self; it is manifest by Experience*
that all Men are not sav'd. But where hath God said or promised that
all Men shall be sav'd. To this there is subjoin'd a Declaration, rather
than a Disputation; and such as is more then sufficiently *free* and *con-*
fident, and in which there appears nothing of that Modesty and Reverence, with which it is fitting sacred things should be handled. Certainly in the Ways and Counsels of God, by which he has determin'd
in general to bring Men to Salvation, there is nothing of Obscurity,
but all things are plain and perspicuous. *He that believes on the Son*
hath everlasting Life, he that believes not is condemn'd already. Christ is
the Light which Enlightens every Man, but the Darkness comprehended it
not. To them who shut their Eyes, even the bright Noonday is but
Darkness. But in the Providence of God about future Events, even
there where Prophecies give something of Light, we willingly confess
there is a great deal of Darkness mingled, but that is what concerns
not the present Question. Lastly, He endeavours to evince by Questions
indeed sufficiently rude, and violent, that God would not have all Men
sav'd. *If God would be known and lov'd by all Men, why hath he not so*
clearly manifested himself, as that no Man can refuse to do so.[60] But an
equal Light is propos'd to the Pious and the Wicked, but these despise
it, and will not suffer that it may exert its Force in their Minds. But
that God did not give an Irresistible Force to that Light, the Reason
is, because he thought it Congruous to his Wisdom and Justice, so to

---

60. Ibid., p. 68.

act in the Business of saving Men, as that their Perdition might justly be imputed to themselves. *If God would have all Men to be sav'd, if he would have all Men come to him, why has he left so many Ruggednesses, and Precipices, and such want of Tracks in the Ways of his Providence?* There is an Answer to this, *Mat.* 7:13, 14. *Acts* 14:22. And in general that Declaration of God may be return'd, which we have in the Prophet *Isa:* 55:8, 9. *My thoughts are not your thoughts, nor my ways your ways.* And I am so fully perswaded of the Wisdom of God, as to judge that the Reason of all that he hath said, or done, is manifest to himself, against all the Petulant Questions of *Jurieu.*

§78. We come next to the Redemption by Jesus Christ; concerning which that there were always different Opinions, no one will easily believe *Jurieu.* He endeavours to assert that to be *Particular,* altho' he grants that it may in a certain Sense be said to be *Universal,* not only by *Merit* and *Sufficiency, but also in respect of Times, as well before as after the coming of Christ,* in respect of *Nations and Degrees of Men, and moreover with respect to all Men in general. For Christ died he grants for Mankind Indefinitely.* (p. 73.) I suspect by the word *Indefinitely,* is intimated Christ is not dead for all, and every one of Mankind. *Yea, he open'd the Gate of Life to all Men, and procur'd a Possibility of Salvation.* Now you may be apt to believe that he is willing to be of our Mind. But he quickly returns to his wonted Mockery. *It is truly said the way is open for all Men to come to Christ, He is the Saviour of all Men under the Condition of Faith.* For he asserts that God is not willing to give Faith to all; which yet whereever it is, is the Gift of God, and does not spring from our natural Powers. Therefore that Condition of Faith is with respect to the Reprobate Impossible. Tho' we admit that Proposition, Christ died for all under the Condition of Faith, in no other Sense then this, That the Benefit or Fruit of his Death is applied to Men by Faith. Which also is the meaning of that noble Expression, *John* 3:16. *God so lov'd the World,* (which word no where signifies only the Elect,) *that he gave his only begotten Son,* even to that World. Therefore on the part of God there is an universal Love, and an universal Redemption. But because God will not snatch Men as by an Engine

Concerning the Universal Redemption by Jesus Christ; and the first Argument of Jurieu against this.

up into Heaven, there is requir'd their Acceptation of those Benefits which is done by Faith, and this God offers to all, *Acts* 17:31. And which every Man can have, provided he does not despise it, when offer'd of God. Then *Jurieu* forms the State of the Controversie. *Whether God gave his Son for that end, with that Intention, with that Purpose, that he might make Attonement for all, and every one of Mankind, or but only for the Elect, and those that are to be sav'd and to believe? The latter is affirm'd by those who hold with the Synod of Dort.* And for them *Jurieu* produces these Arguments. The first is taken (p. 74.) from all the Proofs of the foregoing Assertion, That God Wills that not all Men shall be sav'd. To that end, 1. *The Omnipotence of* God is urg'd. *If God did Will the Salvation of all Men by the Will of his Good-pleasure, he would cause this to be by most efficacious Means, because no Man can resist his Will.* But God does not use his Omnipotence about the Salvation of Men, which he used in Creating the World when *he spake, and it was done.* But he Wills to save Men in a certain Order, that there may be place for Morality. And if the Business of Redemption were to be accomplish'd by Omnipotence, what need were there of a Redeemer. (2.) *He who Wills the end, Wills also the Means, and the Condition, but God does not Will the Condition, that is the Faith and Conversion of all Men: For if he did Will the Condition, he has it in his Power to change the Hearts of Men, without any Injury to his Justice and Mercy.* Concerning this Argument, it is to be observ'd, That God also Wills the Means of Salvation, but he does not Will to impose them upon Men by the full Force of his Omnipotence. And any one may will an end, but yet so as not to will Promiscuously any Means, and any manner of the Application of them. And if God did concur in this Matter by meer Power, he could not, saving his Justice and Mercy, bestow the Means of obtaining Salvation on some, and refuse them to others of those who are equally Miserable and Wicked. Which yet is *Jurieu's* Assertion. (3.) *Because God hath not left that Condition of Faith and Conversion to be fulfill'd by Men alone, but hath taken it upon himself to meet with them, to prevent them, to call them as well inwardly as outwardly. Therefore if he did Will by a Will of Good-pleasure the Salvation of all Men, he would certainly effectually call them all.* But God does indeed effectually call Men, but with such a Degree of Efficacy, as not to take away all Morality in the Business of Conversion. (4.) *If God at present, and at this day did Will the Salvation of all Men, he would Will things altogether contrary; For at present, and at this day he Wills the Eternal Death of a great many from the foresight of their Final Impenitence. Therefore he would Will, properly speaking, the Life and Death of the same Persons at the same time which is absurd.* But these two Wills are not Repugnant to each other; My Supper is prepar'd for all, and none of them shall tast of my Supper who shall despise it. That Goodwill of God towards Mankind in general, is understood to subsist perpetually; but the Effect of it expires, or ceases as any one persists in final Incredulity. But this is what implies no Mutation, or Contradiction in God. For the Will of him who Wills, or Wills not under a certain Condition, undergoes no Change, whether the Condition does exist or not: Because his Will was from the beginning alternative, and so the Argument falls of it self. (5.) *God could not from all Eternity, and before the World was made will the Salvation of all, because he is immutable. But he had chang'd, if he had some time Will'd the Salvation of the Reprobate, for that at present he Wills the contrary. There is not any one Moment in Eternity, in which we can conceive God to pass from Willing the Salvation of all, to Willing the Eternal Death of the far greater part of Men, because in God there is no succession, no Mutation.* This Difficulty is taken away, if it be consider'd that there is at least an Order of Decrees in the Exercise of the Divine Mind. (*p.* 75.) (6.) This Argument is plainly of no force. *The manner of Divine Providence, is to exert it self by Light and Darkness mingled,* therefore God does not Will the Salvation of all Men. (7.) Lastly, *Some places of Holy Scripture* are brought in, by which it is said, *a particular Will of saving Men* is declar'd. Among which is put first that Expression, *Gen.* 3:15. But the Genuine Sense of it is very badly wrested. *Immediately after the Fall, God discriminates Mankind into two parts, the Seed of the Woman, and the Seed of the Serpent; to the Seed of the Serpent, that is wicked Men, he threatens Ruine, and Perdition, and Death. And the Seed of the Woman shall bruise thy Head. To the Seed of the Woman, that is the Faithful, and to them only he promises Victory over the Devil; therefore to them alone*

he promises Salvation. Therefore God did not intend to deliver all Man-
kind from the Serpent; yea, on the contrary he commits part of Mankind
to him, and numbers them among the Children of Satan. Hardly could
any thing more perverse have been devised than this Interpretation.
The Devil under the Form of a Serpent seduced *Eve,* it was not wicked
Men that did this: Therefore God threatens Punishment to him, not
to them. The Seed of the Woman here are not the Faithful, but that
eminent Seed of the Woman, produced without the Concurrence of
Man; compare *Gal.* 3:16. By him the Head of Satan is bruised, not by
the Faithful, whose Power cannot reach so far. Altho' that eminent
Seed of the Woman does receive his Brethren after a manner into a
Communion, or Participation of those things which are here said of
him; which however is not the proper Sense of the place, but a Consequence of what is here said in some measure. Nor are Wicked Men
understood here by the Seed of the Serpent, the Heads of whom it
does not fall to the share of the Faithful to bruise, but rather these, 'tis
manifest, are in this Life obnoxious to the Persecutions and Insults of
the other. Nor is it said that the Seed of the Woman shall bruise the
Head of the Serpent's Seed, but of the Serpent himself. Nor does there
appear any Foot-steps from the Scope of this Place, that God does here
distinguish Mankind into two Parts, since under the Word Woman,
between whom and the Serpent the Enmity is put, all Men are comprehended, who naturally spring from the Woman: But by the Seed
of the Serpent, may be understood those evil spirits who fell together
with Lucifer. The things built upon so bad a Foundation fall of themselves. (*p. 76.*) *This being laid down* (says *Jurieu*) *That the Seed of the*
Serpent is the Company of Evil and Wicked Men, it is certain that the
Messias does not belong to them, who is not promised to them. Also if the
first Promise of Salvation was not universally made to all Men, but par-
ticularly to the Sons of God, (I would know where any mention is made
of Sons of God in that Sentence,) *Then the Will of Saving was not*
universal in God. And lest any Reasonings should be opposed to these
things, he adds for a Sanction to them, *He who argues against these*
things is Contentious. But what Character shall we give to him, who
after this manner interprets Holy Scripture. To *Acts* 13:48. *They believ'd*

as many as were Ordain'd to eternal Life. Georgius Calixtus,[61] in his literal Exposition upon the Place answers. *Ordain'd indeed of God, but it does not therefore follow that they were Ordain'd to this by the Absolute Will of God, which had no Consideration of Means. But rather if God had Ordain'd them to eternal Life, he had regarded that Order, which he himself has Establish'd in the bestowing of Salvation, and the Means by which he Wills that Men should come to Life. So that they who would not reject those Means, but would be obedient to them; (and this very thing also God had from all Eternity foreknown,)* Therefore he ordain'd those to eternal Life. *For whom he foreknew them he Predestinated,* Rom. 8:29. *And we are Elect according to* the Foreknowledge of God the Father, 1 *Pet.* 1:1. That is God *Wills to bestow Life upon them that believe, and Faith to them who do not neglect or repel his Word, but hear and receive it. But now he has foreknown from all Eternity what ever comes to pass in Time. And so he had foreknown that the* Jews *would reject his word, and judge themselves unworthy of eternal Life, as it is in 46. Ver. That the Gentiles on the other side would hear, rejoyce, and magnifie as it is,* Ver. 43. *According to this foreknowledge, therefore he Ordain'd these to eternal Life, but past by, or Reprobated the other. So far therefore is this Place from Establishing any Absolute Decree, that rather it is here clearly declar'd that the Order which God observes, in time of bestowing Faith and Salvation, was so appointed and setled from all Eternity.* In a word, they believ'd, Not whom God had ordain'd to this, but who obey'd and complied with the Divine Order, to which not only Divine Actions, but also some things on the part of Men are requir'd. From the Expression, 1 *Thess.* 5:9. It does not follow that God had Ordain'd some Men to Wrath, much less that he had done this out of a certain Absolute Will and Pleasure. If I should say God has appointed us not to a Brutal Life, but to lead an honest and sociable one, it could not from thence be concluded that God had destin'd some Men to a Brutal Life. The Expression in *Rom.* 9:22. *Georgius Calixtus,*[62] in his literal Exposition, thus explains. *But if God willing to declare his Wrath and*

---

61. See note 4.
62. See note 4.

*Power, namely, because an Occasion is given for the declaring them, has
endur'd with much long suffering the Vessels of Wrath, and so hath by
Accident hardned them; for that Long suffering leads wicked Men to Repentance, as is said before,* Rom. 2:4. *and it is used by God for that end,
but Men by their Wickedness turn it into Evil, and on that Foundation
lay up for themselves a Treasure of Wrath. And so the Patience of God
hardens, not by its self, or from the Divine Intention, but by Accident, and
by reason of the Wickedness of Men. But in this very thing, that 'tis said,
God with much long-suffering bears the Vessels of Wrath, it is sufficiently
shown that he is not the Author, or Cause of such; for neither is there any
Necessity of Long-suffering for the bearing of that which we our selves have
done, and would have to be as it is. And when 'tis added, fitted to Destruction, 'tis not added that they were by God fitted to Destruction.* Beza
*therefore forces the Text, when he writes upon the Place. It may be said
with St.* Paul, *that some Men are by God the maker of them created to
destruction. More rightly,* Theodoret *upon this Place calls those the Vessels
of Wrath, who become such of their own accord; or, as* Theophylact *speaks
by themselves, and their own Propensity, add also by the Work and Instinct
of the Devil. For according to* Basil, *a Vessel of Wrath is he who receives
into himself all the Operation of the Devil as a certain Vessel, and cannot
be applied to any use by reason of the ill smell which it has from Corruption.
And so while he hardens, not indeed properly, and directly, or from his
Intention, but altogether by Accident, by enduring the Vessels of Wrath,
and giving them space for Repentance, since they abuse that Patience of
his he declares to them his Wrath and Power, that this Declaration may
be the end of that Patience not intended, but consequent or obtain'd. But
because Contraries set together do mutually illustrate each other; therefore
if you consider the Vessels of Mercy whom he indeed has prepar'd unto
Glory, his End is the Declaration of his Riches, or of the Greatness of his
Glory towards those Vessels, as is said, Ver. 23. For when he shows his
Wrath against the Unbelievers, his Mercy towards those that believe shines
the more. But the whole Sentence is to be thus understood: If a Potter
without any Injustice, and without being expos'd to the Complaint of any
one, and out of the same Mass of Clay which has given him no Offence,
forms one Vessel to Honour, and another to Dishonour: How can God be*

accused of Injustice; (for this is to be understood in the Sentence, because it is suspended and incompleat) if in bearing with the Vessels of Wrath, he does without any Intention of his harden them, so that in them being already hardned, beside his Intention, by his very Goodness he may show his Wrath and Power, and the greatness of his Grace and Favour towards the Vessels of Mercy? Thus far *Calixtus.* Lastly, in *John* 16:26, &c. the *Jews* are truly said not to be of the Sheep of Christ, but not from the meer Pleasure of God, but by reason of their wicked Reluctancy. Whence all these Expressions may very well consist with the general Will of saving Mankind, because that Will is not Absolute. But if it should be further objected to *Jurieu,* (*p.* 77.) *That God has indeed a general Will of saving Men, and therefore he has laid that universal Law, I Will that all, and every one of those who embrace Jesus Christ be sav'd by Faith:* He has in readiness his distinction between *his Legislatorial, and Decreeing Will;* and that the Means are not prepar'd but for the Execution of the Will of his *Decree,* not for the Execution of the Will of the *Legislatour.* But that Maxim of *Jurieu* has no Foundation at all. Certainly Humane Legislatours do presuppose a Faculty of performing, which if they knew to be absent, and notwithstanding should Establish a Law under a Penalty, they would be thought to commit a manifest Tyranny. But God who is both a Lawgiver, and the Creatour and Disposer of all things, could not, saving his Justice and Goodness command any thing which he has not afforded the Means of performing. Therefore if he would make a Law that all must believe in Christ, but should not afford fit Means for obtaining this Faith, he would only bitterly mock Mankind, and seek an unjust Pretence to damn them. Whence 'tis false that *God as Legislatour, only lays Laws, and commits the Execution and Observance of them intirely to Men:* But he does also afford Strength to fulfil his Law: Not indeed such as shall operate absolutely, but in a certain Order which he has Constituted. *God also when he Wills anything by a Decree, does then sweetly dispose the Means, that the thing Decreed may come to pass:* But yet as the Decree is Absolute or Conditionate, so also he tempers the Efficacy of the Means, that they may sute the Nature of the Decree. *When therefore,* as *Jurieu* proceeds, (*p.* 78.) and says, *That general Will, I Will that all Men should be sav'd, by believing is only Legislatory: The Death of Christ, and his Redemption is not order'd for the Execution of that Will, as a Means, but only so far as that the Law could have no force, unless Christ were first sent, and should die. Otherwise Christ is not dead with that end, that every Man should believe and be sav'd by Vertue of that general Law. For that Law determines nothing concerning the Salvation of Peter or James, or any Man, but only puts the Rule according to which Peter and James shall be judged.* These things are very obscure and intricate, but if they are rightly disentangled, and set in order, they contain nothing of any strength against our Opinion. Our Church teaches that God would have all Men sav'd by Faith in Christ. That is, He Wills to deliver them from the Damnation contracted by the Fall, not by a bare Remission of Sins, but by a Ransom interpos'd, which Ransom he has Constituted to be paid in the Death of his Son. But he hath not Will'd that the Efficacy of that Death should exert it self in that manner, as for Instance, The Sun exerts his Vertue of Shining, which shines upon the Just, and upon the Unjust, and upon them that would not have him shine upon them, and upon them that think nothing of the Benefit: But on the part of Mankind he hath ordain'd a Mean by which that is to be receiv'd, and that is Faith which he offers to Men, but after a Moral, not a Physical or Mechanick manner, so as that at least it is in the Power of Men to reject it. And from the foresight of the Acceptance, or Rejection of this Faith, the Decrees in the Exercise of the Divine Mind are form'd concerning the saving of particular Men. Thus therefore the Death of Christ is on the part of God the universal Mean of saving Mankind, without which God would not bestow Salvation upon any. But because he will not thrust Salvation upon any against their will, that alone is not the Mean that particular Men are actually sav'd, but on the part of Men there is requir'd a Mean of accepting and applying that Benefit, which is Faith: Which since every one has not, 2 *Thess.* 3:2. From thence it is understood that particular Decrees are form'd concerning the saving of particular Persons. Whence we can rightly say that God has absolutely Will'd the Death of Christ as a Mean of saving Men on his part, but he has not absolutely Will'd Faith as a Mean on the part of particular Men, but has left a

Power of Resisting it, that those Acts might be reckon'd among the Number of Moral ones.

§79. The second Argument by which *Jurieu* opposes the universal Redemption by Christ is such as this. *The designing from all Eternity, or that Will which God had before the Creation of the World of Redeeming Men by the Death of Christ, is the same with that Will which God had in that moment of time in which Christ died, and did according to the Divine Counsel, accomplish the Redemption of Mankind.* The Reason brought for this Connexion is, *Because whatever things are done in time by the Will of God, they are done by that same Will which Will'd them before all time; for God is not mutable, God has not one Will when he Decrees, and another when he Works and Executes.* (p. 79.) *But the Will of God in that moment when Christ died, could not be general for the Redemption of Mankind, that is of all, and every one of Men:* The Reason given is, *Because God hath from Eternity fram'd Decrees concerning the eternal Disposal of every Man: And therefore when God at the time of Christ's Death had already from all Eternity Decreed to Damn* Peter *and* James *for their foreseen Impenitence, there could not be a Will in God of Redeeming and Expiating the Sins of* Peter *and* James *by the Death of Christ, unless we will fain in God two Wills contradictory to, and mutually destroying one another.* But the Decrees which according to the Measure of our weak Reason, are conceiv'd to be in God, must not be oppos'd to one another, but be reckon'd Subordinate; nor is it to be thought that what is set in the former place is altogether compleat, and that which is set later is superadded to the former. But all things are to be conceiv'd of as comprehended and dispos'd together. Whence the universal Decree of Mercy, and the Death of Christ does not exhaust all the Counsel of God concerning our Salvation, but the Acceptation, or Rejection on the part of Men comes also into Consideration. That Will of God remains immutable before the Execution, and after it, because in God there is not any such Succession of Time as in created things. Nor does the Will of God which was at the time of the Passion, differ from that which was from Eternity. For the Efficacy of the Death of Christ began to exert it self immediately after the Fall, so that it was from the beginning of the World, set forth for the Salvation of all who should neglect to embrace it. And since that Death must be of infinite value, there could be nothing taken from it at what time soever it happened, as might be done to those Ransoms, the Price or value of which might be divided into Parts. So that this Similitude which *Jurieu* says he is so mightily mov'd with, (*p.* 80.) is greatly a Dissimilitude. And he who has a serious Will to bestow any Good upon another, under the Condition of his Acceptation of it, he has in no wise upon that account two Wills.

§80. The Third Argument of *Jurieu,* (*p.* 82.) is, That *at the time of the Death of Christ there were now* 4000 *Years past over, in which space of time very many, being as without God in the World, and out of the Covenant, perished, and so the greater part of those who were to be damn'd, were already doom'd to eternal Punishment. But since there is no Redemption from Hell, it must needs be that the Passion of Christ for those already damn'd must be in vain, which is an Absurdity. It is more like a monstrous Thing then a Dream, that a Price should be paid for the Life of them who have the least Punishment inflicted on them.* This difficulty is dissolv'd, if it be consider'd that the Merit of the Passion of Christ is of infinite value, and so is not divisible into several Parts, as for Instance, a great Sum of Money is divisible into Thousands or Hundreds: To which on the other side the Price of a certain thing may be equall'd, or it may be determin'd how much the one exceeds the other. Whence, if a thing of Infinite Price is done for another thing, which does not equal the value of that, or exhaust it, we must not therefore say that there was any Prodigality therein, or an unprofitable Profusion of a precious thing. But if the Merit of Christ did belong to a certain part of Mankind, and so were proportion'd to that, so as not to reach any further, it were upon this account Finite: When as the Redemption but of one Man exceeds all Humane Power, *Psal.* 49:7, 8. Therefore the Death of the Redeemer came to pass at length in the fulness of Time, yet by Vertue of the Covenant which God after the Fall made with the first Parents, it has exerted its Force backwards also; and therefore whoever have been damn'd before it, have perish'd for their

The third Argument of Jurieu.

Incredulity, and because they did not put their trust in the Saviour of the World who was to be born. Hence he is said to be the Lamb slain from the beginning of the World, *Rev.* 13:8. And so it suffices to maintain the universal Will of God for bestowing Salvation, that God has reveal'd the way of Salvation to all from the beginning of the World, and that the Perdition of Men comes not to pass by his Absolute Will, but by their own Fault, and Neglect of the way of Salvation. And when afterwards a Ransome of Infinite Price was to be presented, nothing could be diminish'd, or subtracted from it, tho' many before hand had rendred themselves uncapable of the Fruits of it.

The fourth Argument of Jurieu, taken from Vocation.

§81. The Fourth Argument of *Jurieu* (p. 86.) is taken from Vocation, which according to his Opinion is certainly, and without doubt particular. But if the Redemption by Christ were universal, the Vocation ought to be such also. To this purpose he produces the Expression of *Paul, Rom.* 10:14. *Whoever shall call on the Name of the Lord shall be sav'd; but how shall they call on him in whom they have not believed? Or how shall they believe, except they hear? Or how shall they hear without a Preacher? And who shall Preach, except he be sent?* From whence he does, and indeed with Confidence enough conclude, *That the Nations to which there are no Preachers sent ought not, nor are bound to embrace the Gospel, nor can they obtain Salvation by Christ, nor are they to be punish'd for having rejected the Sacrifice of Christ.* In all this there is not one thing deliver'd which is worth any Remark. For why did *Jurieu* from the mention'd place of *Rom.* 10. omit the following *Ver.* the 18*th. But I say, have they not heard? But their sound is gone out into all the Lands, and their words unto the end of the World, Psal.* 19:4. And therefore there is no Reason that *Jurieu* should reject with so much Scorn the Reasoning of our side, which is deriv'd from the first and second Chapters of the Epistle to the *Romans:* As if from the Contemplation of the Divine Works, there is only a way open'd to acknowledge the Eternal Power of God, but that there is not a word there concerning Christ and the Redemption wrought by him. For from that Knowledge which might be attain'd by the Light of Reason which yet remain'd, it might be known that the Worship of Idols was Worship unworthy of God. They might also acknowledge that they were bound to the Worship of God from whom they did daily receive so many Benefits. Therefore when the true Worship of God was continually maintain'd in a conspicuous manner, and of old the Temple at *Jerusalem* was renowned far and near, and afterwards the Gospel was Preached in the most eminent and frequented Places, and the Fame of it was largely spread, they ought indeed without Prejudice, and a Mind confirm'd in the contrary before-hand, to have enquir'd what there was of Solidity in the Doctrines deliver'd at *Jerusalem,* and Preach'd about by the Apostles. See *Deut.* 4:6. So the Queen of *Arrabia* who came from far to know the Wisdom of *Solomon,* 1 *Kings* 10:1. Shall in the last Judgment condemn those who have neglected Christ a greater then *Solomon, Matth.* 42:14. *Luke* 11:31. Compare *Acts* 8:31, &c. But neither is it to be believ'd that it is requir'd to the Universality of the Vocation, that a particular Preacher be sent about into every City, every Town and Village, and every House. As also the same thing is not requir'd to the Promulgation of Humane Laws, the Obligation of which, notwithstanding takes place from the Promulgation of them: But when once the Publication of Edicts is made in the wonted way, it is in vain after that to plead Ignorance. And therefore it is not necessary that they who Establish an universal Vocation, must demonstrate by what Men, or what Day, or in whose Consulship the Gospel was Preach'd, in all, and every Place of the Habitable World: But the universal Expressions may suffice for them: Such as *Mark* 16:15, 20. *Luke* 24:7. *Rom.* 10:18. Altho' we cannot undertake to deny but that God does often proceed in such a manner in the Dispensation of his Call, as that the Cause of it is not perfectly discernable by humane Reason. Of which however no Man may say that it wants a fit Reason, or that it has any such a one as is repugnant to his Goodness and Justice. Nor because we cannot always render a Reason of the Divine Dispensation, should we presently have Recourse to an Absolute Decree. So it is manifest that some Men have repeated Calls from God to Repentance; some again when they have rejected the first Impulse, are after that abandon'd to their Lusts: Which is a thing that may be observ'd concerning whole Nations and Cities. To some the Gospel is Preached time after time, and this Preaching is not ceased till it has taken good rooting. Elsewhere the Grace of God being once offer'd and rejected, is never offer'd again. To some Nations sooner, to others later is the Gospel Preach'd. Of all which things our Men give this Reason: That God foresaw if he had concern'd himself to offer his Grace sooner, or more often to those Persons, yet the same would have been rejected by them, and so that only their Damnation had been encreas'd. And if this Reason does not satisfie any one, yet it may consist with the Divine Justice and Goodness, tho' we cannot perfectly discern it. So the *Tartars,* in truth, the *Indians,* the *Chineses,* the *Americans* are descended from *Noah,* whose Sons having been endow'd with the true Knowledge of God, the Posterity of them were able to have retain'd it after the dispersion of the Nations. But that God will obtrude his Grace upon Men again and again, after it has been once offer'd and refused, is that which I no where read any Promise of. I know that he has exerted that exuberant Repetition of Grace in one place, and has not done it in another: If I am utterly ignorant of the Reason of this Difference, yet I acknowledge God to be just in all his Actions. But neither is it therefore necessary to refer this to an Absolute Pleasure, since God can do that which is above the reach of our Comprehension and understanding, of whom yet we ought to confess that he does all things justly and well. There is no reason that any Pious Person should give himself the trouble to answer the Scoffs of prophane Men. Our Reason must be captivated to the Obedience of Faith: and it is safer for us to follow the Simplicity of Holy Scripture then the counterfeit Subtlety of idle Men.

The fifth Argument of Jurieu. §82. In the 5*th.* place *Jurieu* thus reasons. *If the Redemption of Christ were Universal, Salvation would be Universal too.*[63] For he merited for Men, not only Remission of Sins, and Eternal Life, but also Faith, Grace, Repentance, Conversion, and the Habits of Vertues and Goodworks, and likewise the Condition of the Acceptance, namely, Repen-

63. Jurieu, *De Pace,* p. 91.

tance and Conversion. From whence it should follow that all Men should be actually sav'd. But to these things the Answer is easie. God Wills that all Men should be sav'd, but not after an irresistible manner as things are wrought in the Kingdom of Nature, and where the Laws of Motion take place: but in a certain Order, and so as that there may be a Morality existent in the Business of Conversion, and so that the Fault of Damnation may be laid upon Men themselves. Therefore the Business of Salvation and Conversion, is not to be measur'd by the Omnipotence of God, or by the manner used by God in the Creation of things, where he only said, let it be, and it was so. But in the Conversion of Men, God enters into Covenant, he invites, admonishes, asks, threatens, the Power of Resisting still remaining in Man, *Psal.* 95:8. Whence Christ did merit, 'tis true that Men might be able to accept the Efficacy of his Death, but yet so as that he does not compel them, nor dispose them by an Indispensible Necessity to accept of it. And *Jurieu* trifles with the word *necessary Grace,* (p. 92.) Christ did by his Death merit the Grace necessary to Salvation, that is that without which it cannot be obtain'd, or laid hold on, but not such Grace as brings an inevitable Necessity. And it is certain that the Death of Christ belongs to all, but a great part of Mankind miss of the Benefit of it by their own Fault.

§83. In the sixth place *Jurieu* thus Argues: *God,* (says he) *before-hand knew that very many of Mankind would perish for not having perform'd the due Obedience to the Law of Nature written in the Hearts of the Gentiles; and that very many would not obey the Gospel. The appointment of a Redeemer would have been unprofitable to both these sorts. There are but three Ends only for which God hath sent the Redeemer. (1.) That he might declare his Good-will to Man. (2.) That he might save them that believe. (3.) That he might render the rest unexcusable, who despise this Salvation. With respect to the first end, an Universal Redemption would be altogether unprofitable, because the Good-will of God to Men is sufficiently declar'd by the Salvation of those Men that are Elected. For they are the best and the most valued part of Mankind, and in them is suffi-*

The sixth and seventh Arguments of Jurieu.

ciently fulfill'd whatsoever is promised to all Mankind.[64] But whether or
no God has sufficiently declar'd his Good-will to Mankind, cannot,
and ought not to be judg'd from that which *Jurieu* thinks sufficient in
the Case, but from that which the Holy Scripture hath reveal'd to us;
from whence alone we must be directed to judge in this Matter. But
that does not say God so lov'd the *Elect,* but God so lov'd the *World.*
And it has seem'd worthy of the Goodness of God, That there should
be an universal Redemption, that he might testifie the abundant Power
of his Grace. Which is not to be accounted unprofitable, because many
perish, any more than the Rain may be said to be so, which falls upon
places that are not capable of bearing any thing, or the Sun who plentifully sheds his Light upon all parts. Also it is not necessary to our
Purpose to examine, whether or no the Good-will of God to Men be
a necessary Affection. For it is enough for us to know that God hath
declar'd himself a Lover of Mankind, and indeed that he has declar'd
that Affection with more glorious Proofs of it towards Men, then towards the Angels, in that the Saviour *took not on him the Nature of
Angels, but of the Seed of* Abraham, *Heb.* 2:16. Which *Philanthropy,*
however, because it has Justice join'd with it, is able to set a Measure
to its own Effects, where it is arrogantly rejected, because God will not
snatch Men to Heaven, whether they will or no, but will bring them
to it in a moral manner. *Jurieu* adds, That, *An universal Redemption is
altogether of no use for the Manifestation of the Philanthropy in God; for
it is no Mercy to offer Salvation to him who cannot receive it.* But God
offers to all so much Grace as suffices to Conversion, and he really
gives it, if they do not of their own accord refuse it. Yet *Jurieu* confesses,
That Impotence to receive it not to be natural; such as is, for Instance,
that of Stones, Trees, and Brute-beasts, *but Moral, yet nevertheless insuperable, and which cannot be overcome but by the Divine Grace.*[65]
Which things in a good Sense may be admitted. The Impotence of
Men to the Converting of themselves, is indeed insuperable, that is by
the Powers which remain in the Corrupted Nature of Man: But which

64. Ibid., p. 92.
65. Ibid., p. 94.

may be overcome by the Grace of God which is offer'd to all, unless they wickedly neglect or reject it, but which yet leaves the Morality of the Action. And it is distinctly observ'd by some, that as there is in Man a double Corruption: The one born with him, which follows from the common Pollution, and the other contracted by every Man; so the Grace of God which always accompanies his Call, is sufficient to overcome the former, but the Corruption of Manners contracted by particular Men, is not always overcome by the first Impulse of Divine Grace, but it may, and ought to be mended by, and overcome by the Endeavour of Man. Whence we also see the Gospel Preached to several Men at the same time with different Effects, according as they are possess'd with Evil Habits which they have contracted. See *Acts* 17:21, 32, 34. They who were wont to spend their Time and please themselves with hearing some new thing call'd *Paula* Babler: Those who were less Corrupted stagger'd at his Discourse: They who brought to the hearing him, no hindrance which they had contracted were converted. So *Acts* 24:25, 26. The Speech of *Paul* with *Felix* profited nothing, because he regarded nothing but the getting of Money. So *Acts* 26:25, 26. *Festus* was altogether possess'd with the Prejudice of the *Roman* Superstition: *Agrippa* was nearer touch'd by the Grace of God, had not Honour hindred him, and that external Magnificence which seem'd to him not consistent with the Discourse of *Paul*. Also I know not from whence it appears to *Jurieu*, that God Wills not to bestow his Grace upon the *Tartars* and *Chinese*. In truth there are whole Nations of the *Tartars* which profess the Christian Faith, and are Subject to the Empire of the *Muscovites*. Nor do all the *Chineses* abhor the Christian Religion; unless we will have it that all the Relations of the Jesuites about that Matter are meer Lies. The second End which *Jurieu* Establishes of sending the Redeemer, the *Salvation of the Godly* is true, but not adequate. As for the third End which *Jurieu* mentions, that of *rendring the Wicked unexcusable*, It is to be observ'd, that it is only spoken of Natural Knowledge, *Rom.* 1:20, 21. But 'tis no where said that the Saviour Redeem'd all, that the Wicked might be unexcusable, that is, that they might become the worse, and the more miserable. It is moreover wrong said that the end of sending the Saviour, was that the

Reprobate might be unexcusable. For to do a thing with such an End belongs to him who wishes Evil to others, and lays Snares for them. But the unexcusableness it self, as I may say, follows the Contempt and Neglect of offer'd Benefits. But it may be rightly said, that if there be an universal Redemption, God hath omitted nothing on his part for the Conversion of Men: So that these cannot possibly lay on him the Cause why they are not converted and sav'd, when the Revelation of a Salvation to be obtain'd by the Redeemer, has been once and again made to Mankind. Which Knowledge when the Posterity of those to whom it was given do suffer to perish from among them, this is not by any Fault of God. But wicked Men to whom the Doctrine of Salvation is declar'd, would justly be excusable, if from the Absolute and Eternal Appointment of God, no Remedy were provided for them against the Native Hardness of their Hearts.

In the seventh Place, (*p. 95.*) *Jurieu* produces what is said, *John* 10:11, 15. *The good shepherd giveth his Life for the Sheep, I lay down my life for my sheep.* John 17:9, 20. *I pray thee for those whom thou hast given me; not for the world, but for those who shall believe on me through their preaching.* Concerning which, and the like Expressions in general it is to be observ'd: That from one or two Expressions all things cannot be deduced; and that one ought not to be oppos'd to all the rest, but all things are to be digested into an Agreement one with the other. And the Expressions urg'd do not contain the whole Method of our Salvation, but only a particular part of it. And in the former Expression Christ shows himself a much more faithful Pastour then they were, who in that time pretended themselves to be such, to whom he opposes that saying. Such are describ'd, *Jer.* 23:1, 2, &c. *Ezek.* 34:2, &c. *Mat.* 23:2, &c. Nor does there appear any Exclusive in this Place; nor is it denied, but that there was a Ransom paid by the Saviour for them who perish by their own Fault. So in the other Saying, Christ only denies that He in that Valedictory Speech Pray'd for the World; but he does not deny that he was about to give himself a Sacrifice for the whole World. So from this that Christ Prays for his Disciples, and those who should be converted by them, that God would preserve them in the Truth, that they might be one among themselves, it does not follow that his Death does not belong to others. As it does not follow, A Master bestows his Blessing at parting to his tractable Disciples, therefore he did not bestow sufficient Pains upon those who are untractable. And if indeed in that place Christ did not pray for the Wicked, yet he did this on the Cross, *Luke* 23:34. *Isa.* 53. *ult.* But neither is the Prayer of Christ appointed by God to be the Expiation of the Sins of the World, but his Passion and Death. Nor does it follow Christ then did not Pray for the Reprobate, therefore he has not Will'd that they might be sav'd, in a certain Establish'd Order. But by what Authority will *Jurieu* prove what he has deliver'd: *The words signifying Universality, must not be urg'd in opposition; The word* [All] *prefixed to the Preaching of the Gospel, must create no Prejudice against the particular Grace of God.* But why not? Or as if these Sayings were less express, and without Ambiguity, and Equivocation, then those in which he places the Strength of his Cause: Where however there is no mention so much as in a word of that which is in question. Lastly, *Jurieu* endeavours to destroy our Opinion, even from the Hypothesis of our Men. (*p.* 96.) He says, It is common with us to say, *That Christ died for all, and every Man, but not absolutely, but under the Condition of Faith.* But I on the contrary, say, That this Position never came into the Mind of any of our Men, and has either no, or a very absurd Meaning. For what is it that we say? That Christ died for all not absolutely, but under the Condition of Faith? No, but this is our Opinion, Christ died for all, but only they who believe do really receive the Fruit of his Death. Yet perhaps *Jurieu* had before his Eyes that Position of our Men, God hath Elected Men to Salvation, not by an Absolute Will, but under the Condition of foreseen Faith. Which differs as widely as can be from that Position which He would fasten upon us. Also God hath no where said I give my Son for all under the Condition of Faith. For we think it not Repugnant to the Divine Perfection, seriously to Will the Salvation of all; but for the attaining of which a certain Order is fixed; and that this should be purchas'd by a Price that is of value sufficient for all: And yet that he foreknows that all will not attain it, and who these are that will not; because God in the Holy Scriptures, from whence all these things are learn'd, has in express words thus declar'd himself. Also we believe it very well agreeing with the Goodness of God, that he should not leave any Man without a Remedy, and Mean of obtaining Salvation: But also that it agrees with his Wisdom not to proceed in this Matter with an Absolute Power, but that he should leave so much of Power in Man, that there may be a Morality remaining in this Affair, and that so Men may be judg'd to have, as it were a Negative Vote about their Salvation.

The Places of Scripture Vindicated.

§84. For a Conclusion *Jurieu* endeavours, (*p.* 98.) to elude those Expressions of Scripture which our Men oppose to the Particularism. But if Cavils of that sort may be admitted, it will not be difficult to invent a Divinity to which the whole Context of Holy Scripture is Repugnant, and yet to recommend it as drawn out from thence. As the *Socinians* begin with evading some Expressions by little Distinctions, and empty Interpretations, and from thence proceed so far as to take away from Christian Religion all that is mysterious, to convert it into a meer Moral Philosophy. *When Christ is said to be the Saviour of the World, or the Saviour of Men, or of all Men, this must be understood indefinitely, not universally.*[66] But from whence does *Jurieu* fetch that Imperious *must be.* Why have not our Men more right to say that ought to be understood universally, not indefinitely, from the Opposition, from the Context, and from the whole Tenour of Scripture. So likewise because *Jurieu* is so pleas'd the word σωτηρ, 1 *Tim.* 4:10. must not signifie a *Saviour,* but a *Preserver* or *Keeper,* who averts Corporal Dangers; and if indeed in that place that word may admit of this signification, shall therefore the words σωζειν to save in all other places, be the same thing as to free from Corporal Danger and σωτηρ or the Saviour be such an one as performs such a Deliverance, or Conservation? To the Expression, 1 *John* 2:2, that he may evade it, a very poor Cavil is made use of, (*p.* 99.) *Christ is a Propitiation, not for our Sins only, but for the Sins of the whole World,* that is, *Not only of us the Believers, who are now, and at present living, but for those of all Ages past and to come.* But

66. Ibid., p. 98.

let *Jurieu* show but one place where this word has this Sense. And why is the word World? *John* 3:16, eluded by another Cavil, and a Refuge taken against it in the distinction of a *Legislative* Will of God? And where this distinction will not do, at length the *Philanthropy*, and *Will signified* is feign'd. If this manner of Interpreting be allow'd, what certainty of Doctrine can be fetch'd from Holy Scripture. That the Saying, *Isa.* 5:4. may be enervated, *What could have been done more to my Vineyard that I have not done?* That it is to be Interpreted *of External Means, Benefits, Chastisement, Compellations, not of saving and internal Grace.* But how fine would the Sense of that Place be, if we would say, In that Similitude there were applied efficacious Means for the producing of Fertility, but in that which is insinuated by the Similitude of a Vineyard that is in the People of *Israel,* there were efficacious Means afforded, but for fashion sake only, and that were void of all Virtue, and were Illusory. That he might Cavil against the Expression in *Mat.* 23:37. A new Subtilty is used, that we may not believe God speaks with Men, so as Men of good Morals speak with one another. He says, *If he spoke those things as a Man, there is nothing to hinder, but that they may signifie a real Affection with which he often truly desir'd the Salvation of the* Jews. So then, those things which Christ has spoken to us as Men, may be accounted as seriously spoken. *But if he spoke them as God, it is to be understood of the Will signified contradistinct to his Good-pleasure.* But we believe even those things possible to be spoken by God seriously and sincerely, and so as that the Divine Essence is not thereby obnoxious to Change or Passions. Lastly, When in *Heb.* 6:4, 5, 6. and 2 *Pet.* 2:1. It is expresly intimated that Christ Redeem'd also those, who but for a time only believe, and do afterwards deny the Faith, and never resume it, he does not want a Cavil for this too. To wit, *That the Temporary Righteousness of these Men proceeded from the Merit of Christ, as the Cause of it: Not that Christ was willing to Redeem them by his Death from eternal Death, but that he merited for them this Temporary Righteousness, that they falling from this might serve for an Example to the Faithful, and truly Godly, to make them take heed of a grievous Fall and Apostacy.* But what Foundation can there be shown from the Text for so violent an Interpretation? And that Christ while he died for these, had another Intention then about those who persevere in the Faith. By such Answers, perhaps the Mouths of young Students may be stop'd; and where, that they may urge the more forcibly, they may be pronounced with the severe Countenance of a Master, and an imperious Voice, they may have some regard. But with those who are wise, and who search the Scriptures with Reverence, such things excite either Indignation or Pity. And he who disputes in such a manner proves his Heart not to be upon Truth, but upon Victory at any rate, or that he may not be said to have been altogether reduced to Silence.

§85. From thence *Jurieu* proceeds to explain and vindicate the Decree of Absolute Predestination, according to the Mind of the Synod of *Dort*.[67] About which the Sum of the Matter seems chiefly to turn upon the Order of the Divine Decrees, or in what order these are to be placed in the Exercise of the Divine Mind. Where we indeed did presuppose this in the beginning, That since the Business of Salvation cannot be clearly searched out by the Principles and Powers of Reason, that which God has Decreed concerning it must be known from his Revelation, or from his Works which confer something towards it. But since the laborious and subtle Engine of an Absolute Decree recommended by the Synod of *Dort,* is no where extant in the Holy Scriptures, and which the very Anxiousness of the Structure, and the number of the Divisions renders suspected, the simplest and safest way of knowing what God hath Will'd and Decreed, will be to inspect what he hath actually done. Since therefore it is confess'd by all that God is from all Eternity a Being most perfect in himself, and most happy, and self-sufficient, In the first place we conceive him to have Will'd this, That he would manifest his Majesty and Glory to Works produced by him, and would Communicate of his Goodness to them: So as that the

Concerning the Order of the Divine Decrees.

67. The Synod of Dort (1618–19) was held in order to settle the serious Arminian controversy in the Dutch Reformed Church. In 1610 Dutch followers of Jacob Arminius had presented to the States General a remonstrance in five articles, directed against the strict Calvinist doctrine of predestination. The Synod of Dort rejected the remonstrance and set forth the orthodox doctrine on this and associated points in the "Canons of Dort."

Glory of God, and the Revelation of the Divine Majesty is the beginning and end of all things. But as he truly Created Man upright, holy, and capable to attain Eternal Felicity, and such, as that no necessity, either Extrinsick, or Intrinsick, manifest, or hidden should oblige him to abdicate or loose that State, so he decreed to create him such. For the contrary is repugnant to the Goodness of God, and it is manifestly better never to exist, then to exist with this Law, and Necessity, that it must be always Ill with one, and so the Benefit of Creation by such a Law as this would have the place of the highest Cruelty. Altho' on the other hand, neither was there any Indispensible Necessity, but that Man might of his own accord throw himself from that Original State. But that he might not rashly will this it seem'd good to God to strengthen that State by a Covenant made with Man, which was the most sacred of all Moral Obligations. If this Covenant had been always kept by Man, there had been no Diminution of the Divine Majesty and Glory. If at the most his Judiciary, and Vindicative Justice could not have had an Object of Man, yet God might have gain'd sufficient matter for the glorifying of this under the name of Justice from the Punishment of the Devils. Yea, the Majesty of God had remain'd safe, if there never had been any one upon whom Punishment might take place. On the contrary, many of the first of the *Reform'd* Party did in the first place among the Decrees of God, even before the Fall, set this, That God Will'd to show his Mercy and Justice; for the attaining which End he would Create Men, and procure their Fall, that so there might be an Object for the Exercise of both. Which Doctrine is indeed the most absurd, and contrary to all Reason, while the Decree of exercising Justice is set before the Decree of Creation. For Justice, as it is among Men, is a Vertue respecting another. So that even in God it cannot be understood unless there be for Objects of it Creatures capable of Vertue and Sin. For Justice in God cannot be otherwise conceiv'd of, then as that of a Ruler and Judge, *Gen.* 18:25. *Rom.* 11:35. and so it supposes those that are subject. But tho' the Punitive Justice supposes Creatures Culpable, there had been no Diminution of the Divine Majesty if such an Object had never been existent upon which such Justice might exert it self. Certainly God Created Man for eternal Life, *Wisd.* 1:13, 14. 2:23,

24. And when he punishes Men, he is said to do his strange Work. Among Men also a Prince may retain his Majesty, even tho' he never commands any Man to be punish'd. For tho' there be no exercise of the thing, the Right and Power may be safe. Absurdly also is the Salvation and Damnation of Men set as an ultimate end, since they are Means which may serve to an End, namely, the Manifestation of the Divine Majesty and Glory. The following Doctors of the *Reform'd Party* therefore, and the Synod of *Dort* themselves, that they might after some manner soften the horrid Opinion of their Predecessours, they cut off part of their System, and set the Fall before their absolute Decree, abstracting by whose Fault, or Impulse Mankind fell into that. Which however is that which ought to be first look'd into by those who would search this Doctrine to the Foundation, since it cannot be but those who contemplate these Matters must carry their Minds to the State and Condition which Mankind were in before that Fall, since that Fall is not accounted by any one the Original State. But supposing the Fall, it does not appear by any one place of Holy Scripture, that God propos'd to himself in his Prescience, all that were to be born of the first Parents, and of them now being all infected with the same Pollution did pass by some, and suffer them without Remedy to perish in their Misery, and follow others with his Mercy, for whom he has prepar'd Means of Salvation. But on the contrary, immediately after the Fall a new Covenant is propos'd, in which there appears no Exception, and by which a Way is opened for the Salvation of all. And perhaps some Pretence might have been found for the Doctrine of Pretention, by an Absolute Will, if that Decree could be said to have been made concerning those who by their own Fall precipitated themselves into that Misery, to wit, *Adam* and *Eve,* that one of these should be allow'd Mercy, and the other be suffer'd to perish in the Misery which they had voluntarily Contracted: But that this Pretention should be extended to those who were afterwards to be born, who have not sinned after the Similitude of *Adam*'s Transgression, that is equally Repugnant to the Divine Goodness, as if he had destin'd them from the beginning by an Absolute Will to eternal Torments, without any regard to Sin. For it was not in their Power to hinder but that they must be born,

but if the Covenant of God be refused by those that are born; that is what may afford Matter for Imputation. Therefore the first Decree concerning the Fall, is concerning the making a Covenant with Men in the Mediatour; who by bruising the Serpent's Head should prepare a way for their Salvation. And that Decree since it involves a Covenant, cannot be conceiv'd to be Absolute without great Absurdity. Certainly it is in no wise order'd by that Decree on which the Covenant with Man is founded, that Men should either obtain eternal Life, or die the Death from an absolute Will and Pleasure of God: But there is included under it a Performance requir'd on the part of Man, if thou wilt always observe the Law of God thou shalt live, If thou dost eat of the forbidden Tree thou shalt die. Whereas 'tis superfluous and illusory to enter into Covenant about that which God had determin'd to procure by an unavoidable Necessity, and by his meer Will and Pleasure. And the Case is the same with the Covenant after the Fall. Where if God out of his Absolute Pleasure, and without Respect, not only of any Merit on the part of Men, but also without regard to the not rejecting his federal Grace, would destine some of those who were in the common Filthiness of Sin to eternal Life, what need had there been for preparing Means of so great Price, and Value. And to provide that those Benefits should be declar'd to Men already Reprobate were a new Cruelty, when nothing could come from thence but the Encrease of their Infelicity. But neither does any thing appear in that Covenant, which may argue that certain Men are excluded from it by any Absolute Decree. Further, as that Covenant is free, and made without any Respect to Merit on the part of Man, so also God has yielded himself ready, and prone to give Power to embrace it to all; for as much as without this that Covenant must have been still unprofitable to Men fallen into that Misery. But yet that the Covenant might retain the true Nature of such a thing, and that neither the Salvation of Men, nor their Perdition should come to pass like the Operation of an Engine, or by the Laws of Natural Motion, there must be left to Men at least a Faculty of refusing this Covenant. Whence, on the part of Man there is nothing else requir'd to his coming under this Covenant but Faith, and that not consider'd as a Vertue, but as a Mean of Accepting it, which also it self God is ready to give to those who do not refuse as it were the first Motions of his Grace. But they who do not accept the Covenant, do by their own Fault remain in their damnable State. When therefore God hath Decreed to bestow Salvation upon fallen Mankind by that Covenant, he hath also Decreed to give eternal Life to those particular Persons who do not reject, but accept of that Covenant; or, which comes to the same thing, to give eternal Life under the Condition of Faith, the rest being left for their rejecting of the Covenant, that is for their Incredulity, in a damnable State, which of it self leads to Perdition. All which things are clearly intimated, *John* 3:16, 17, 18. 1 *John* 4:9, 10. But when God has propos'd this Covenant out of meer Goodness and Mercy, that he does invite Men seriously into it, and afford Strength and Means proper for the embracing of it, the same Goodness and Faithfulness of God will not suffer us to doubt. For what Cause can be imagin'd to induce a most free Agent, him who owes nothing to any one, who is subject to no one, that he should mock Men by obscure and ambiguous Expressions, and by words differing from the secret Sense of his Mind, and by that illusion should do nothing else but increase their Infelicity. And this is that which we suppose to be the most simple Order of the Divine Decrees about the Salvation and Predestination of Men, and most agreeing with right Reason, and the sacred Writings.

§86. *Jurieu* on the contrary endeavours by some Reasons to have it denied that there is any Respect of Faith, or of the Acceptance, or Nonacceptance of the Federal Grace which is an Ingredient of the Decree of Predestination. Among those of the first is (*p.* 104.) *That the Appointment to Glory is before the Preparation of Grace, or before Faith and Conversion in the Order of the Decrees. For the last in Execution is first in Intention. A right and wise Mind, first thinks of the end, and after that prepares the Means: Eternal Salvation is the End, Faith and Conversion the Means which lead to that End. Therefore God first thinks of the End, that is the Eternal Glory of Men, afterwards of preparing the Grace by which they are to be brought to life, and so the Decree of Election is Absolute.* But this Reasoning is weak enough, which is built upon Phil-

Whether or no there be a Predestination without any Respect to Faith.

osophick Rules, which for the most part admit of Limitations and
Exceptions. Let us suppose that a Mind in a right Condition would
first determine concerning the End, and then concerning the Means:
But it is not to be thought that the Decree of the End must always be
first compleated, and then another Decree must be Establish'd concerning the Means; and that the former must be fully finish'd, without
any thought of the Means, and that being fixed afterwards, the
Thoughts must be carried to the Means. But regularly the ordering of
the Means is an Ingredient in the Decree of the End. And it is rather
accounted absurd to determine any thing barely concerning the End
before the Means are thought on. And such a real distinction of the
Decrees of the End, and of the Means argues an Imperfection of the
Understanding, and so it cannot be in God, to whom all things present,
past, and future are as it were at one Prospect beheld. Therefore it is
not only not Repugnant, but also altogether agreeing to Reason, that
the Condition of accepting the Covenant, should immediately influence into the Decree. Yea, it seems contradictory to say that God had
first absolutely Decreed to give this or that Man Glory, and afterwards
to Decree concerning the Means. For that which God could absolutely
give, and without any respect, saving his Goodness and Justice, what
need is there for so operose Means towards the obtaining it? If God
could decree eternal Glory to Man fallen into Sin absolutely, that is,
without any respect, what need was there of the Passion of his Son? If
the Potter can from his absolute Will form out of the Clay a Vessel to
Honour, what need is there that he should make a Covenant with that
Vessel, and urge that Vessel with Promises, Exhortations and Threat-
nings to be willing to admit of that Honour? Nor is the other Reasoning more forcible. (*p.* 105.) *Predestination has no Cause, but depends
solely on Good-pleasure.* But this is the thing in question. Who indeed
can deny that the Cause of it is the infinite Goodness and Mercy of
God, together with the Merit of the Saviour satisfying the Divine
Justice. We also deny that there is any external meritorious Cause on
the part of Men, nor do we pretend Faith to be such an one. Further,
If indeed *Faith, Conversion, Repentance, and Good-works are the Effects
of Predestination:* It does not thence follow that the Decree of Predes-

tination is Absolute. For let us suppose a Father has Decreed that his Son shall apply himself to the getting of Wealth. And for a Mean of this he chuses Merchandise, and upon that account Merchandise is an Effect of the Decree concerning the Prosecution of Wealth. Must we therefore say that Merchandise cannot be an Ingredient in the Decree of applying the Son to the Prosecution of Wealth? Further, we say that foreseen Faith, not good Works does enter into the Decree of Predestination: Because since God is pleas'd by the Intervention of a Covenant to save Men, the Nature of a Covenant cannot be understood to be without Faith, that is without Acceptance, or Refusal, which is what cannot be said concerning good Works, or Sanctification, tho' these always accompany Faith as the Fruits of it. Whence the Faithful are said to be created and prepar'd to good Works. Tho' in this *Jurieu* is mistaken, that he opposes to our Men those things which do not regard them but the Papists. Such as is that which he says in his Fifth Argument *concerning the foreseen Condition of the good use of our Free-will.* The Third Argument is taken from the Salvation of Infants, who die before the use of Reason, by whom it appears from the whole Context, he means the Baptized Infants of Christians. About which we need not give our selves any trouble before *Jurieu* declares what he thinks of the Effect of Infant Baptism. For our Men say that by Baptism Faith is bestow'd upon them, and they cannot put any Obstacle of Grace in the way, because they have not yet the use of Reason. And if *Jurieu* thinks it *fit* for him to deny that a full Act of Faith can be produc'd in Infants before the seventh Year of their Age, I would fain know from whence he would prove that any Infant can before the full use of Reason be sav'd. The *Examples of the Thief on the Cross, of* Zacchaeus *and* Paul, which *Jurieu* mentions in the fourth place, (*p.* 106.) are besides his Purpose, nor can any thing be drawn from them that is contrary to our Opinion. Nor does his Fifth Argument more press us: *If the Election of God were made upon foreseen Faith, it is not God that Elects and separates, but Man separates himself;* and so Man hath cause of Glorying, which yet *Paul* denies him. But according to our Opinion, Man does not separate himself by his own Strength, and so he has not cause of Glorying: Since he receives all good things from without himself. There is no more remains to us but the Faculty of refusing the Things offer'd, because without this the Nature of a Covenant could not exist. Lastly, *Jurieu* produces some Expressions which make no thing against us. That in *John* 15:16. may perhaps be oppos'd to the Papists, but it does not regard us. But we may rightly say Christ chose his Apostles not absolutely, but upon the foresight of their accepting his Vocation. But he did not elect, or chuse that rich young Man, who, when he heard that all his Goods must be relinquish'd that he might follow Christ, went away from him sorrowful. *Mat.* 19:22. From the Expression, *Eph.* 14. *God hath chosen us in Christ that we should be holy:* So far is it that any thing can be drawn, which is contrary to our Opinion, that it is rather very much confirm'd from thence. For why is it not said God hath Elected us from his absolute Will, but in Christ who profits not unless we embrace him by Faith: And whom moreover God does not Will that they should afterwards live in Sin, but *that they should be Holy,* and so bring forth the Fruits of Faith. The Expression also, 2 *Thess.* 2:13. Establishes our Opinion: *God hath chosen us from all Eternity in the Belief of the Truth.* The same thing is to be thought of what is said, *Eph.* 1:11. which must be compar'd with 2 *Tim.* 1:9. Where that Purpose is said to respect Christ, and so Christ and the Faith, which apprehends him in no wise to be excluded from the Counsel of the Divine Will concerning our Salvation, but rather must be included in it. And to do all things according to the Counsel of his Will, is not the same thing as to do all things from an absolute Pleasure, without the Intuition of, or respect to any thing whatever. Concerning what remains, *Jurieu* says rightly, (*p.* 108.) that the Purpose in *Paul* signifies a Will in opposition to the Merit of Works. But that is never oppos'd to Faith. Also nothing can be gather'd from the Expression, *Acts* 13:48. that is against us. *As many as were Ordain'd to eternal Life believ'd.* Indeed they were Ordain'd, but not by an absolute Decree of God, but because they would accommodate or conform themselves to the Order appointed by God for them who shall obtain Salvation. In the *9th.* Chapter of the Epistle to the *Romans,* where the Reform'd were wont formerly to place the chief Strength of their Cause, *Jurieu* seems to acknowledge that there is not much Defence to be expected. Yet he produces the 11*th.* Verse of the fore-mention'd Chapter. But the words there, *when they had neither done Good nor Evil,* show that they are unjustly apply'd to the present Question, for as much as Man fallen into Sin, is set as the Object of Predestination, and so when he had already done something that was Evil. Further, those words, *The elder shall serve the younger,* do manifestly argue that he Treats not concerning Election to Salvation, or of Reprobation, but of the Temporal Prerogative which *Jacob* and his Race enjoy'd beyond *Esau* and his Posterity. Add. *Gen.* 27:29, 37, 40. As also *Jurieu* acknowledges that *Jacob* and *Esau,* do not here signifie single Persons, but whole Nations. But he will have it notwithstanding that they are Types of Election and Reprobation. But if that should be admitted, the third of the Comparison ought to be sought only in the Denial of any Respect to good Works, not to Faith. But we utterly deny *that what God did towards Esau and Jacob,* with respect to temporal Prerogative, *he can do the same consistently with his Justice towards other Men* in the Matter of Election and Reprobation. For God may without the Consideration of any Merit assign one a larger, and another a straiter Measure of Temporal Goods: But he cannot consistently with his Goodness and Justice condemn any Man to eternal Torments without any Consideration of Merit. Nor is it more true that the whole *Idumean* Nation was reprobated by God, so as that they should not partake of eternal Life, then that all and every Person of the Descendants of *Jacob* were among the Elect. It is certain that the *Idumeans* being subdued by the *Jews,* receiv'd their Religion. So the Similitude of a Potter ought not to be applied but to Temporal Prerogatives, and the denial of them. In the Expression, *Rom.* 8:30. is shown in what Order the Execution of Salvation is perform'd, but it is not there said that Predestination is made without any Intuition of the Acceptance of Vocation. Lastly; the Exclamation, *Rom.* 11:33. does not regard only those things which are discoursed on in the immediately foregoing Chapter; but those which *Paul* had deliver'd concerning the Business of Man's Salvation through the whole Epistle. In truth there are many things, no less deep and profound which go before the 9*th.* Chapter, so as that they might justly carry Men to the Admiration of them. But in truth there were nothing worthy of Admiration, if God had without any respect chosen some to eternal Life, and had pass'd by others no worse in themselves then they, and if so the naked Will of God had stood for a Reason of his Actions. For that such a manner of Acting seems more becoming an insolent Tyrant, then the wise and mild Moderatour of the Universe. As *Suetonius* mentions it among the Specimens of a barbarous Nature in *Caligula*:[68] That he set himself in the middle of a Company of Prisoners, and without any regard to their Crimes, sent one part of them to be devour'd by the wild Beasts, and sav'd the other alive. On the contrary that Temperament of Divine Mercy and Justice is worthy of Admiration, and unsearchable by humane Reason.

§87. As for what concerns Reprobation: We think it hardly agreeing with the Goodness and Justice of God, that it should be only for the Sin which is common to all Men. But because God so lov'd the World, even when fallen into Sin, as to send his only begotten Son for their Salvation, there can be no other Cause of Reprobation, but the not accepting the Federal Grace. *He that believes not is condemn'd because he believeth not in the Name of the only begotten Son of God,* out of whom there is no Salvation. The Reasons which *Jurieu* brings on the contrary are weak enough. The ways of God which are said to be unsearchable do not belong to Reprobation, but the whole Method of Salvation. Tho' we have before said we do not deny but that a distinct Reason is not to be given by any Man of all those things which a disorderly Curiosity may enquire about in this Matter. As, for Instance, Why this Nation should be sooner, and that later call'd? Why some Men are call'd time after time, others only but once, and never have the Grace offer'd them which they have once refused. But it does not follow, that because we are ignorant of the Cause of such things, that God has done them without respect to any thing, and for his meer Will and Pleasure. And we also deny that the value of the Divine Mercy is lessened by our Opinion. For both our Salvation, and the Means in

Of Reprobation.

---

68. G. Suetonius Tranquillus, *De vita Caesarum: Caius Caligula.*

order to it, are intirely from God, who gives also the Acceptance of them; *He gives to will and to do.* But he exercises a special Favour towards the Elect, in that he endows them with a more plentiful Degree of his Favour, when they have not rejected but receiv'd the first Grace according to that, *to him that hath shall be given.* That which is said, *Rom.* 9. *God hath mercy on whom he will have mercy,* does not infer any absolute Decree, nor is Faith excluded by that Will. Nor does it follow from 1 *Thess.* 5:9. That God has by his meer Will dispos'd of some to Wrath.

Of Irresist-
ible Grace. §88. After this in Chap. 7 (*p.* 112.). *Jurieu* disputes many things concerning Free-will, and effectual and irresistible Grace, the most of which do not touch our Church; some things concern a few of our Men, and either particularly him against whom he disputes, or those whose undue and unconsider'd Expressions ought not to be imputed to the whole Church. For which *Jurieu* might have spar'd that Note, *The Augustan Brethren are here contrary to one another,*[69] if he would have remembred how great Dissentions there have been among the *Reform'd,* and still are about this Matter. But that the Divine Grace does not act in an irresistible manner in the Conversion of Men, many Expressions of Scripture do prove, and many Examples of those who have not only repuls'd the first Degrees of Grace, but of those who also after it had long taken Possession of them, have cast it away again, and fallen into the most heinous Sins; and because a Moral and Federal Way of dealing with Men, cannot consist with such an irresistible Force, since God does not Will to save Men by the Force of his Omnipotence, but in a certain Order, the Powers of Grace being so attemper'd, as not to turn Man into a sort of Engine. Altho' this also is a Fruit of Conversion and Regeneration, that the Faithful are more and more confirm'd in Goodness, and the evil Power of resisting is by little and little weakned, by which at length they bravely overcome the Temptations of the World, the Flesh and the Devil, and willingly follow

---

69. Jurieu, *De Pace,* p. 126.

the Conduct of Divine Grace, 1 *Pet.* 5:10. But *Jurieu* seems willing (*p.* 124.) to acknowledge the Resistibility of Grace, as I may speak, while he says, *That not only the external Graces are rejected but also the Internal, and the Motions excited by the Holy Spirit, and so the Grace is rendred ineffectual.* But soon after, *in effectual Grace he distinguishes the Effects for the producing of which it is destin'd and given of God, from the Effects to which it allures and exhorts only. For Instance, there is a Grace he says which is call'd the first, which does really excite good Motions, and creates a Desire of a new Life, and that solicites; exhorts, invites to a full and perfect Conversion, but it invites only by Suasion, so does not perfect this.* He pronounces therefore; *That the Grace of God is never refuted, with respect to those Effects for which 'tis design'd, and given of God, but is often resisted with respect to those Motions to which it only sollicits and exhorts.* But it is not enough to invent some little distinction, but the Foundation of it ought to be demonstrated from the Holy Scriptures. Further, it does not consist with the Sincerity with which God deals with Men, that he should exhort and invite only to any thing without having a Mind truly to give the thing, to knock at the Door, and yet not be willing to come in. Lastly, *Jurieu* makes every Grace irresistible with respect to those Effects for which it is destin'd and given of God. In which thing he takes away all Morality from the Conversion of Man. And so according to *Jurieu's* Hypothesis it is falsly said, That *Man is the cause that the Grace of God is uneffectual,* which yet was given of God for no other end, then for a vain Exhortation, or Impulse, when there is no Power in Man of his own for his Conversion. We on the other side say, God is always willing to add more Grace to them who refuse not the first Degree of Grace; and so he is always ready to give a sufficient Measure of Grace, provided Man does not reject the first Degree, nor the Encreases of it by his own Wickedness. We say too that Man cannot be accounted guilty of a new Fault, if he does not admit the Grace of God, but rejects it, by which God did not intend to work a full Conversion in him. From these things therefore I think it will manifestly appear to any one who can free his Mind from Prejudices, that our Men do not want what to oppose to the Principles of the Reform'd, which is more then those Principles, agreeing with the constant Tenour of Holy Scripture, and the Conception or Idea which we thence learn to form of Almighty God. Nor do I doubt but if that Matter were calmly and solidly debated, without Cavils and Impertinent Digressions, it might be brought so far, as that there should be no place to proceed further, and so it might come to pass that by disputing the thing, an end of these Controversies might be found.

Why there is little Benefit of Disputing.

§89. Since we have gone thus far, it may not be amiss briefly to make some Observations on those things which *Jurieu* has thought fit to say concerning the making Peace among Protestants. He therefore in the beginning presupposes that a naked Debate or Disputation would be of no use to the making of Peace: *Because no Party will recede from its Right; none will confess it self overcome; never will one Party suffer it self to be as it were led in Triumph by the other.*[70] We confess very many are of that Disposition, especially those who are posses'd with the Scholastick Stiffness, as that they will peremptorily defend the Opinion which they have once taken up, and will rather even disturb the Common-wealth, then depart from the Opinion which pleases them, especially if there be no other Concern in them but for a vain Applause. Yet because, but one part of a Contradiction can be true, and they who dispute from the same Principle, must at length come to that beyond which they can go no further: They who only seek the Truth ought not to think it a shame to yield themselves conquer'd, and therefore to put away their Errour. And when many erroneous Opinions in the Civil law, Medicine and Philosophy are at length destroy'd by disputing, why may not the same thing be done in Divinity? Especially when in the Points of Faith, Ambition, and the Preposterous Concern to maintain an Authority, ought by no means so far to prevail as to make us rather part with Truth then with a false Opinion. And as no Man hardly can be so foolish as to be unwilling to be freed from his Disease, lest he should seem to have been sick; so he can hardly be in his right

---

70. Ibid., p. 138.

Mind who would chuse to continue in his Errours, lest he should seem
to have err'd. When we ought rather to rejoyce no less at the putting
away an Errour of the Mind, then at a Deliverance from a distemper
of the Body. Therefore there is so little profit usually from disputing,
not from the Nature of the Controversies, as if they would not be
examin'd to the bottom; but from a Disease of Mind which is familiar
with those who profess the Study of Divinity, who had rather confound
Heaven and Earth together, then seem to have been in an Errour.
Nevertheless it is easie for those who can free their Minds from Prejudice to see when a Controversie is examin'd throughly, on which side
the Truth must stand. And so the disputes which are solidly manag'd
may not want their Fruit, altho' he that is truly conquer'd, who it is
presupposed is not to be commanded in the Case, cannot be compel'd
to confess his Errour; whose Obstinacy however being destitute of
Reason will deservedly be despised.

§90. Then *Jurieu* delivers four ways of Reconciling and Uniting divided
Parties. Of which the first is, *If one part would Abdicate its Principles,*
and way of Worship, in a word its Religion, and pass over to the other.
An Example of which there was in the ancient Church, when having
Abdicated Arianism both parts joyn'd, and by common consent Establish'd the Truth of *the same Substance.*[71] But *Jurieu* pronounces
(*p.* 141.) that this way of Reconciling Protestants, is neither *possible* nor
just. As he is not to be heard who would be a Mediator of Peace between
the *Spaniards* and *French,* if he should propose such Conditions of
Peace as this, That the former should deliver themselves, and all that
is theirs into the Power of the latter. And formerly in *France* they were
receiv'd with scorn, (*p.* 142.) who invited the *Reform'd* to a Reunion,
with this Law, that they should return into the Bosom of the Church.

Concerning the Abdicating of former Principles.

71. Arianism (called after Arius, c. 250–c. 336) denied the divinity of Christ and
was one of the most widespread and divisive heresies in the history of Christianity.
A series of ecumenical councils (the first at Nicea, 325) were convened to solve the
problems raised by Arianism. Only with the Council of Constantinople in 381 was
the Nicene orthodoxy on the Trinity secured in the Church.

In which very thing they sought the Ruine of the *Reform'd* Religion under the Name of Peace and Union: When nevertheless a War is wont to be laid down between two contending sides, by something yielded, and something retain'd. We on the other hand say, That as this way of Uniting those that disagree would be the most perfect, if one part laying aside their Errour would come over to the other, so it is neither impossible nor unjust. For even *Jurieu* himself acknowledges it is what can be, from the Example of the Extinction of Arianism, when nevertheless it is not to be doubted but heretofore the *like Substance* was no less dear to the *Arians,* then now the Absolute Decree is to the *Reform'd,* and the things which follow from thence. And why cannot a Mind free from Prejudice acknowledge that the Opinion which has hitherto pleas'd, does not agree with the genuine Sense of Scripture? Especially when the Contention among Protestants is only about the Truth of Principles, to which if a Man will prefer his Authority, he is guilty of a rash Contentiousness. Nor is the Strife among them, as it is between them and the Papists about Dominion and Wealth. Therefore it is absurdly too that he instances in the War between the *Spaniards* and the *French.* For these contend for Countries and Empire, and so about such things as can be divided into parts, but not about any Temporal Emolument, so not about the external Government of the Church: About which there is so great a Contention between the Church of *England* and the Presbyterians there, who yet both go under the Name of the *Reform'd.* When our Men would readily endure that whatever Government of the Church is receiv'd in any place, and no less that the Ceremonies to which they have been accustomed, should be retain'd. It is also a weak thing to compare what is requir'd by the Papists of the *Reform'd* in *France,* with what we desire towards the Uniting of Protestants. For they went about to draw these under the Dominion of Antichrist, and to the Profession of Principles that ought to be abhor'd. We wish that they would dismiss a few Principles unknown to the first Ages of the Church, and brought into it at length by *Augustine* through the heat of Dispute. But yet if the *Reform'd* pretend that they are not convinced of Errour by our side, they may not absurdly desire that a friendly and solid Debate be first held by

Writings, rather then Discourse. Since, lastly, as *Jurieu* himself acknowledges, many of the *Reform'd* prefer the Opinion of our Men before the *Particularism,* but so as that they are unwilling to have the liberty of thinking otherwise taken from them; whose Communion, too the *Particularists* do not shun,[72] and therein show they reckon that Principle not to be a Fundamental; why at length can they not proceed altogether to abandon that *Particularism,* if it shall be demonstrated by our side that that Principle is not only repugnant to the Scriptures, but also has very many hard Consequences attending it?

§91. The second way of Reconciling Controversies, *Jurieu* says is this (*p.* 146.) If it be shown that the Dispute is only about words, and inconsiderable Matters, and which are not of so much worth as that a Division should be made about them. Where we readily grant this, that there have been many Disputes among Divines which have proceeded only from an Ambiguous Sense of Words, or in which the Difference has been about words, when they were agreed in the thing. Also after that many Philosophick Questions came to be mingled with Divinity, and especially that under the Times of the Papacy the Scholastick Theology Clouded the Christian World, there arose an infinite Crop of unprofitable Disputes which had been better buried in eternal Silence. But this also we acknowledge, if any one will examine any Controversie to the bottom; this in the first place must be enquir'd into: What things the Parties agree in, and what they differ about. For if the main Matters be agreed between them, the lesser ones may be wink'd at, provided the Strength of the Cause does not lie hid in these, nor any such thing, as from whence the rest may be indirectly overthrown, and provided the other Party does not deal unsincerely, and yield some things in show which it may elude afterwards by Reserves and Exceptions. Also if any Questions are at length drawn into such Subtlety, as that it can hardly be discern'd wherein one Opinion differs from another, certainly 'tis better to set such Questions aside altogether.

Of the Strife about words.

---

72. Particularists adhere to the decree of absolute predestination.

Therefore if on both sides Men would deal sincerely, there might be something done, which were not to be despised, and were worth the Labour, in this way, towards at least the diminishing of the Controversies. Nor does the Reason of *Jurieu* seem proper why he will not insist long upon this way, which is, *Because it is not accommodate enough to the Strength and Capacity of all Men.*[73] For so much the rather is it fitting that those few should apply their Endeavours to it who are possess of such Accurateness and Equity as is necessary for scattering the Darkness of Prejudices. Certainly they who seriously seek the Peace of the Church ought least of all to mind those Men who are of a troublesome Nature, and who cannot endure that the Matter of Debate should be taken out of their Hands; and who from their Childhood even to gray Hairs have spent their time in debating unprofitable Questions, and who have their Minds so possess'd with vain things, as that nothing can be more displeasing to them, then if one should demonstrate that they have through their whole life with great Endeavour only trifled. But we therefore think this way will not suffice, because the Controversies that we have hitherto been discoursing about, do not lie meerly in words, but concern the most weighty Matters; namely, what Conceptions Man ought to form to himself of Almighty God, and what Confidence he ought to place in his Promises: Which the Distinctions of the Secret and the Reveal'd Will, and of the Sign and the Good-pleasure do extreamly weaken.

Of Toleration. §92. The third way of Reconciling Controversies, *Jurieu* will have to be: *If while the Controversies remain entire, both Parties keeping their Principles, and maintaining them, a Concord be however preserv'd, by Vertue of those things which are agreed between the Contending Parties, a Liberty being left to every one by a mutual forbearance to think what they will.* Where we do indeed easily yield to *Jurieu*, that in the *United Provinces* they transgress in excess in the Tolerating all sorts of Religions.[74] And that while this is endeavour'd, by some especially, that the

---

73. Jurieu, *De Pace*, p. 150.
74. This point was already addressed by Pufendorf in his *Introduction to the History of the Principal Kingdoms and States of Europe.* This led to a controversy

things necessary to be believed may be brought into as narrow bounds as may be, there may almost nothing of Christianity be remaining in Religion. Perhaps too I would not deny but that with many of our Divines there may be found too warm a Zeal, and such as is wanting in Knowledge and Discretion; by which they are often carried to inveigh against Principles which they do not themselves well understand, and against which they receiv'd a Hatred from others who are no wiser than themselves; or who do at least so manage Controversies, as that they seem rather to afford Matter to cherish them eternally, then to apply their Endeavours towards the lessening of them. Nor will I much oppose that which is presupposed by *Jurieu,* (p. 152.) That *without Forbearance, Piety and Peace cannot be preserv'd in the Church,* provided that be not extended too far. But that is what cannot be commended in *Jurieu* that he should alledge the Example of the *Roman* Church, to prove that Toleration by it. For all the Institutions of this Church tend, not to the Establishment of Divine Truth, but to confirm an unlawful Dominion introduced with the Pretence of Christian Religion. If they can but be safe here, there is with them little care what becomes of other Matters. But the Doctrine of the Omnipresence of Christ is so explain'd by our Men, that the Obsolete Reproach of Ubiquity ought not to be repeated, since our Men stretch that Doctrine no further then the express Sayings of Scripture lead us, and as that they may not divide the indissoluble Conjunction of Natures in one Person. Much less is it fitting that the absurd Saying of *Flacius*[75] should be brought out of the dark, and mention'd to the Reproach of our Churches after an Age and half, which was imprudently thrown out in the Heat of Dispute, and more imprudently defended; and which had I believe not one follower, and which with the Author is long since vanish'd. Yea,

---

with the Calvinist theologian Jean Le Clerc about the usefulness of diversity of religion in a state. See Pufendorf, *Kleine Vorträge,* ed. D. Döring, 467–87; Simone Zurbuchen, "From Denominationalism to Enlightenment: Pufendorf, Le Clerc, and Thomasius on Toleration," in *Religious Toleration: "The Variety of Rites" from Cyrus to Defoe,* ed. John C. Laursen (New York: St. Martin's, 1999), 191–209.

75. Matthias Flacius Illyricus (1520–75), German Lutheran reformer. Leader of the strict Lutherans, he disputed with Philipp Melanchthon (1497–1560), objecting to the latter's compromise with the Roman Catholic Church about nonessentials.

and many think him injur'd in the Opinion which is imputed to him commonly, as being a Person that thought right, tho' sometimes he spoke unfitly. Further, that he may the more easily perswade the Forbearance of his *Particularism,*[76] *Jurieu* would not have it made odious by the bad *Consequences* which our Men are wont to deduce from it, and which the *Reform'd* on the contrary do neither admit nor see. (*p.* 165.) But we on the contrary say that as from true Premises a false Conclusion cannot follow, provided it be rightly form'd: So if it be rightly form'd, and any thing Evil does follow from the Premises, it must needs be that one of the Premises is in fault. Nor is that Fault taken away by this, That the Authors of the Premises deny that they see the Consequence, much less if by an Obstinacy of Mind they will not admit it. For he who Establishes any Proposition is accountable, not only for that, but also for all those things which by a necessary Consequence are thence deduced. And therefore if our Men can deduce any thing that is Ill by Lawful Consequence, and without Cavil, or Calumny from the Doctrine of *Particularism,* they who are addicted to this Opinion are bound to answer for it, altho' they should say they do not admit that Consequence; since that were all one as to yield the Premise, and deny the Conclusion; unless a good Reason can be given why the latter should be thought not rightly inferr'd from the former. Further, he says, If the Doctrine of *Particularism* be truly Erroneous, yet *the Foundation of the Faith is not weakned thereby;* or that Errour is not a Fundamental one. What seems to us true concerning this Matter may be gather'd by what has been said above. Indeed for that Errour alone I would not doubt of the Salvation of any Man. Yet I deny that it can consist with a Genuine System of Divinity. Those things which *Jurieu* largely disputes with his Adversary, it is not to our purpose particularly to examine, since we take a course very different from his. Nor do we think it follows, because prophane Men, and those who take upon them to Reason about Divine Things without the Scriptures, are wont to make as many Objections against our Opinion, as against

76. See note 72.

the *Particularism,* that therefore one Doctrine is no better then the other, nor comes any thing nearer to the Mind of Holy Scripture. And if any one would regard the Cavils of prophane Men, he might give heed to the *Turkish* Argument: God hath not a Son, because he hath not a Wife. Nor did *Paul* therefore cease to Preach Christ Crucified, because that Doctrine was to the *Jews* a Stumbling-block, and to the *Greeks* Foolishness. But neither are we bound to approve of that which *Luther* in the beginning, or some others of our Churches have thought about this Matter; since we have not sworn to his, nor any other Doctor's words, but do acknowledge the Scripture alone to be above all Exception. And if we grant that *Luther* follow'd the Opinion of the *Particularists,* and that it was not for many Years cast out of our Churches, (which yet we leave to be more strictly enquir'd into by those that Will,) and that *Aegidius Hunnius*[77] was the first, or was among the chief of those who recall'd the ancient Doctrine, and that which was receiv'd in the first Ages before *Augustine,* and introduced it into our Churches and Schools; yet we reckon this so far from being a Disgrace to us, that we rather account it a Matter worthy of Praise to have chang'd the Opinion which we had formerly receiv'd for one that is better. And therefore when the *Reform'd* may see that their Absolute Decree does so much hinder Concord, the earnest Desire of which they in words profess, why do they not cease to contend for this, as they would do for all that may be dear to them? What the Adversary of *Jurieu* has judg'd concerning the Doctrine of *Amyraldus,*[78] and some other of the *French-men,* these things cannot prejudice our Churches. And besides that his Doctrine is sharply oppos'd by others of the Reform'd, our Men also have long since observ'd, that they as well as others agree in the Center of the Doctrine of Predestination, and the Means of Saving, and the Decree of Reprobation with the rest, with

77. Aegidius Hunnius (1550–1603), orthodox Lutheran theologian.

78. Moïse Amyraut (1596–1664), French Calvinist and eminent professor of theology at the Academy of Saumur, established in 1598 by the French Reformed Church and abolished by Louis XIV at the revocation of the Edict of Nantes in 1685.

this only difference, that *Amyrald* and his Companions suspend the Execution of the Decree, not the Decree it self upon an impossible Condition, and that which is absolutely denied to the Reprobate by an eternal Decree, namely, *If they can believe.* Which God is absolutely unwilling that they should be able to do, and absolutely will'd that they should not be able to do. So as that their Temperament is Vain and Illusory. Which will sufficiently appear if you consider what *Jurieu* writes concerning their Opinion. (*p.* 225.) What *Jurieu* shows at large, that there were many Differences about the Doctrine of Grace after *Augustine's* Time, which however did not break out into a Schism; does not oblige us to a blind Forbearance. Since from that time the Christian Doctrine began to be involv'd in a great deal of Darkness, and the Sum of Divinity was commonly made up of vain and subtle Disputations. But he rightly says, (*p.* 239.) That *in the first Ages after Christ, before any Corruption was brought into the Church there was no Contention about Predestination, and the manner of the Divine Grace. Then the good and pure Christians did not attempt to Penetrate and meddle with these secret things of God. It were to be wish'd that at present the Doctors would use more Modesty, and abstain from such curious Disquisitions.* But why do not the *Reform'd* suffer this to be said to them. Lastly, His eighth Argument (*p.* 240.) for perswading Toleration: That the *Reform'd,* if our Men would bear with the *Particularism,* would be willing on their side to Tolerate other Errours of ours; is what we think has no Place in a Matter of Faith. Whereas it would make much more for Concord if the Errours of both sides were put away. Tho' we hardly acknowledge those to be Errours which *Jurieu* would in compensation take away. For we profess a *Real Presence* indeed of the Body of Christ in the Lord's Supper, but not a *Carnal* one. We think there may be said to be a *Corporal Presence of the Body,* tho' it is not obvious to the Senses. Nor do the Consequences which the Papists joyn here concern us who only depend upon the words of the Institution. Nor is there any danger that from our Opinion the Eucharistical Bread should be again ador'd, and afford Matter for Idolatry. Such an Ubiquity as some of the *Reform'd* would fasten upon our Churches there is none of us that does not abhor. Also there is none of us that acknowledges *the*

humane Nature of Christ to be become Omniscient, Omnipotent, or Om-
nipresent in this Sense. As if these Idioms were become Properties of
that Nature, but because in the Person of the Word they are Communicated to it. Lastly, The Controversies of our Men about the Necessity of good Works, were in the bottom meerly Contentious about
Words; and in truth the Merit of them has not been excluded but from
the Articles of Justification; and if any have err'd, it comes to pass by
their not being able rightly to distinguish the Articles of Justification
and Sanctification. But those things which *Jurieu* has largely discours'd
concerning Toleration, (we mean the Ecclesiastical one,) might perhaps
have found place before the Separation was made between our
Churches and the Reform'd: But after that is come to pass there is
need of a new sort of Transaction.

§93. The Fourth and last way of Composing Controversies, *Jurieu* Of Silence.
accounts to be, *If all Occasions of Dissention be taken away, and com-*
manded to be banish'd: If the Controversies be suppress'd and buried in
Silence: If those things in which the Parties agree be publickly taught, and
the rest be held in silence, and so if there be a silence impos'd upon Dis-
putations. But these things, as it seems to us, do need some Qualification. For before all things it should be enquir'd whether or no from
those Principles in which both Parties agree a full System of Christian
Doctrine can be form'd, and such as is in all Parts consistent with it
self? And whether the Points that remain in Controversie do neither
directly nor obliquely destroy that System? Those things being laid
down, it may be certainly judg'd that the Questions which remain are
Problematical, and do not enter into the Faith, about which tho' every
Man may abound in his own Sense, yet it were better that they were
utterly suppress'd in Silence, 1 *Tim.* 6:4, 5. 2 *Tim.* 2:16, 23. *Tit.* 3:9.
But if any Controversies enter into the System of Theology, and so are
accounted to belong to the Integrity of Christian Doctrine, it cannot
be that the Doctors should be commanded to hold an entire Silence
about them. But this however may be enjoyn'd, and also ought to be
so, that in them they do only follow the Holy Scripture as the Guide;
that they put away all fierce and evil Dispositions in the management

of them; that they treat about them modestly and honestly without Sharpness, or the love of Cavelling; that every where Prudence, Courteousness, and Moderation bear sway. But if any Principle does truly belong to the Integrity of Christian Doctrine, there does not appear any Reason why it should be conceal'd from the Vulgar; for as much as in that very thing it would be rendred suspected. For why should not all the Counsel of God be declar'd to Men, *Acts* 20:27. 2 *Pet.* 1:19. I think indeed he were but a foolish Preacher who should take upon him to fill his Peoples ears with the Terms and Distinctions of the Schools which are made use of on both sides. But that the Doctrine of our Men concerning Predestination may be propos'd in clear Expressions to the People with much more Fruit then the Principles of the *Reform'd*, I think is what no Man can have the Confidence to deny, who will but consider both without Prejudice. And to what Purpose are those words of *Jurieu: There is none of us who does not often Inculcate to his Auditours the Love of God to Men, and his Goodness and Clemency, his Propensity to show Mercy, and his desire to do good to all. But concerning that hidden profound Providence according to which he denies his Grace to very many, we speak soberly, least unwary or wicked Men should thence take occasion to attribute to God things unworthy of him.* That is, Concerning the Will of the Sign, which is empty and Illusory, we make a great noise; of the Will of the Good-pleasure which is serious and efficacious, we say little, because the Repugnancy of those Wills thwarts the common Sense of Mankind, and from thence doubtfulness and Aversation towards God, are more apt to arise then any trust in him, or due Veneration for him. As also *Jurieu* will not easily perswade any Man that is truly Pious to receive those things which he feigns concerning the Universality of the Redemption accomplish'd by Christ, (*p.* 225.) yet in general we easily grant that the Methods propos'd by *Jurieu* for the Reconciling of Controversies, (*p.* 260.) which are *a kind Interpretation of Principles, Mutual Forbearance and Silence,* are things that may have some Effect towards allaying the Fierceness of Men's Minds, and preparing the way to an Agreement. But the Roots of the Dissention can never be taken up by them. Thence *Jurieu* spends a particular Chapter, which is the 12*th*. in prescribing Means of Promoting and Consummating the Work of Reconciliation, and the Conditions of a Godly Union. But these, tho' not in themselves very difficult, and tho' they may seem in part neither unjust nor absur'd, yet he who considers narrowly the Genius of the present Age, and the Disposition of the Men whom that Matter concerns, will easily acknowledge that those things can hardly be attempted with any Fruit, or reach the desir'd End: And I believe but very few of either Party would consent to the Conditions by him propos'd. Nor would the Schism be taken away if both parts should subscribe the *Augustane* Confession: Since this difference is, indeed, from the Papists, but does either not at all, or but lightly touch the most of the Controversies between the Protestants. Lastly, The Confession which *Jurieu* adds at the end as common to all the Protestants, our Men truly would not hastily admit; for as much as he insinuates there under Obscure, ambiguous, and loose Expressions, those very Principles which the Controversie is about.

§94. All these things being weighed it seems to me that this Dissention cannot be taken away at once, or in the twinkling of an Eye. But the Remedy must be expected from time: The process of which may produce much for the Reconciling the Minds of both sides. In the mean while this would very much promote the Affair: If not only the Protestant Princes, notwithstanding these Controversies, would set themselves to defend the common Cause against the Papists who are equally Enemies to both, but also the Divines of both Parties would industriously oppose the common Enemy. If these would mildly and modestly handle the Controversies which are among them, abstain from inhumane Hatred, Cavils, Calumnies, and damning one another, and not omit the Duties of Christian and Brotherly Charity towards each other for their disagreeing Opinions. Lastly, If they would not contend, or strive which shall overcome the other by disputing, so much as which of them shall with greater endeavour conform their Lives to the Precepts of Christ: So it might be hoped that the Spirit of Peace would

The Conclusion.

heal by degrees the exasperated Minds of Men, so as that casting away what is Vain and Erroneous, they might conspire in the Unity of the Faith.

If any thing in this Work is fallen from me, disagreeing with the Genuine Sense of Holy Scripture, beside my Intention, let it be as not said.

S. D. G.

F I N I S.

SELECTED BIBLIOGRAPHY

Works by Samuel Pufendorf with the Titles under Which They Appeared in English

De statu imperii Germanici (*The Present State of Germany*) by Severinus de Monzambano (Pufendorf). 1667.

De jure naturae et gentium libri octo (*The Law of Nature and Nations*). 1672.

De officio hominis et civis juxta legem naturalem libri duo (*The Whole Duty of Man According to Natural Law*). 1673.

Basilii Hyperetae [Pufendorf's] *Historische und politische Beschreibung der geistlichen Monarchie des Stuhls zu Rom* (An Historical and Political Description of the Spiritual Monarchy of Rome, never translated into English). 1679. Later included in the following work.

Einleitung zu der Historie der vornehmsten Reiche und Staaten so itziger Zeit in Europa sich befinden (*An Introduction to the History of the Principal Kingdoms and States of Europe*). 1682–86.

De habitu religionis christianae ad vitam civilem (*Of the Nature and Qualification of Religion in Reference to Civil Society*). 1687.

Jus feciale divinum sive de consensu et dissensu protestantium exercitatio posthuma (*The Divine Feudal Law: Or, Covenants with Mankind, Represented*). 1695.

Studies Related to Religion and Theology

Dingel, Irene. "Recht und Konfession bei Samuel von Pufendorf." In *Recht-Macht-Gerechtigkeit*, ed. Joachim Mehlhausen (Gütersloh: Kaiser, Gütersloher Verlagshaus, 1998), 516–40.

Döring, Detlef. *Pufendorf-Studien: Beiträge zur Biographie Samuel von Pufendorfs und zu seiner Entwicklung als Historiker und theologischer Schriftsteller* (Berlin: Duncker and Humblot, 1992).

————. "Untersuchungen zur Entwicklung der theologischen und religionspolitischen Vorstellungen Samuel von Pufendorfs." In *Religion und Religiosität im Zeitalter des Barock*, part 2, ed. Dieter Breuer (Wiesbaden: Harrassowitz, 1995), 873–82.

Duchhardt, Heinz, and Gerhard May (eds.). *Union–Konversion–Toleranz: Dimensionen der Annäherung zwischen den christlichen Konfessionen im 17. und 18. Jahrhundert* (Mainz: Philipp von Zabern, 2000).

Hunter, Ian. *Rival Enlightenments: Civil and Metaphysical Philosophy in Early Modern Germany* (Cambridge: Cambridge University Press, 2001).

Otte, Hans, and Richard Schenk (eds.). *Die Reunionsgespräche im Niedersachsen des 17. Jahrhunderts. Rojas y Spinola–Molan–Leibniz* (Göttingen: Vandenhoeck & Ruprecht, 1999).

Rabe, Horst. *Naturrecht und Kirche bei Samuel von Pufendorf* (Cologne: Böhlau, 1958).

Zurbuchen, Simone. "Samuel Pufendorf's Concept of Toleration." In *Difference and Dissent: Theories of Toleration in Medieval and Early Modern Europe*, ed. Cary J. Nederman and John C. Laursen (Lanham: Rowman & Littlefield, 1996), 163–84.

————. "From Denominationalism to Enlightenment: Pufendorf, Le Clerc, and Thomasius on Toleration." In *Religious Toleration: "The Variety of Rites" from Cyrus to Defoe*, ed. John C. Laursen (New York: St. Martin's Press, 1999), 191–209.

INDEX

Note: Page numbers followed by *n.* and a number indicate material in footnotes.

Abarbeneles, Isaacus, 79–80, 80 n. 33

absolute decree. *See* predestination

abstinence: from covetousness, 121; from evil, holiness of life and, 118–20; from revenge, 120

acquiescence to will of God, 121

"Advertisement" (Dorrington), xviii, 3–4

Against Julian of Eclanum (St. Augustine), 51, 51 n. 23, 142 n. 43

Against the Letter of Manichaeus Called Fundamental (St. Augustine), 55, 55 n. 31

Against Two Letters of the Pelagians (St. Augustine), 142 n. 43

agreement: on fundamental articles of faith, 23, 60, 127; in new covenant (*see* new covenant); not to contradict nature of Christianity, 14–15; theological, among Protestants, 60, 127

Alexander V, Pope, 155 n. 47

Alexander VI, Pope, 46 n. 21

Alfonsus, King of Aragon, 173

altars, composition of, 153, 155

Amyraut, Moïse, 221 n. 77, 221–22

Anabaptists, 57

Anglican Church. *See* Church of England

The Annals (Tacitus), 29 n. 6

Anne, Queen of England, xviii

antecedent will of God, 170, 171, 172

apostles: chosen by Christ, 209; drawn to faith in Christ, 176; preaching by, 107, 193

Apostles' Creed, 57–58

arbitrators, controversies committed to, 52

Arianism, 215 n. 71, 215–16

Arius, 215 n. 71

Arminus, Jacob, 202 n. 67

articles of faith: disputed, Pufendorf on, xii–xiii; ordination of clergy as, 45–46; questions remaining about, 58–60; used by priests for procurement of wealth, 42, 44–45. *See also* fundamental points of faith; *specific articles of faith*

atonement, through superficial religion, futility of, 33

Augsburg Confession (1530): controversies over, 52, 52 n. 25, 130–31, 225; Protestant/Catholic reconciliation and, 38 n. 14, 38–39

Augustine, Saint, 51, 51 n. 23, 54, 54 nn. 28–29, 55, 55 n. 31, 142, 142 n. 43, 143, 216, 222

authority: diminution of, feared, 24–25; of Holy Scripture, denied, 128; of pope, dependence on temporal power, 31

baptism, sacrament of: exorcism retained in, 152, 153–54; faith and, 110, 208; infant baptism, 39, 111, 119, 153–54, 208; as initiation into new covenant, 109–11; Original Sin and, 153–54; renunciation of sin and, 110–11

Bellarmine, Robert Francis Romulus, 43, 43 n. 18
bishops. *See* priests
body of divinity. *See* theology, system of
Borgia, Cesare (Duke of Valence), 46, 46 n. 21
Bossuet, Jacques-Bénigne, xv, 44, 44 n. 19
Boulliau, Ismael, 30, 30 n. 7
Brett, Thomas, xix, xix n. 12
Bullinger, Heinrich, 152, 152 n. 46

Caligula, Caius, 211, 211 n. 68
Calixtus, Georgius, 24, 24 n. 4, 186–88
call to salvation: in general terms, 177, 178; reprobates called, 165 n. 50, 165–67; secret will of God and, 178–79
Calvin, John, 130
Calvinist/Lutheran reconciliation. *See* Lutheran/Calvinist reconciliation
Calvinists: dissension among, regarding grace, 212; on Eucharist, 135, 136–37; on freedom of will, 147–48; German, rights of, xi, 131; obstinacy of mind in, 157; on omnipresence of body of Christ, 133; order of divine decrees and, 203–4; on predestination, 127, 141–42, 148–52; theological agreement with Lutherans, 60; on will of God, 150, 151
candles, use of, 153, 155
"canons of Dort," 202 n. 67
Catholic/Protestant reunion. *See* reconciliation between Protestants and papists
causality: not occurring with prescience, 163; prescience of God not to be construed as, 146–47, 163, 169
celibacy of priests, doctrine of, 45
ceremony: in Jewish state, 32–33; in Roman Catholic Church, 33
charity, 120, 177–78
Charles II, King of England, 17 n. 1
Charles IX, King of Sweden, 17–18 n. 2
Charles XI, King of Sweden, ix, 129
chastity, 121
Christian religion: based on Scriptures,

xii; belief in Holy Trinity as foundation of, 91–92, 109; circumcision improper to, 81–82; differences within, 13; reconcilement of dissension in, 14–15; right of Christian citizenship, 110–11, 114–15, 126
Chronicle of the Saxons and Some Neighboring Peoples from 1500 to 1593 (Chytraeus), 52, 52 n. 26
Chronicon Saxonicae et vicinarum aliquot gentium: ab anno Christi 1500 usque ad 1593 (Chytraeus), 52, 52 n. 26
church: ancient, consent to interpretation of Scriptures, 54 n. 30, 54–55; external things of, modesty in, 156; government of, 156–57; judgment in matters of faith belonging to, 27; as kingdom of God, 126; primitive (*see* primitive church). *See also specific denominations*
Church of England, 17; communion with reformed churches, 153–54; controversies with Presbyterians, 216; Lutheran Church and, xviii, 3–4; relationship with dissenters, xviii
church union conference (Hanover, 1683), xv, xvi
Chytraeus, David, 52, 52 n. 26
Cicero, Marcus Tullius, 92, 92 n. 36
circumcision, as mark of universal covenant, 81–82
civil law: promulgation of, 193; regarding testaments and covenants, 103–4
civil toleration, of Roman Catholic Church, 38
Clement IX, Pope, 30–31 n. 9
clergy: conferences of, to decide disputes (*see* conferences); garments of, 153, 156; offering given to, 152, 154; ordination of, 45–48; permission to marry, 45, 47; requirements of, 19. *See also* priests
Commentary on the Epistles of the Apostle St. Paul (Calixtus), 24 n. 4
commonwealth: peace of, political toleration and, 46; religion contrary to peace of, 19–20; revenues for preserva-

tion of, 30–31, 30–31 n. 9; usefulness of religious diversity in, 218–19 n. 74

Commonwealth of Israel. *See* Jewish state

communion: of Anglican Church with reformed churches, 153–54; heresy in, 49–50; maintaining, 21; man not be cast out from, 23–24, 58–59; physical, Eucharist as, 138; sacrament of (*see* Eucharist, sacrament of); virtual communion, 39, 57

concupiscence, 69

conditional will of God, 167–69, 171

conferences, to decide disputes, 26–27; princes solicited to send representatives, 50; questions to be examined in, 50–52

confession of faith: formal *vs.* material, 40–41; Lutheran, 38 n. 14; Protestant/ Catholic reconciliation and, 40–41. *See also* Augsburg Confession

confession of sins: forgiveness and, 44–45; private, 152, 154; as superficial religion, 33

consent: disputes resolved by, 26–27; to interpretation of Scriptures, 54 n. 30, 54–55; mutual, in new covenant, 75–76

Constance, Council of (1414), 155 n. 47

Constantinople, Council of (381), 37–38 n. 13, 215 n. 71

Consultation About Making Peace Among Protestants (Jurieu), xiv, 152, 157 n. 48, 157–58, 159–63, 165 n. 50, 165–67, 194 n. 63, 212 n. 69, 218 n. 73

contentment, 120–21

Contra epistolam Manichaei quam vocant fundamenti (St. Augustine), 55, 55 n. 31

controversies: advantage of common enemy and, 60, 130–31; over ambiguous sense of words, 217–18, 223; over Augsburg Confession, 52, 52 n. 25, 130–31, 225; calm debate of, 213–14, 216–17, 225–26; cherishing, 219; committed to arbitrators, 52; concealment of truth and, 224; contentious persons and, 218; disputation of, useless, 214–15;

over doctrine of transubstantiation, 124–25; over efficacy of Scriptures, 63; over emoluments, 28–31, 216; ending (*see* reconcilement of differences); over Eucharist, 134–39; over fundamental articles of faith, 51–52, 129–32, 218; over good works, 223; of lesser importance, 152–157, 217–18; mitigated by time, 25; particular, 132; over personal union, 98; over person of Christ, 132–34; points of, over primacy of pope, 43; about principles, deciding, 25–27; between Protestants and Catholics, 28, 43; about revenues, 50–51; sources of, 216; in system of theology, 139–42, 223–25; temporal interest and, 25

conversion: by covenant, 195; grace and, 212–13; morality in, 183–84, 195; by sufficient grace of God, 196–97, 213

corruption of mankind: double corruption, 197; following the Fall, 73–75, 204; put off by regeneration, 112–13

Council of Constantinople (381), 37–38 n. 13, 215 n. 71

Council of Nicea (325), 37–38 n. 13, 215 n. 71

Council of Trent (1545–63). *See* Trent, Council of

covenants between God and man, xiii, xvii–xviii; with Abraham (*see* particular covenant with Abraham); breach of, as sin, 70; civil law regarding, 103–4; conversion by, 195; faith as component of, 208; feudal, proportion in, 72; first covenant (*see* original covenant); freedom from death and, 70–71; idolatry and, 77–78; mankind as beneficiary of, 66–67; with Moses (*see* particular covenant with Moses); mutual obligation in, 64, 72–73; nature of, 66–67; with Noah after flood, 80; original state of mankind and, 203; as part of system of theology, 63–66; second covenant (*see* new covenant); time for acceptance of, 66

covetousness: abstinence from, 121; evils of, 11–12
creation, decree of, 203

damnation, cause of, 148
d'Aulnoy, comtesse Marie-Catherine Le Jumel de Berneville, 33 n. 10
death: freedom from, by covenant, 70–71; of Jesus Christ (*see* Passion of Christ)
De baptismo contra Donatistas (St. Augustine), 54, 54 n. 29
decretive will of God: difference between law and decree, 174–75; efficacy of means and, 188; immutability of, 190–91; kinds of decrees, 170; legislative will and, 159–63, 188; predestination and, 159–60
De Doctrina Christiana (St. Augustine), 54, 54 n. 28
De habitu religionis christianae ad vitam civilem (Pufendorf), ix–x, ix n
De jure belli a pacis (Grotius), 90, 90 n. 35
De Jure Naturali et Gentium Juxta Disciplinam Ebraeorum Libri Septem (Selden), 109, 109 n. 38, 111, 111 n. 39
denial of self, 121
De oratore (Cicero), 92, 92 n. 36
De Pace inter Protestantes ineunda consultatio . . . (Jurieu), xiv, 152, 157 n. 48, 157–58, 159–63, 165 n. 50, 165–67, 194 n. 63, 212 n. 69, 218 n. 73
De Potestate summi pontificis in rebus temporalibus adversus (Bellarmine), 43, 43 n. 18
De rebus gestis Friderici Tertii, Electoris Brandenburgici, post Primi Borussiae Regis Commentariorum Libri Tres, complectentes annos 1688–1690. Fragmentum posthumum ex autographo auctoris editum (Pufendorf), 17 n. 1
De Trinitate (St. Hilary of Poitiers), 54, 54 n. 30
De vita Caesarum: Caius Caligula (Suetonius), 211, 211 n. 68
Die Reunionsgespräche im Niedersachsen des 17. Jarhunderts. Rojas y Spinola–Molan–Leibniz, xiv–xv n. 6

disciples. *See* apostles
dissension: on mere principles, 24–25; reconcilement in Christian religion, 14–15; relationship of dissenters with Church of England, xviii; about rule and liberty, 40
divine decrees: absolute (*see* predestination); decree of creation, 203; decree of election, 206–11; decree of reprobation, 221 n. 78, 221–22; kinds of, 167, 170, 203; laws contrasted, 174–75; order of, 202–6; prescience of God proceeding from, 169–70
The Divine Feudal Law (Pufendorf), x, xvi n. 7, xvi, xvii, xviii, 3–4
divine revelation: Adam's knowledge of God by, 68; as frame of religion, 32; harmony and uniformity in, 62–63; reason shows rightness of, 62
Döring, Detlef, xiii n, 30–31 n. 9, 218–19 n. 74
Dorrington, Theophilus, xvii, xvii nn. 10–11, xviii
Dort, Synod of (1618–19), 183, 202, 202 n. 67, 204
Duchhardt, H., xvi n. 9
Dutch Reformed Church, 202 n. 67

Easter, observation of, 21
ecclesiastical courts: controversy committed to, 52; to decide disputes, 26–27; matrimonial cases in, 51
ecclesiastical peace, 58, 59
ecclesiastical toleration, x, xii, 16, 21; of errors in religion, 21; Lutheran/Calvinist reconciliation and, 218–23; reconcilement of differences under, xii
The Eclogues (Virgil), 139 n. 42
Edict of Nantes (1598), 29–30 n. 7, 221 n. 78; on liberty of conscience, xi; revocation of, reaction to, ix–x
the elect: according to prescience of God, 186; Christ as savior of, 183; fulfillment of God's promises in, 176; God's favor given to, 212; universal redemption and, 196

election, decree of: as absolute, 206–7; faith and, 206–11; man separates self from, 208–9

emoluments, controversies over, 28–31, 216

"Epistola ad Amicum super exercitationes posthumas Samelis Puffendorfii de consensu et dissensu protestantium" (Leibniz), xv–xvi, xvi n. 7

Ernst August, Duke of Hanover, xv

errors in religion: admission of, truth and, 214–15; casting away, unity and, 225–26; consequences of, 128–29; conviction of, 27; ecclesiastical toleration of, 21; error of particularity, 148, 150, 151; innocent error, 137; maintained out of envy or pride, 24–25; mutual toleration of, 222–23; nature of Eucharist, 42–44; particularism, as fundamental error, 220–21; refusal to admit, 22–23, 41, 214–15; rejection of, 143–44; of Roman Catholic Church, 35–36, 41; transference of guilt, 79–80

eternal life: bestowed upon believers, 186, 206, 209–10; mankind created for, 71–72, 203–4; not promised before Christ, 86; original covenant and, 69–72; predestined, Passion of Christ unnecessary for, 207; union of faithful with Christ and, 126

Eucharist, sacrament of: Calvinist views of, 135, 136–37; controversy over, 134–39; equivalence or substitution in, 138–39; idolatry of eucharistical bread, 222; Lutherans on, 135–36; maiming of, 49–50; as obstacle to reconciliation, 42–44; permission from pope to celebrate, 47; person of Christ and, 132–34; as physical communion, 138; presence of Christ's Body and Blood in, 102–3, 123–24, 125, 222; Protestant beliefs about, 44; Roman Catholic abuses of, 155 n. 47; round wafers used in, 152–53, 154–55; substance of, not dependent on beliefs of man, 135; as symbol of new covenant, 122–24; as

symbol of perfect Christian union, 42–43; transcending reach of human reason, 139; transubstantiation and (see transubstantiation, doctrine of)

evil. See sin(s); wickedness

exorcism, retained in sacrament of baptism, 152, 153–54

external religion: internal religion contrasted, 31–35; modesty in, 156

faith: baptism and, 110, 208; bestowed by God, 186; as condition of redemption, 189–90, 199, 205–6; covenants and, 90, 108, 208; in covenant with Christ, 90; decree of election and, 206–11; denial of, after belief, 201–2; entwined with repentance and virtue, 117–18; foreseen, redemption and, 199–200, 208–9; foundation of: controversies of lesser importance to, 152–57, 217–18; —, overthrown by denial of Scripture, 128; impossible for reprobates, 182; Jesus Christ as the Savior and, 182–83; matters of, judgment of church in, 27; as means of salvation, 205–6; perseverance in, redemption and, 201–2; principles of, in Holy Scripture, 49; reason in obedience to, 137, 194; repentance and, 119; sacrifice unacceptable without, 79; salvation and, 59–60; in the Savior yet to come, 81; union with the Savior and, 93

Fall, the: corruption of mankind following, 73–75, 204; obligation of sanctity and, 74–75; Original Sin contracted from, 73–74; predestination and, 204; procured by God, in Calvinist theology, 203–4; shame of, 69–70

false religion, punishment of treason for, 83–84

festival days, 153, 156

Flacius (Matthias Flacius Illyricus), 219 n. 75, 219–20

force: religion not to be propagated by, 13, 14, 20; salvation not given by, 146, 181–82

Frederick III, Elector of Brandenburg-Prussia, ix, 17 n. 1, 129

Frederick William I, King of Brandenburg-Prussia, ix, 129

freedom of will: Calvinists on, 147–48; in nature of mankind, 65, 68–69; negative liberty, 65–66, 168, 171, 200; Pelagianism and, 142, 142 n. 43; to refuse salvation, 145, 146, 148–49, 182; seducement to evil and, 69; theology and, xiv; true worship and, 65–66; will of God and, 158, 161, 164

"From Denominationalism to Enlightenment: Pufendorf, Le Clerc, and Thomasius on Toleration" (Zurbuchen), 218–19 n. 74

fundamental points of faith: agreement on, 23, 60, 127; celibacy of priests, 45; composition of, 58–59, 127–29; controversies over, 51–52, 129–32, 218; denial of, by fanatics, 57–58; doctrine of justification, 44–45, 47, 108, 115–18, 223; ecclesiastical peace and, 58; nature of, 24; Protestant/papist reconciliation and, 41–42; reconcilement of differences and, xii, 41–42; retained by Roman Catholic Church, 39–40. See also articles of faith

George I, King of England, xviii, xix

"Gerard Wolter Molan und seine Stellung zum Projekt einer kirchlichen Union" (Ohst), xvi n. 9

Germany: liberty of religion in, xi; Protestant Reformation in, 130–31

Gesammelte Werke (Pufendorf), xiii n

Glorious Revolution, xviii, 17 n. 1

God: covenants between God and man, xiii, xvii; as creator of mankind, 67; desire to save all sinners, 166, 168, 170–71, 173–74; elect and, 176, 212; faith bestowed by, 186; freedom to inflict pain, 168–69; goodness and clemency of, 151–52; goodwill of, 167, 168, 170–74, 184, 195–96; hardness of heart against sin, 181–82; immutability of, 184, 190–91; inducements by, 64–65;

Jews and, 82, 84–85; kinds of decrees of, 170; kingdom of Christ subjected to, 101; knowledge of, by divine revelation, 68; liberty of man and, 165, 167; love of, 70, 116; man's contempt of, after Fall, 73; means of salvation supplied by, 201, 211–12; as mediator of new covenant, 93–94; mercy promised by, 180; moral behavior of, 145–46; natural knowledge of, insufficient, 61; obedience to, regeneration and, 116–17; omnipotence of, imposition of will and, 183; omnipresence of, 133; omniscience of, 62–63; Passion of Christ appointed by, 199–200; patience of, 187–88; power of, moderated, 163–64, 165, 170; preaching and, 106–7, 166–67; prescience of (see prescience of God); purpose of, particular redemption and, 195–98, 199; reason insufficient for knowledge of, 61–62, 144, 172–73, 193, 202; refusal of salvation and, 184, 205–6; religion not imposed by force, 64–65; requirements for veneration by man, 61–62; right of dominion over mankind, 72–73; speaking with mankind, 201; unbecoming for man to question, 134; will of (see will of God)

goodwill of God, 167, 168; man's unbelief and, 184; predestination dependent upon, 207–8; sufficiently declared to mankind, 195–96; universality of, 170–74

good works: appeal to, in Last Judgment, 117; controversies over, 223; legal works contrasted, 100; meritorial power of, 142–43; not essential to covenants, 208; as positive holiness of life, 118, 120–22; sanctification of regenerate and, 116; virtue of, 51

Gospel, repentance required in order to receive, 107

government: of church, 156–57; liberty of religion granted by concession of, xi; toleration by concession of, 16–18 grace: conflict between Lutherans and Calvinists over, xiii–xix, 139; conversion and, 196–97, 212–13; dissension among Calvinists regarding, 212; doctrine of, differences in, 222; without inevitable necessity, 195; irresistible, 172–73, 212–14; predestination and, 139, 141, 143; questions of, 127; reprobation caused by refusal of, 211–12; sufficient for conversion, 196–97, 213; universality of, 148–50, 152

Gregory of Nazianzus, 37–38 n. 13

Gregory XII, Pope, 155 n. 47

Grotius, Hugo, 90, 90 n. 35

Gualther, Rudolf, 152, 152 n. 46

guilt, 79–80

hardness of heart: God's, against wickedness, 181–82; man's, against redemption, 197–98

Hartung, Gerald, 17 n. 1

hatred, arising from differences in religion, 13

head, uncovering in worship, 153, 156

Henry IV, King of France and Navarre, 29–30, 29–30 n. 7

heresies: Arianism, 215 n. 71; in Communion, 49–50; disappearance of, 16; Pelagianism, 142 n. 43; punishment for, 155 n. 47

Hertzberg, E. F. de, 17 n. 1

hierarchy: of presbyters, 50; share in advantages of, 29; withdrawing from subjection to, 29–30

Hilary of Poitiers, Saint, 54, 54 n. 30

Hildebrand, Joachim, 56, 56 n

holiness of life and manners: abstinence from evil and, 118–20; condition of mankind and, 121–22; as consequence of justification and regeneration, 117; faith and repentance entwined with, 117–18; fall from grace and, 74–75; good works and, 118, 120–22; as obligation of original covenant, 115; perpetual penance and, 119–20; required of Jews, 83

holy sacraments: baptism (see baptism, sacrament of); Eucharist (see Eucharist, sacrament of); matrimony, sacramental nature of, 50, 51

Holy Scriptures: absolute decree not found in, 202; authority of, denied, 128; charged with falsehood, 23–24; Christianity based on, xii; conference on reconciliation and, 53–54; consent to interpretation of, 54 n. 30, 54–55; efficacy of, 63; faith and, 49, 128; as guide to reconcilement of differences, 223–24; knowledge of Holy Trinity derived from, 91; knowledge of personal union in, 98, 103; as law of final judgment, 100; Lutheran theology and, 157–58; means of interpretation of, 54 n. 30, 54–55; not all writings necessary to salvation, 22; principles of faith in, 49; remission of sins promised in, 105–6; secret will of God differing from, 179; transubstantiation not acknowledged in, 102–3; as treasury of divine revelation, 63; truth of, determining, 26; on universal redemption, 196; universal salvation as doctrine of, 152

Holy Trinity, 39; baptism done in name of, 109; belief in, as foundation of Christian religion, 91–92, 109; concept of, not to be overexamined, 92, 95; condition of Father and Son in, 94; denial of, covenant overthrown by, 92–93; mystery of, in new covenant, 90–93; Nicene orthodoxy of, 215 n. 71; understanding of, xiii, 68. See also personal union

hope, 120

Huguenots: liberty of religion and, xi; toleration of, renounced, ix–x. See also Calvinists

human nature: intemperance of, 11–12, 22–23; of Jesus Christ (see personal union); participation in kingdom of God, 99–100, 153–54; pride and obstinacy of, 25. See also mankind

humility, 120
Hunnius, Aegidius, 221, 221 n. 77
Hunter, Ian, xvi n. 8
Huss, John, 155, 155 n. 47
hymns, sacred, 153, 156

idolatry: covenant and, 77–78; of eucharistical bread, 222; Jews fallen into, 86;
Jews to live separate from idolaters,
80–81, 84; sacrifice by idolaters and,
138
ignorance: of day of judgment, 101; salvation and, 59–60, 144
Illyricus, Matthias Flacius, 219 n. 75,
219–20
images in churches, 153, 155–56
In Acta Apostolorum Expositio Litteralis
. . . (Calixtus), 24 n. 4
inducements: God's government of man
by, 64–65; by pope, to gain princes'
submission to Rome, 48, 56; to salvation, 145–46
indulgences, sale of, schism and, 52
inefficacious will of God, 157–58
infants, salvation of: baptism and, 39, 111,
119, 153–54, 208; Eucharist and, 124
Innocent XI, Pope, xv
intemperance, as cause of calamity, 11–12
intercessions, as superficial religion, 33
internal religion: external religion contrasted, 31–35; purity of mind and, 32
Introduction to the History of the Principal
Kingdoms and States of Europe (Pufendorf), 218–19 n. 74
Israel. *See* Jewish state

James II, King of England, 17, 17 n. 1
Jesus Christ: actions required by new
covenant, 105–6; conceived of virgin,
94–95; corporal presence of body of,
133–34, 222; death of (*see* Passion of
Christ); divestiture of mediatorial office, 100–101; divinity of, Arianism
and, 215 n. 71; doctrine of faith in savior to come, 80–82; dual nature of, as
God and man in one, xiii, 95, 98; final

judgment and, 100; God's purposes in
sending, 195–98; mankind as heirs to,
104–5; manner of drawing disciples to
faith in, 176; merit of, indivisible,
148–50; methods of propagating religion, 13–14; nativity of, confined to
Jews, 82; offices of, under new covenant, 105–6; omnipresence of body of,
133–34, 219; prayers of, 198–200; as
preserver rather than savior, 200; rejection as savior, by Jews, 87; as sacrifice
for mankind, 87–90, 94–95, 102,
198–200; as savior of all, on condition
of faith, 182–83; union of faithful with,
126. *See also* God; personal union
Jewish religion: interwoven with commonwealth, 86–87; nature of, 86; prescribed by God, 84; sacrifice in, 138
Jewish state: according to covenant with
Moses, 82–83; false religion as crime
against, 83–84; religion interwoven
with, 86–87; under yoke of ceremonies, 32–33
Jews: beliefs of, 79; captivity in Babylon,
86–87; captivity in Egypt, 84–85,
122–23; under God's protection, 82; religion prescribed to, by God, 84; reluctancy of, 188, sanctity of life and
manners required, 83
John III, King of Sweden, 17–18 n. 2
judiciary proceedings. *See* ecclesiastical
courts
Jurieu, Pierre, xiv, xiv n. 5, 152; on abdication of principles, 215–17; on conditional will of God, 167–69; on condition of faith, 182–90; on divine
decrees, 202–11; evasions of, 200–202;
on future contingencies, 169–70; on
immutability of God, 190–91; on irresistible grace, 212–14; on Passion of
Christ, in vain, 191–92; on prayers of
Christ, 198–200; on preaching,
192–94; on reprobation, 165 n. 50,
165–67, 211–12; on silence, 223–25; on
strife about words, 217–18; on toleration, 218–23; on universal goodwill of

God, 170–74; on universality of salvation, 194–95; on universal redemption, 195–98; on uselessness of disputation, 214–15; views of Lutheran/Calvinist reconciliation, 157 n. 48, 157–58; on will of God, dual nature of, 159–63, 174–82

Jus feciale divinum sive de consensu et dissensu protestantium (Pufendorf), ix, ix n

justice, decree of, 203

justification by faith alone, doctrine of: effect of new covenant, 108; as fundamental article of faith, 44–45, 47; performed instantaneously, 115; sanctification as fruit of, 115–18; sanctification distinguished from, 223

kingdom of God: church as, 126; human participation in, 99–100, 153–54

kingly office of Jesus Christ, 106

Kleine Vorträge und Schriften. Texte zu Geschichte, Pädagogik, Philosophie, Kirche und Völkerrecht (Pufendorf), 30–31 n. 9, 218–19 n. 74

Lamb of God, paschal lamb representing, 85

Last Judgment: appeal to good works in, 117; day and hour of, unknown, 101; eternal life and, 126; as part of office of mediator, 100

Laursen, John C., 218–19 n. 74

The Law of Nature and Nations (Pufendorf), ix

The Law of War and Peace (Grotius), 90, 90 n. 35

Le Clerc, Jean, 218–19 n. 74

legislative will of God: to bind men's actions, 174–75; decretive will and, 159–63, 188; equity of, 174; impediments to, 171–72; means of performing and, 188, 205; as metaphorical, 160–61, 162; obligation and, 162; as tyranny, 161–62, 175

Leibniz, Gottfried Wilhelm, xv–xvi, xvi n. 7

"Leibniz als Verfasser der 'Epistola ad amicum super exercitationes posthumas Samuelis Puffendorfii de consensu et dissensu protestantium'" (Döring), xvi n. 7

Le Jumel de Berneville, Marie-Catherine, comtesse d'Aulnoy, 33 n. 10

Leopold I, Holy Roman Emperor, xv, 34, 34 n. 11

Levitical worship, 32–33, 79

Lewis, John, xix n. 12

liberty: betrayal of, peace and, 51; of conscience, xi; dissension about, 40; evangelical, not to be renounced, 55–57; in interest of princes to retain, 29–30; maintained by sovereign, 19; of man, God and, 165, 167; negative liberty, 65–66, 168, 171, 200; prescience of God and, 169–70; right to, 16–17; unconstrained, 167–68; wickedness permitted by God and, 164

liberty of religion: bought with blood, 56; Peace of Osnabrück and, 17, 131, 131 n. 41; Protestant, prejudged, 49; ways of enjoying, xi

Louis XIV, King of France, ix–x, 34, 34 n. 11, 221 n. 78

love of God, 70, 116

love of neighbor, 70, 116

Luther, Martin, 57, 103, 130, 143, 221

Lutheran/Calvinist reconciliation, xiii–xiv; abdication of principles as means of, 215 n. 71, 215–17; controversies about words and, 217–18; controversies of lesser importance and, 152–57; defense against common enemy and, 225–26; through ecclesiastical toleration, 218–23; issues of grace and predestination, xiii–xix, 127–32; Jurieu's views of, commentary on, 157 n. 48, 157–58; through silence, 223–25; system of theology and, xiii; uselessness of disputation and, 214–15

Lutheran Church: Church of England and, xviii, 3–4; confession of faith in, 38 n. 14; on Eucharist, 135–36;

Lutheran Church (*continued*)
German, rights of, xi, 131; on omnipresence of body of Christ, 133, 219;
opposition to particular redemption,
200–202; principles of, xviii; relics of
popish rites in, 152–53; as Swedish
state religion, 17–18 n. 2; theological
agreement with Calvinists, 60; theology of, Holy Scriptures and, 157–58;
views on predestination, 127–28,
140–41, 145–47

Machiavelli, Nicolo, 46 n. 21
mankind: agreement of Christ with, in
new covenant, 90; as beneficiary of
covenants with God, 66–67, 126; capable of morality, 173; Christ as man,
new covenant and, 94–95; comfort of,
principle of universality and, 148–51;
corruption of, 73–75, 112–13, 197, 204;
creation of, purpose of God and, 203;
crime of, expiated in new covenant,
75–76; depraved nature removed by
regeneration, 112–13; divided into two
parts, 184–85; expectation of God's
truth, 145–46; fault of, for refusing salvation, 148, 178, 182, 192; first man in
natural state of purity, 68–69; forgetfulness of covenant, 77; as free agent,
sin and, 170; freedom of will in nature
of, 65, 68–69; God's dominion over,
72–73; God's goodwill declared to,
195–96; God speaking with, 201; human bodies, body of Christ and,
133–34, 222; ignorance of day of judgment, 101; immortal soul of, 67; incorporation with Christ through Eucharist, 124; initiation of own salvation,
142 n. 43, 196, 213; Jesus Christ as sacrifice for, 87–90, 94–95, 102, 198–200;
means to perform God's law, 188, 205;
nature of, predestination and, 141–42;
new covenant published to, 106–7;
prescience denied to, 66; proofs of
God's love for, 196; reduced to machine by predestination, 65–66, 168,

173; requirements of new covenant
upon, 107; resistance to will of God,
159; as sons of God, 104–5, 113–14, 185;
state of, after fall from grace, 73–75;
wicked (*see* reprobates); wickedness of,
as cause of calamity, 11–12. *See also* human nature
Mary, Queen of England, xix, 17 n. 1
masses, sale of, 33–35, 47, 50–51
matrimony, sacramental nature of, 50, 51
May, G., xvi n. 9
means of salvation: determination of end
and, 206–7; faith as, 205–6; new covenant as, 74, 145, 204–5; Passion of
Christ as, 189–92; supplied by God,
201, 211–12
mediator of new covenant: actions required of Christ, 105–6; attributes of
mediatorial office, 97–103; divestiture
of office of, 100–101; God as, 93–94;
interposition of, 75–76, 87; as judge,
100; kingdom of God and, 99–100;
knowledge not belonging to, 101;
mankind as heirs of, 103–4; nature of,
93, 97; personal union and, importance of, 95, 96–97
meekness, 120
Mémoires de la cour d'Espagne
(d'Aulnoy), 33 n. 10
mercy: promised by God to believers,
180; vessels of mercy, 187–88. *See also*
grace
merit: of Jesus Christ, indivisible,
148–50; of men, predestination contradictory to, 143, 158, 210; meritorial
power of good works, 142–43; of Passion of Christ, 191–92; as superficial
religion, 33
*Method to Restore an Ecclesiastical Union
Between the Romanists and the Protestants* (Molanus), xv, xvi
*Methodus reducendae unionis ecclesiasticae
inter Romanenses et Protestantes* (Molanus), xv, xvi
ministers. *See* clergy
miseries of mankind: abuse of religion

and, 12–14; breach of covenant and, 70; intemperance as cause of, 11–12; satisfaction of Savior and, 115–16

modesty, in external things of church, 156

Molanus, Gerard Wolter, xv, xvi

morality: mankind capable of, 173; moral behavior of God, 145–46; place in salvation of mankind, 183–84, 195, 200, 213

Münster, Treaty of. *See* Treaty of Münster.

music, 153, 156

mysteries: of Eucharist, 135; of Holy Trinity, 90–93; of personal union, 96–97

natural law, theory of, x

new covenant: actions required of Jesus Christ, 105–6; agreement of Christ with mankind, 90; agreement of God the Father with the Son, 87–90, 100; agreement with feudal contract, 118; conflict with predestination, 127–28; effect on doctrine of justification, 108; Eucharist as symbol of, 122–24; faith as essential condition of, 108; initiation into, by baptism, 109–11; interposition of mediator in (*see* mediator of new covenant); means of salvation in, 74, 145, 204–5; mutual consent in, 75–76; mystery of Holy Trinity in, 90–93; no man excluded from, by absolute decree, 205–6; perfection and execution of, 87; promulgation of, 76–78; prophecies of, 77, 106–7; publication of, 106–7; regeneration resulting from, 111–15; religion arising from, 78–80; remission of sins in, 78–80, 108; repentance required by, 107; sacrifice as symbol of, 78–79, 104; sacrifice of Christ required of, 93–94; salvation of souls obtained by, 74, 86, 145; the Savior as man and, 94–95; sum of requirements of mankind, 107; testament contrasted to, 103–5; union of members of, 126; universality of,

148–49; way of salvation revealed in, 191–92

Nicea, Council of (325), 37–38 n. 13, 215 n. 71

"non-jurors," xix

obedience to God, 116–17

obligation: holiness of life and manners, 115; legislative will of God and, 162; love of God and neighbor, 116; mutual, in covenants, 64, 72–73; of particular covenant with Moses, 83–84, 93; perpetual, of primitive church, 78; of sanctity, the Fall and, 74–75

obstacles to reconciliation: Eucharist as, 42–44; submission to Roman Catholic Church as, 39–40, 42

obstinacy of mind: conviction of error in spite of, 27; in Lutherans and Calvinists, 157; refusal to admit error and, 22–23, 41; Scriptures charged with falsehood, 23–24

Oecolampadius, Johannes, 152, 152 n. 46

Of the Nature and Qualification of Religion in Reference to Civil Society (Pufendorf), 18, 18 n.3

Ohst, Martin, xvi n. 9

On Baptism Against the Donatists (St. Augustine), 54, 54 n. 29

On Christian Doctrine (St. Augustine), 54, 54 n. 28

On Marriage and Concupiscence (St. Augustine), 142 n. 43

On Nature and Grace (St. Augustine), 142 n. 43

On the Grace of Christ and on Original Sin (St. Augustine), 142 n. 43

On the Law of Nature and of Nations According to the Doctrine of the Hebrews (Selden), 109, 109 n. 38, 111, 111 n. 39

On the Merits and Remission of Sins and on the Baptism of Infants (St. Augustine), 142 n. 43

On the Orator (Cicero), 92, 92 n. 36

On the Perfection of Man's Righteousness (St. Augustine), 142 n. 43

On the Power of the Pope in Worldly Affairs (Bellarmine), 43, 43 n. 18
"On the Relation of Christian Religion to Civil Life" (Pufendorf), ix n, ix–x
On the Soul and Its Origin (St. Augustine), 142 n. 43
On the Spirit and the Letter (St. Augustine), 142 n. 43
On Trinity (St. Hilary of Poitiers), 54, 54 n. 30
opinions: erroneous, needless questions on, 58–60; of priests, contrary to public safety, 19–20; of primitive church, erroneous, 21; truth of, 22–23; unreasonable pride in, 12–13
Oration I (Gregory of Nazianzus), 37–38 n. 13
order of worship, 156
ordination of clergy: as article of faith, 45–46; permission of pope for, 47–48
original covenant: eternal life and, 69–72; holiness of life and manners as obligation of, 115; man's immortal soul and, 67–68; universality of, 148; violation of, by Adam, 70, 72–73, 74
Original Sin, 73–75; denial of, 142 n. 43; sacrament of baptism and, 153–54; satisfaction of the Savior and, 115–16
original state of mankind: the Fall and, 204; strength of, covenants and, 203
Osnabrück (Osnabrug), Peace of, 131, 131 n. 41
Ottoman Empire, 34 n. 11

Palladini, Fiammetta, 17 n. 1
papal bull, on Turkish war, 30–31, 30–31 n. 9
papal infallibility: as foundation of pontifical monarchy, 40; inability to admit error and, 35–36; Protestant inability to accept, xvii
papal kingdom, 40
particular covenant with Abraham, 80–82; doctrine of savior to come, 81; rite of circumcision as mark of, 81–82; rites of, 122–23; temporary nature of, 86, 87
particular covenant with Moses: to establish Jewish state, 82–83; obligations of, 83–84, 93; paschal lamb as symbol of, 84–85; rites of, 123; temporary nature of, 86–87
particularism: doctrine of predestination and, 217, 217 n. 72; as fundamental error, 220–21
particular redemption: God's purpose and, 195–98, 199; Lutheran opposition to, 200–202; universal preaching and, 192–94
paschal lamb: sacrament of Eucharist and, 122–23; sacrifice of, 84–85
Passau, Treaty of (1552), 41 n. 16, 41–42, 46, 48
Passion of Christ: as appointed by God, 199–200; efficacy of, 190–91; merit of, 191–92, as universal means of salvation, 189–92; unnecessary, if eternal life predestined, 207
patience, 120
patience of God, 187–88
patriarchal rights of pope, 48–49
peace: betrayal of liberty and, 51; of commonwealth, toleration and, 46; ecclesiastical, 58, 59; love and endeavor for, 120; of state, religion contrary to, 19–20
peacemakers, 14
Peace of Osnabrück (Osnabrug), 17, 131, 131 n. 41
Peace of Westphalia (1648), xi, 131 n. 41
Pelagianism, 142, 142 n. 43
Pelagius, 142 n. 43
penance, 33, 119–20
persecution, 13
personal union: body of Christ and, 133–34; concept of, not to be overexamined, 96, 98, 102–3; consequence of, 97; of divine and human in Christ, 95; human nature of Christ and, 97–103, 133–34; in mediator of new covenant, 95, 96–97; nature of, 96–97
Phillip IV, King of Spain, 34
physicks, perfect understanding of, 68
piety, disagreement for sake of, 37, 37 n. 13

political toleration, 15–18; by concession of government, 16–17; excess of, 218–19, 218–19 n. 74; limited, 18–20; in own right, 16–17; peace of commonwealth and, 46; as remedy for evil, 15–16; sovereign and, x–xi; universal, 18

pontifical monarchy, papal infallibility as foundation of, 40

pope: authority of, dependence on temporal power, 31; bishops subject to, 46; consent of, to interpretation of Scriptures, 54 n. 30, 54–55; inducements to princes, 48, 56; infallibility of (*see* papal infallibility); multiple claimants to office of, 155 n. 47; patriarchal rights of, 48–49; power to permit reconciliation, 46–48; primacy of, controversy over, 43; Protestants unwise to trust, 52–53. *See also specific pontiffs*

power of God, moderated, 163–64, 165, 170

prayer, love of, 121

preaching: by apostles, 107, 193; different effects of, 197; directed indifferently toward all, 166; effect of predestination on, 178; in name of God, 106–7; in places appointed by God, 166–67; universal *vs.* particular, 192–94

predestination: decree of, not absolute, 207–8; dependence on goodwill of God, 207–8; effect on preaching, 178; the Fall and, 204; grace and, 139, 141, 143. *See also* predestination, doctrine of

predestination, doctrine of: Calvinists on, 127, 141–42, 148–52; conflict between Lutherans and Calvinists over, xiii–xix, 139–42; consequences of, 143–44; contradictory to merit of men, 143, 158, 210; cruelty of, 151–52, 165–66, 175, 203; decretive will of God and, 159–60; God's freedom to inflict pain and, 168–69; inadmissibility of, 145–48; Lutheran views on, 127–28, 140–41, 145–47; man reduced to machine by, 65–66, 168, 173; new covenant, conflict with, 127–28; origin of

doctrine, 142–44; particularism and, 217, 217 n. 72; prescience contrasted with, 163; remonstrance against, 202 n. 67; salvation and, 140–41, 142

Presbyterian Church, 216

prescience of God: conditional decrees and, 167; denied to mankind, 66; elect established by, 186; foreseen faith, redemption and, 199–200, 208–9; future contingencies and, 169–70; nature of, 163–65; not to be construed as causality, 146–47, 169; proceeding from previous decrees, 169–70

pretention, doctrine of, 204–5

pride, unreasonable: error maintained because of, 24–25; in opinions, 12–13

priestly office of Jesus Christ, 106

priests: bishops subject to pope, 46; celibacy of, 45; lies for profit, 118; opinions contrary to public safety, 19–20; pride and obstinacy of, 25; procurement of wealth by, 34, 42, 44–45, 47, 50–51

primitive church: erroneous opinions of, 21; Eucharist and, 124; perpetual obligation of, 78

The Prince (Machiavelli), 46 n. 21

princes: of different religion from people, 17–18; interest of, to retain liberty earned, 29–30; maintenance of liberties granted, 19; submission to Rome, 36–37, 48, 56

principles: abdication of, 215 n. 71, 215–17; deciding controversies about, 25–27; dissension over, 24–25; of faith, in Holy Scripture, 49; fundamental, of religion, 76; of Lutheran Church, xviii; principle of universality, 148–51; for reconcilement of differences, 224–25

private confession of sins, 152, 154

prophecies: in Holy Scriptures, 63; of new covenant, 77, 106–7; that God would have all men saved, 180

prophetic office of Jesus Christ, 106

Protestant Act of Succession (1689), xix

Protestant Reformation, 129–32

Protestants: attempts to reunite with Roman Catholics, xiv–xv; controversy over personal union, 98; points of controversy with papists, 28, 43; reunification of, xiv, 3–4; submission to Rome, 36. *See also* reconciliation between Protestants and papists

public safety, religion contrary to, 19–20

Pufendorf, Esaias, xiii, xiii n, 30

Pufendorf, Samuel, xiii n; background of, ix; on disputed religious articles, xii–xiii; on political toleration, x–xi; on religious dissent, x; on toleration, ix–x, xii, 218–19 n. 74; view of Molanus's *Methodus,* xvi–xvii, xvi n. 9

Pufendorf-Studien: Beiträge zur Biographie Samuel von Pufendorfs und zu seiner Entwicklung als Historiker und theologischer Schriftsteller (Döring), xv–xvi n. 7

punishment: for heresies, 155 n. 47; for neglect of paschal lamb, 85; not exercised against man, 203–4; proportion of, to sin, 72–73; of treason, for false religion, 83–84

purity of mind (heart): ceremony useless to obtain, 33; first man in natural state of purity, 68–69; internal religion and, 32

Quakers, 57

questions of faith, revenues dependent upon, 51–52

ransom. *See* sacrifice

readiness to forgive, 120

reason: belief in revealed religion and, 62; Eucharist beyond reach of, 139; fanatics departed from, 57; following, 11; insufficient for knowledge of God, 61–62, 144, 172–73, 193, 202; in obedience to faith, 137, 194. *See also* understanding

reconcilement of differences: in Christian religion, 14–15; difficulty of achieving,

16; ecclesiastical toleration and, xii; fundamental articles of faith and, xii, 41–42; Holy Scriptures as guide to, 223–24; between Lutherans and Calvinists (*see* Lutheran/Calvinist reconciliation); methods of, xiv; mixed with toleration, 23–24; perfect, 22–23, 28–29, 35–37; principles for, 224–25; between Protestants and Catholics (*see* reconciliation between Protestants and papists); truth and, 21–23, 224; universal or fundamental, 15

reconciliation: of dual will of God, 174–82; of sects, attempted, 57–58

reconciliation between Protestants and papists, 37–57; attempts, xiv–xvi; Augsburg Confession and, 38 n. 14, 38–39; conditions for council of reconciliation, 53–54, 55; conference unlikely to be held, 50, 53; confession of faith and, 40–41; desirability of, 37–38; doctrine of justification and, 44–45, 47; ecclesiastical courts and, 52; evangelical liberty not to be renounced, 55–57; fundamental articles of faith and, 41–42; impossible without destruction of one church, 56–57; means of interpreting Scriptures and, 54 n. 30, 54–55; obstacles to, 39–40, 42; ordination of clergy and, 45–46, 47; power of pope to permit, 46–48; promises demanded of Protestants, 48–50; Pufendorf's views of, xvi–xvii; questions to be decided, 50–52; sacrament of Eucharist and, 42–44; unlikely to occur, 52 n. 26, 52–53

redemption: faith as condition of, 189–90, 199, 205–6; man's hardness of heart against, 197–98; particular (*see* particular redemption); perseverance in faith and, 201–2; prescience of God and, 199–200, 208–9; of temporarily righteous, 201–2; universal (*see* universal redemption)

reformed party (churches). *See* Calvinists

refusal of salvation: covenant unable to

exist without, 209; faculty of, allowed by God, 205–6; as fault of mankind, 148, 178, 182, 192; freedom of will and, 145, 146, 148–49, 182; God's foresight of, 184; subsequent offers and, 193–94. *See also* reprobates; salvation

regeneration, 111–15; corruption put off by, 112–13; grace as fruit of, 212–13; making mankind sons of God, 113–14; necessity of, 111–12; obedience to God and, 116–17; performed instantaneously, 115; sanctification as fruit of, 115–18; understanding received by, 113, 114–15

Regulae circa christianorum omnium ecclesiasticam reunionem (Rojas y Spinola), xv

Relation du voyage en Espagne (d'Aulnoy), 33 n.10

religion: acceptable to God, 70; arising from new covenant, 78–80; changing, by concession of government, 18; contrary to peace of state, 19–20; fundamental principle of, 76; solid *vs.* superficial, 31–35

religious differences: methods of removing, 15; miseries of mankind and, 12–14

religious diversity, overcoming, temporary means of, xi

Religious Toleration: "The Variety of Rites" from Cyrus to Defoe (Laursen), 218–19 n. 74

remission of sins: in new covenant, 78–80, 108; required of Savior, 105–6

repentance: entwined with faith and virtue, 117–18; reparation of damage and, 119; required by new covenant, 107; suffering as path to, 187

reprobates (reprobation): called to salvation, 165 n. 50, 165–67; caused by refusal of grace, 211–12; condition of faith impossible for, 182; decree of reprobation, 221 n. 78, 221–22; inexcusable, 197–98, 204–5

revelation. *See* divine revelation

revenge, abstinence from, 120

revenues: affected by controversies, 50–51; articles of faith used for, 42, 44–45; for preservation of commonwealth, 30–31, 30–31 n. 9; from sale of masses, 34, 47, 50–51; virtue of good works and, 51. *See also* wealth

A Review of the Lutheran Principles (Brett), xix, xix n. 12

righteousness, temporary, 201–2

Rival Enlightenments: Civil and Metaphysical Philosophy in Early Modern Germany (Hunter), xvi n. 8

Rojas y Spinola, Cristoforo, xv

Roman Catholic Church: abuses of Eucharist, 155 n. 47; articles of faith and (*see* articles of faith); attempts to reunite with Protestants, xiv–xv; compromise with, about nonessentials, 219 n. 75, 219–20; controversies among Protestants and, 130–31; corruptions of, Protestant Reformation and, 129–30; degeneration from primitive purity, 39–40; as distinct state, 20; fall of, 30; German, rights of, xi; inability to admit error, 35–36, 41; James II and, 17 n. 1; masses for souls of dead as abuse of, 33–35; opinions contrary to public safety, 19–20; Pufendorf's view of, xvi; submission to (*see* submission to Roman Catholic Church); tyranny of, 38, 39

rosaries, 33, 33 n. 10

round wafers in Eucharist, 152–53, 154–55

Rules Concerning the Ecclesiastical Reunion of All Christians (Rojas y Spinola), xv

Sabbath, observance, of 83

sacrifice: of Christ for man, 87–90, 94–95, 102, 198–200; delivery from damnation by, 189; of paschal lamb, 84–85; as superficial religion, 32–33; as symbol of new covenant, 78–79, 104

salvation: from beginning of world, revealed, 191–92; of believers, Redeemer and, 195; call to (*see* call to salvation);

salvation (*continued*)
expectation of, demonstrated by baptism, 110; force and, 146, 181–82; Holy Scriptures and, 22, 152; ignorance of Gospel and, 59–60, 144; impossibility of attaining, cruelty of, 175; impotence to receive, moral, 196–97, 213; inducements to, 145–46; of infants and children, 39, 111, 119, 124, 153–54, 208; initiated by man, 142 n. 43, 196, 213; invitation to, will of God and, 172–73, 178–79; means of (*see* means of salvation); new covenant and, 74, 86, 145, 191–92; not all religions useful for, 21–22; not willed by force of omnipotence, 212; place of morality in, 183–84, 195, 200, 213; possible for all, 173–74; preaching to all mankind, 192–94; predestination and, 140–41, 142; price of infinite value for, 149; promise of, 185; proposed in manner of law, 164–65; refusal of (*see* refusal of salvation; reprobates); universality of, 194–95; way of, 181

Samuel Pufendorf und die europäische Frühaufklärung. Werk und Einfluss eines deutschen Bürgers der Gelehrten republik nach 300 Jahren (1694–1994) (Palladini and Hartung), 17 n. 1

sanctification, 115–18, 223

Saumur, Academy of (1598–1685), 221 n. 77

schism: Council of Constance and, 155 n. 47; evangelical liberty not to be renounced, 55–57; sale of indulgences and, 52

Scriptures: *See* Holy Scriptures

A Second Review of the Lutheran Principles (Brett), xix, xix n. 13

secret will of God: call to salvation and, 178–79; Holy Scripture differing from, 179; ignorance of, 177–78

sects, reconciliation of, attempted, 57–58

Seidler, Michael J., 17 n. 1

Selden, John, 109, 109 n. 38, 111, 111 n.39

serpent, seed of, 184–85

shame, of Fall, 69–70

Sigismund, King of Sweden, 17–18 n. 2, 30, 155 n. 47

sin(s): fall from grace, shame of, 69–70; inclination to further sin and, 73; moral impossibility of avoiding, 69; Original Sin, 73–75; putting aside (*see* holiness of life); remission of (*see* remission of sins); removed by regeneration, 112–13; renunciation of, baptism and, 110–11; violation of covenant, by Adam, 70, 72–73, 74; of whole world, Christ as sacrifice for, 200–201. *See also* wickedness

slavery: in Egypt, deliverance from, 84–85; freedom from, purchased by Christ, 89–90

Socinians, 57, 101, 101 n. 37, 139, 200

Socinus, Faustus, 101 n. 37

sons of God, mankind as: as heirs to Jesus Christ, 104–5; promise of salvation and, 185; by regeneration, 113–14

soul, inner man residing in, 113

sovereign(s). *See* princes

spiritual bodies, not liable to alteration, 71

state. *See* commonwealth

subjects: exclusion from privileges of, 18; right to liberty, 16–17

submission to Roman Catholic Church: articles of faith and, 42; Augsburg Confession and, 38–39; necessary for reconcilement, 36–37; as obstacle to reconciliation, 39–40, 42

superficial religion, Roman Catholicism as, 35–36

Tacitus, P. Cornelius, 29, 29 n. 6

teachers, knowledge required of, 128

temperance, 121

temple of Solomon, 85

temporal interest (advantage): controversy and, 25; as God of popish clergy, 31; points of religion and, 28; temporal prerogative, denial of, 210

Test Act of 1673, 17 n. 1

testament, covenant contrasted to, 103–5

theology, system of, xii–xiii; absolute decree irreconcilable with, 144; complete, ecclesiastical peace and, 59; controversies in, 139–42, 223–25; controversies referred to, 132–34; covenant included in, 63–66; entire, denial of, 57–58; increase in bulk of, 58; not necessary to encompass all points, 128; particularism inconsistent with, 220–21; points presupposed to, 61–62; questions in, 22; reconciliation of Lutherans and Calvinists by, xiii; revealed religion in, 62; superfluous questions banished from, 26; on which all Protestants may agree, 127

Thirty Years' War, 131 n. 41

Tiberius, 29, 29 n. 6

time: for acceptance of God's covenants, 66; controversy mitigated by, 25

toleration: limited, xi–xii, xviii; "political" and "ecclesiastical," x–xi; reconcilement mixed with, 23–24; universal, xi; universal or fundamental, 15. See also ecclesiastical toleration; political toleration

Toleration Act of 1689, xviii

Tranquillus, G. Suetonius, 211, 211 n. 68

transubstantiation, doctrine of: abhorrent to Lutherans and Calvinists, 135–37; absurdity of, 136, 155; not acknowledged in Scriptures, 102–3; not to be overexamined, 125; sharp controversy over, 124–25; symbolic of perfect Christian union, 42–43, 44

Treaty of Münster, 131 n. 41

Treaty of Passau (1552), 41 n. 16, 41–42, 46, 48

Tree of the Knowledge of Good and Evil, 72–73

Trent, Council of (1545–63): decrees of, not to be appealed to, 53; on divine right of bishops, 46; renunciation of, demanded, 56; Roman Catholic error continued by, 41, 41 n. 15, 49, 54

Trinity. See Holy Trinity

truth: admission of error and, 214–15; of call to salvation, 179; discerning, 25–26; reconcilement of differences and, 21–23, 224; retaining saving truth, 14, 15

Turkish argument, 221

"'Turkish Judgment' and the English Revolution" (Seidler), 17 n. 1

Turks: Ottoman Empire, 34 n. 11; Venetian war with, 30–31, 30–31 n. 9

Two letters to . . . Viscount Townsend, xix n. 13

tyranny: legislative will as, 161–62, 175; reprobation of sinners as, 211; of Roman Catholic Church, 38, 39

understanding: of Holy Trinity, xiii, 68; imperfection of, impossible in God, 207; perfect, by first man, 67–68; prescience as work of, 163; received by regeneration, 113, 114–15. See also reason

Union–Konversion–Toleranz. Dimensionen der Annäherung zwischen den christlichen Konfessionen im 17. und 18. Jahrhundert (Duchhardt and May), xiv–xv n. 6, xvi n. 9

universality: of God's promises, fulfillment of, 176; of grace, 148–50, 152; principle of, 148–51

universal redemption: condition of faith and, 182–83; declared in Holy Scripture, 196; particular redemption and, 195–98, 224; universality of salvation and, 194–95

Valence, Duke of (Cesare Borgia), 46, 46 n. 21

Venetian Commonwealth, war with Turks, 30–31, 30–31 n. 9

vessels of mercy, wrath toward unbelievers and, 187

vessels of wrath, patience of God and, 187–88

vices: alleviated by virtue, 121–22; evil proceeding from, 121; indulgence in,

vices (*continued*)
external religion and, 32. *See also* sin(s); wickedness

A View of the Principles of the Lutheran Churches; shewing how far they agree with the Church of England: Being a Seasonable Essay towards the Uniting of Protestants upon the Accession of His Majesty King George to the Throne of these Kingdoms (Dorrington), xvii, xvii n. 10

Virgil, 139 n. 42

virtue(s): decree of justice and, 203; faith and repentance entwined with, 117–18; good works (*see* good works); having no place in primitive state, 116; vices alleviated by, 121–22. *See also specific virtues*

vocation. *See* preaching

war: arising from differences in religion, 13; virtues as cure of, 121–22

wealth, procurement by priests: articles of faith used for, 42, 44–45; by sale of masses, 33–35, 47, 50–51

Westphalia, Peace of (1648), xi, 131 n. 41

The Whole Duty of Man According to Natural Law (Pufendorf), ix

wickedness: abstinence from, holiness of life and, 118–20; deliverance from, 89; God's heart hardened against, 181–82; patience of God and, 187; permitted by God, liberty and, 164; political toleration as remedy for, 15–16; proceed-

ing from vices, 121; seducement to, freedom of will and, 69; seed of serpent and, 184–85; used to good end by God, 164. *See also* sin(s)

William of Orange, King of England, xix, 17 n. 1

will of God: absolute decree contrasted, 209, 211–12; acquiescence to, 121; antecedent, 170, 171, 172; Calvinists on, 150, 151; conditional, 167–69, 171; contradiction in, 160, 162–63, 172, 190; decretive (*see* decretive will of God); double, reconciliation of, 174–82; dual nature of, 159–63, 174–82; inefficacious, 157–58; invitation to salvation and, 172–73, 178–79; known by works, 202; legislative (*see* legislative will of God); man's freedom of will and, 158, 161, 164; man's impenitence and, 184; prescience contrasted, 163; resistance to, 159; to save men, place of morality in, 183–84; secret (*see* secret will of God)

words, ambiguous sense of, 217–18, 223

worship: acceptability to God, 78; Levitical, 32–33, 79; public, 79; true worship, 65–66, 193

Wycliff, John, 155 n. 47

Zeitschrift für Kirchengeschichte, xv–xvi n. 7

Zurbuchen, Simone, ix n, 18 n. 3, 218–19 n. 74

Zwingli, Huldrych, 130

This book is set in Adobe Garamond, a modern adaptation by Robert Slimbach of the typeface originally cut around 1540 by the French typographer and printer Claude Garamond. The Garamond face, with its small lowercase height and restrained contrast between thick and thin strokes, is a classic "old-style" face and has long been one of the most influential and widely used typefaces.

Printed on paper that is acid free and meets the requirements of the American National Standard for Permanence of Paper for Printed Library Materials, z39.48-1992. ∞

Book design by Louise OFarrell, Gainesville, Florida
Typography by Impressions Book and Journal Services, Inc., Madison, Wisconsin
Printed and bound by Edwards Brothers, Inc., Ann Arbor, Michigan